T0370845

## NEW SURVEYS IN THE CLASSICS

Regular subscribers to the journal *Greece & Rome* receive a volume in the New Surveys in the Classics series as part of their subscription. The following volumes are also available to purchase as books.

Volume 38 *Epigram* (ISBN 9780521145701)
Volume 37 *Comedy* (ISBN 9780521706094)
Volume 36 *Roman Oratory* (ISBN 0521687225)
Volume 35 *The Second Sophistic* (ISBN 0198568819)
Volume 33 *Reception Studies* (ISBN 0198528655)
Volume 32 *The Invention of Prose* (ISBN 0198525234)
Volume 31 *Greek Historians* (ISBN 019922501X)
Volume 30 *Roman Religion* (ISBN 0199224331)
Volume 29 *Greek Science* (ISBN 0199223955)
Volume 28 *Virgil* (ISBN 0199223424)
Volume 27 *Latin Historians* (ISBN 0199222932)
Volume 26 *Homer* (ISBN 0199222096)
Volume 25 *Greek Thought* (ISBN 0199220743)
Volume 24 *Greek Religion* (ISBN 0199220735)

To place an order from within the United States, Canada and Mexico please contact Cambridge Customer Services toll free via +1 800 872 7423 or by email via information@cup.org/. For orders outside of North America please call + 44 (0)1223 325566 or email via ukcustserve@cambridge.org/.

## THE CLASSICAL ASSOCIATION

The Classical Association has a worldwide membership and is open to all who value the study of the languages, literature, and civilizations of ancient Greece and Rome. It creates opportunities for friendly exchange and co-operation among classicists, encourages scholarship through its journals and other publications, and supports classics in schools and universities. Every year it holds an annual conference, and it sponsors branches all over the country which put on programmes of lectures and other activities.

The Classical Association has about 3,500 members. Members receive the *Presidential Address* once a year and a newsletter, *CA News*, twice a year. They may also subscribe at substantially reduced cost to the Classical Association journals *Classical Quarterly*, *Classical Review*, and *Greece & Rome*.

For more information and a membership application form please contact the Secretary, The Classical Association, Senate House, Malet Street, London WC1E 7HU (tel: +44 (0)20 7862 8706, e-mail: office@ classicalassociation.org). The Secretary can also give information about the reduced journal subscription rates, and about the Association's other occasional publications.

Cover illustration: the frontispiece (artist unknown) to J. W. Mackail's books on the *Greek Anthology*, beginning with his *Select Epigrams from the Greek Anthology: Edited with a Revised Text, Introduction, Translation and Notes* in 1890 (London: Longmans, Green). A lady gardener, her clothes a mix of sensible outdoor gear and classical drapery, bends to pluck a flower - or root out a weed? - from the *Anthology*'s drifts.

*Greece & Rome*

NEW SURVEYS IN THE CLASSICS No. 38

# EPIGRAM

BY
NIALL LIVINGSTONE AND GIDEON NISBET

*Published for the Classical Association*
CAMBRIDGE UNIVERSITY PRESS
2010

# CAMBRIDGE
## UNIVERSITY PRESS

University Printing House, Cambridge CB2 8BS, United Kingdom

Cambridge University Press is part of the University of Cambridge.

It furthers the University's mission by disseminating knowledge in the pursuit of education, learning and research at the highest international levels of excellence.

www.cambridge.org
Information on this title: www.cambridge.org/9780521145701

© The Classical Association 2010

First published 2010 (Greece & Rome 55)

*A catalogue record for this publication is available from the British Library*

ISBN 978-0-521-14570-1 Paperback

# CONTENTS

# ACKNOWLEDGEMENTS

A short book owes as many debts as a large one, but leaves itself less space to acknowledge them. Francesca Sapsford, currently writing her PhD on Martial, helped compile the bibliography. She also lent her expertise to an undergraduate seminar series on Greek epigram in reception, 'Inventing the Ancient Greeks', taught by Gideon Nisbet to undergraduates in the Institute of Archaeology and Antiquity at Birmingham in 2008–9. The students who participated in this seminar were an invaluable test audience for the ideas presented in our fifth chapter, and we thank them collectively for their positive feedback and encouragement. Niall Livingstone also taught an undergraduate course on Greek epigrams, inscribed and literary, at Birmingham in 2000–1, and would similarly like to thank the students involved for exciting discussions which sowed the seeds of many of the ideas in Chapters I and II. Begoña Ortega of the University of Burgos, our guest as an Honorary Research Fellow at Birmingham in July 2009, was a congenial early audience for some of the ideas herein. We gratefully acknowledge the contributions of the series editor, John Taylor; our copy-editor, Hester Higton; and our editor at the Press, Phil Jones. We also thank Liz Clements and Diana Spencer, for their constant support. While this has been a shared project, GN was essentially responsible for the Prologue and Introduction and for Chapters III, IV and V, and NL for Chapters I and II.

A thing, whose match or in the depths profound
Of ocean, or on earth, can ne'er be found;
'Tis in an instant born, its growth of limb
Does Nature order by the strangest whim:
Tis ten, and is a giant form appears;
Tis ten middle age a smaller size it wears;
And now again, its day of life nigh o'er,
How wondrous! 'tis gigantic as before.

'A strange sort of creature that', said Lysiteles; 'and one I shall hardly hit upon. Great in its childhood, little in its prime, and big again at last. Ah! I have it', he suddenly exclaimed; 'one need only look at the gnomon; it is the shadow, which is great in the morning, and then contracts, till, towards evening, it again increases.' 'Tis guessed it', cried the whole party, and Lysiteles received a festia and a kiss.

'Now Charicles', said he, 'it's your turn to guess'?

Not hostile fate, nor yet immortal thine,
Soothes once of human race doom;
Still o'er me she moves, nor sets again;
Ever and living to the gloomless term:
For herald to tread our most familiary.

'Your riddle is somewhat vague and obscure', said Charicles after a little consideration; 'but if I mistake not, the solution is sleep, isn't it? But you should have made it plainer. Now solid, Euctemon, he proceeded, 'my riddle is full of contradictions. Beware of the penalty. As for the penalty, I can get over that, but you surely won't deprive me of your kiss.' 'By the live, cried

them', 'there is one thing we have forgotten. Suppose the riddle is not solved, must the next try to guess?' 'Not so', said Ctesiphon; 'whoever can guess it first gets the riand and kiss; but if he guesses wrong, let him drink the fine.' This was agreed to, and turning to Euctemon, Charicles spoke thus:

Know the mother, that a tiny brood
Within her bosom keeps securely mewed;
Though voiceless all, beyond the ocean wide
To distant realms their still small voices glide;
For, far away, whome'er it address they seek
Will understand, yet no one hears them speak.

This proved too much for Euctemon's acumen. Hard as he tried to unriddle the mystery of the dumb speakers, it was all of no avail, and he had to drink the fine. 'I know', cried Stephanus; 'it is the city; and her children are the speakers, who cry out so that their voice may be heard far across the sea in Asia and Thrace.' A roar of laughter followed. 'But, Stephanus', said Charicles, 'did you ever see an orator that was dumb? he must then be impeached thrice for personation, and condemned.' 'Salt water', screamed several voices; and, though he tried hard to get it, Stephanus was forced to drink off the goblet of hymn. 'I will tell you the meaning of the enigma, Ctesiphon now said; 'it is a letter, and its children that it conceals within it are the characters, which, mute and voiceless, speak only to him to whom the letter is addressed.' 'Bravo', cried Glaucon; 'how ever will you find room on your head for all the leaves that you're earning to-day'? It was now Euctemon's turn. 'You'll have to drink too, said he to Nausicrates, who had mean-

* This riddle, one of the best works to use diagram devices for riddle, is proposed in the Sappho of Antiphanes; Athen. x. p. 450:

# PROLOGUE: AT THE SYMPOSIUM

We are at a symposium in the house of Lysiteles of Athens in the last month of the 111th Olympiad, 328 BCE. The guest of honour is Charicles, a handsome and athletic young Athenian of good family, lately returned from abroad. Dinner has been lavish – the finest Copaic eels and the largest sea pike, Boeotian in their luxury – but this has now been cleared away. The slaves have distributed garlands of myrtle and roses, the pretty flute-girls have struck up their tune, and the symposiarch, master of festivities, has declared his rules for the mixing and drinking of the wine (old Chian, and chilled with snow). Next comes the question of entertainment. The company immediately rejects philosophy and gambling, but Ctesiphon's proposal is taken up with enthusiasm: they will play at riddles, each expressed in the form of a short and witty poem. These, then, are *epigrams*.

In this short book we offer a concise account of what epigram is, how it began, how it reached us, and why it is worth getting excited about (Introduction). Beginning with the earliest examples on stone (Chapter 1), we explore epigram's rise to prominence as a literary genre in the Greek world after Alexander (Chapter 2), and investigate its journey from Hellenistic culture into the very different world of Rome (Chapter 3).

Greek epigram did not end when Latin epigram began; instead it mutated, while still maintaining the pretence that nothing had changed. Latin epigram, meanwhile, went its own strange way, and the genre continued to flourish in both languages right through into Late Antiquity and beyond (Chapter 4). Through the *Greek Anthology* (Introduction) and the collected works of Martial, the remains of ancient epigram continued to exert influence in the Renaissance and after.

So many of these short poems survived that any translation had to be selective; any account of the genre had to leave some things out and emphasize others. As the new mass readership of the Victorian age began to discover the classics through cheap translations and popular handbooks, this propensity for intense editorial activity became a blessing and a curse. Epigram could be used to tell *any* story about the ancient past (and of course this applies to our own account as well). In a culture that looked to Greece and Rome to confirm its own ideals and truths, new narratives could be dangerous; the 'wrong' selection of epigrams could and did provoke moral panic, as our final chapter (Chapter 5) reveals.

One can see the anxiety begin to stir at Lysiteles' symposium. These poems look like epigrams, a literary form which very much belongs there; but they are *not* real ancient poems. Nor is this a real symposium – but it is the next best thing, or ought to be. In fact, the gathering at Lysiteles' house is taken from an educational novel by a German classics professor, Wilhelm Becker. *Charicles, or Illustrations of the Private Life of the Ancient Greeks, with Notes and Excursuses* was first published in English in 1846 in the translation of the Revd Frederick Metcalfe, a Fellow of Lincoln College in Oxford and by all accounts quite a character (his entry in the *Oxford Dictionary of National Biography* makes fascinating reading). Metcalfe abridged as he went along, aggressively cutting back the indigestible detail of the professor's scholarly apparatus to make his version of *Charicles* less of a grind.[1]

Metcalfe's version is itself now practically unreadable, but he had his finger on the pulse of his society: his *Charicles* (unlike Becker's) stayed in circulation through sixty-odd years of editions and imprints, answering a real need. Becker himself had never actually visited Greece, but his classical reading was prodigious, and he aimed at nothing less than a total recreation of daily life in the autumn years of classical Athens. (His earlier work, *Gallus*, had done the same for early Augustan Rome.) *Charicles* immersed its readers in an educational virtual reality, every detail of which was determined by the relevant ancient texts. Each striped cushion, each tiny basket is justified and documented with direct quotation of the original Greek. The smattering of local colour in our opening paragraph – Copaic eels, snow-chilled wine – gives only the smallest hint of *Charicles'* obsessive completism, even in Metcalfe's stripped-down version for the Anglophone market. In its desire to present a total simulacrum of antiquity to the visual imagination of its readers, it resembles nothing so much as the elaborate moving panoramas that dominated the visual culture of the mid-nineteenth century. Immersing their

---

[1] Metcalfe's mutilations of Becker, savage even by the standards of his age, were partly directed at making *Charicles* physically shorter to please his publishers; his fellow dons pestered him to restore some of the cut material in subsequent editions (Becker 1895: v).

socially inclusive audiences in worlds that they could never visit for real – scenes of Arctic exploration were a favourite – and enhanced by ingenious special effects, these carnivalesque touring spectacles were always accompanied by a barker, whose scripted patter of plausible detail glossed the spectacle as a compressed education, offering a total experience that could not be had from mere book-learning. *Charicles'* aim is the same. Becker is always *Professor* Becker in Metcalfe's introductory banter; the panorama showmen called themselves 'professors' too.[2]

Total simulation, of course, was not the same thing as the whole truth and nothing but the truth; Metcalfe's speeded-up *Charicles* cut not only the redundant citations but also Becker's juicier appendices.[3] There were certain things that the British public was not ready to see in its ancient Greece, any more than they expected their Arctic panoramas to show their navy's finest succumbing to scurvy and the temptation of cannibalism. No mention, then, of what other services those flute-girls might be contracted for; and certainly no hint of pretty boys, for reasons that we will explore later.

But these strategic omissions were Metcalfe's, not Becker's. Figure 1 shows some of Becker's pseudo-epigrams in their translated publication context. In the surrounding material, the author's mania for accuracy shines through, undiminished by Metcalfe's showmanship. Why then has he broken his own rules this one time and *faked* a whole sequence of Greek epigrams? And why has he taken the trouble, when there are thousands of real ones to hand in the *Anthology*?

We must begin by looking at *how* he has faked them. As his footnotes acknowledge, Becker's pseudo-epigrams are cut down and adapted from fragments of Athenian tragedy and Middle Comedy of the fourth century BCE – the period of *Charicles*, with Plato a recent memory. Becker's underlying problem is chronological: at this date,

---

[2] On the 'Arctic spectacles' in particular, but with more general relevance, see Potter 2007.

[3] Metcalfe brags of his bowdlerizing 'labours' as an improving update at Becker 1895: ix–x: 'It has...been deemed advisable to depart occasionally from the author's principle of ὀνομάζειν τὰ σῦκα σῦκα; by an over-tenacious adherence to which his narrative has here and there become offensive to good taste, without much being gained thereby. Accordingly, one entire Excursus has been left out, and the one on the ἑταῖραι [*hetairai*, courtesans] much curtailed, though the translator rather regrets the necessity of making the latter omissions.' The missing Excursus is about pederasty, although Metcalfe is careful not to say so. He even goes into Greek to 'call figs, figs' (ὀνομάζειν τὰ σῦκα σῦκα), the classical equivalent of 'calling a spade a spade'. Metcalfe retains what he decently can of the *hetairai*, not from prurient interest but because of the light they throw on the awful consequences of loveless Athenian marriages – how very unlike the home life of our own dear Queen.

epigram does not yet exist outside of inscriptions on stone. Literary epigram will be the defining genre of the symposium, but *not yet*: the great names of the Hellenistic period – Callimachus, Posidippus, Asclepiades – are a generation or more in the future. If Becker wants to populate his symposium with epigrams, he must make them up himself from the remnants of writers who have nothing to do with epigram at all.

Now that we know what he is doing, the questions become if anything more acute. *Why* does Becker feel the need to push sympotic epigram back into the fourth century, where he knows it does not belong? (We suggest one likely motivation in our Introduction.) And why *these* epigrams, cut implausibly from Athenian cloth, when he could have taken his pick of hundreds of anonymous *Anthology* originals? Our final chapter will revisit Becker's Victorian epigram-factory and suggest some possible answers.

In the meantime, we must begin by defining what it is we mean by 'epigram'. What is this genre that provoked the respectable nineteenth century into an orgy of fibbing?

# INTRODUCTION
## ROCK, PAPER, SCISSORS

### Rock

Epigram: EPI-GRAMMA, a text written or incised upon something. 'Inscription' is one obvious translation of the root meaning, and epigram began with inscriptions: texts carved in stone to fix cultural memory. Epigram and epigraphy, the modern study of inscriptions, are two sides of the same linguistic coin. The classical Greek epigraphic habit manifested itself across many different contexts. Inscriptions broadcast the laws and decrees of the city-state, the *polis*, and secured the meaning of monuments and tombs against a forgetful future. Cut into trophies and statues, they celebrated victory in war and sport. Inscriptions were unavoidably costly in skilled labour, and competed for the attention of the passer-by with many others of their kind. Official decrees and honorific inscriptions were as long as their elaborate phrasing dictated, but for more personal messages these factors could combine to create a pressure to keep the text short and to the point. A small minority of these inscriptions were in verse.[1]

In the Hellenistic age, cultural nostalgia for 'old' Greece seems to have impelled the compilation of collections of these verse inscriptions as part of the local lore of the traditional Hellenic heartland. These collections were nothing inherently special, and were not compiled with the intention of launching a literary genre. Writing up the verse inscriptions of Nemea or Olympia was, instead, a small part of a wider antiquarian project by which the court intellectuals of rival dynastic centres, predominantly Alexandria and Pergamum, sought to maximize the cultural capital of their local regimes.[2]

This antiquarianism encompassed other, more properly literary genres – didactic epic, universal history – as well as new kinds of textual

---

[1] For an indication of statistics, see Bing and Bruss 2007b: 3.

[2] In Krevans' bracing formulation, '[the] kings collected objects (art, books) and creatures (zoological specimens, scholars). The scholars collected information' (Krevans 2007: 131).

tools: dictionaries, summaries, lists, and digests. Knowledge of the past was power over it. Callimachus and others launched an information revolution of cataloguing, systematization, and scholarship, directed towards mastery over a prestigious period of shared history that was already becoming 'classical' in the sense in which we use the term. A new standard system of education turned the texts of this classical period into the basis of an enduring literary canon. In schoolroom and gymnasium, the canon now transmitted a ring-fenced legacy of shared knowledge and values – *paideia* – that increasingly defined Greek identity in a cosmopolitan world of diaspora.[3] This is the version of Greek literary culture that Rome later appropriated – a classical core packaged as heritage by Hellenistic scholarship.

## Paper

The genre of epigram was not a part of this canon, and could claim no place in the schoolroom of *paideia* (however useful its retrospective focus might have been there); it was a new arrival.[4] The scholars' handbooks of locally derived verse inscriptions somehow became the template for books of short poems of a kind not seen before. They quickly became popular, attracting major literary figures such as Callimachus, Philetas, and Nicander. A poet could now become famous as a 'fashioner of epigrams' – *epigrammatopoios* – although he might not yet refer to his poems under that name. There may have been residual resistance to calling a poem 'epigram' when it was no longer composed for inscription, regardless of its formal similarity to actual inscribed texts.[5]

Certainly, epigram's mutation from an epigraphic archive into an active literary genre was not an obvious development. The editors of a major recent collection on Hellenistic epigram plausibly suggest that these poets were attracted to epigram precisely *because* it was outside the traditional canon (as, for instance, pastoral had been before

[3] A useful survey of Hellenistic education is supplied by Cribiore 2001.

[4] Wissman 2002 accounts for the near-total absence of epigram in papyri identifiable as ancient school-texts. Epigram's use in the Victorian schoolroom (on which, see Ch. 5) thus stands in pointed opposition to ancient practice.

[5] On epigram's Hellenistic popularity, see Cameron 1993: 3. On nomenclature, see Bing and Bruss 2007b: 1 n. 4; but cf. 14–15 on a third-century-BCE decree identifying Posidippus as an ἐπιγραμματοποιός, 'epigram-maker'. On the implicit tension between inscribed ἐπίγραμμα and formerly-inscribed ἐλεγεῖον ('elegy') in Thucydides, see Petrovic 2007a: 55.

Philetas and Theocritus) and because mainstream genres such as epic and tragedy had always been about performance first and text second. Epigram offered the scholar-poets an experimental workspace that gave unique priority to writers and readers.[6]

The limited evidence available to us makes it seem likely that the new literary epigrammatists typically arranged their books by thematic category.[7] We would not expect this arrangement in an original poetry book (although we might in a compiled anthology), and Latin authors such as Catullus and Martial did not adopt it when they wrote epigram in imitation of the Hellenistic poets; perhaps it reflects the organization of those lost collections of local verse inscriptions. As we will see in the case of the Milan Posidippus, organization by category did not rule out artistry in the details of arrangement, and the choice of categories could itself demonstrate creativity.

Arrangement by category also plays to epigram's strengths as a genre of short, occasional poetry. *Epi-* in Greek carries the same double sense as its English translation. Epigrams were now no longer (or not only or primarily) incised physically *upon* a monument, slab, or statue-base; they were composed 'upon' a topic, as responses to a set theme or given occasion. Inscriptional epigram had always been brief and formulaic. As a literary form, these same qualities encouraged participation and creative variation. Anyone could have a go: staying in metre for four lines was not an impossible challenge even for novice writers.[8] In a genre built on formula and variations on a standard theme, individual poems practically wrote themselves. It was easy to get sucked into tinkering with an old chestnut, working the changes in search of a satisfying new twist.

A well-known example is the cycle of poems on Myron's *Cow*. This famous statue stood in the Agora at Athens; later it was moved to Rome (Plin. *NH* 24.57). At some point, poets started writing epigrams about it. These are *epi*-grams in a complex sense: written

---

[6] Bing and Bruss 2007b: 7.

[7] Gutzwiller 1998: 28–36, with the benefit of a sneak preview of the 'Milan Posidippus' papyrus (discussed later in this introduction), remains properly cautious about extrapolating from its structure in an unqualified way. The further papyrus examples that she surveys are broadly compatible with a default practice of organization into categories, but there could well have been significant exceptions. Gutzwiller plausibly suggests that Callimachus arranged his own epigrams alphabetically (1998: 38–40).

[8] Epigrams tend to have an even number of lines because the typical metre is the elegiac couplet; four lines is the typical length of surviving poems in the *Greek Anthology*, our main source for Greek literary epigram. How this *Anthology* came into existence will become clear as the introduction progresses.

'upon' the *Cow* as a topic for literary composition, but also playing
with the idea that such a poem might end up incised *upon* the statue
(or its base) as an accompanying inscription. This playful ambivalence
is absolutely typical of the genre.[9] Literary epigrams know they come
from stone, and are forever throwing out hints of making the return
trip; but thematic variation within the collection gives the lie to their
epigraphic nostalgia. In the real world, the statue can carry only one
caption; the ninth book of the *Anthology* gives us an unbroken run
(*AP* 9.713–42) of thirty-one possible versions, enough to cover the
statue's plinth several times over. Successive epigrams find new ways
to stress how utterly realistic the statue is, but make the scenario of
inscription increasingly unrealistic. The effect of paradox is surely
intentional; sequences like these almost parody the idea of authentic
inscriptionality:

> I am Myron's little cow, and I am set up as a dedication upon a pillar.
> Oxherd, use the goad on me and drive me home to the herd.

> Oxherd, pasture your herd at a distance, in case you should drive off
> Myron's little cow with your cows, thinking it to be alive.

> Myron lied: he did not sculpt me, but drove me off from the herd as I
> grazed, and bound me to a stone base.

> If Myron had not fastened my feet to this stone, I would have been driven
> to pasture with the cows as a young cow myself.

> Myron set me up here, his little cow: but the herdsmen throw stones at me,
> thinking that I have wandered from the herd.[10]

To ask whether or not Myron's statue ever carried an actual verse
inscription is practically beside the point. Literary variations such as
these circulate far more widely than any notional epigraphic original,
which – forever fixed to its inscriptional context – remains of interest
only to scholarly collectors and the most dedicated of tourists. We
might take this further: Peter Bing suggests that ancient readers only
become interested in inscriptional epigram *at all* through encounters
with literary imitations such as the Myron's *Cow* poems. By this

---

[9] For thoughtful consideration of a single such poem from several angles, see Petrovic and
Petrovic 2003.
[10] *AP* 9.713 (Anon.), 715 ('Anacreon' – clearly a false attribution), 719 (Leonidas), 720
(Antipater of Sidon), 731 (Anon.). All translations in this book are the authors' own unless
otherwise indicated.

provocative account, the literary texture of faux-inscriptional epigram made it much more interesting than the real thing.[11]

It was also more accessible and inclusive, for readers and writers alike. The first and last of our *Cow* examples are anonymous. There are some big names in the overall sequence – Antipater, Dioscorides, Marcus Argentarius, Philip – but many of the poems are transmitted with no name attached, and some of these will have been one-off compositions by amateurs. (Each poem in the *Anthology* has an individual heading or 'lemma' stating its authorship, to the editor's best knowledge; often it is *ΑΔΕΣΠΟΤΟΝ*, 'Anon.') Later in the same book (*AP* 9.793–8), a single author – Julian, a Roman Prefect of Egypt – supplies another six poems on exactly the same topic. By his time, people had been composing epigrams 'on' Myron's *Cow* for hundreds of years.

### Scissors

Two of the poems in the earlier sequence (*AP* 9.738–9) are also by Julian, and this ramshackle structure hints at the *Anthology*'s difficulties as our main source for Greek literary epigram. It is important to know a little about its origins and history. The first books to include literary epigrams by multiple authors were Hellenistic; we catch late echoes of them in papyri from Greco-Roman Egypt, discussed in Chapter 4. One major multi-author collection was known as the *Sōros* – 'the Heap', suggesting winnowed grain. Given the title, it was probably not arranged according to an obvious logical or artistic scheme. The *Anthology*'s famous early source and structural prototype is instead the *Stephanos* or *Garland* of Meleager of Gadara, a poet and prose satirist of the early first century BCE.

As his title suggests, Meleager arranged his *Garland* (which ran to several book-rolls) according to a definite scheme, weaving together poems by many hands. A marginal note in the Palatine manuscript of the *Anthology* states that he abandoned the arrangement by category (as used in books by a single author), instead ordering his selection alphabetically by the first letter of the first word of each poem; but Alan Cameron has shown that the surviving traces in the *Anthology*'s text

---

[11] Bing 2002, elaborating on the curious absence of encounters with inscriptional epigram in the touristic scenarios of the Greek novel, but he may overstate his case: for further consideration of the readership of inscribed epigram see our first chapter.

make this impossible. Instead Meleager transferred the conventional scheme of organization by category, previously reserved for books by a single author, to the broader ambit of a multi-author anthology. He also appears to have scaled the categories up: each category now filled a whole book.[12] The *Garland* included Hellenistic greats such as Callimachus and Euphorion, but also earlier poets such as Sappho and Archilochus: their shorter work was now appropriated retrospectively, giving the upstart genre a ready-made genealogy of 'classics'. None of Meleager's authors was later than the third century BCE – with the notable exception of Meleager himself, who asserted editorial privilege by including his own admittedly excellent work.

Meleager's mission statement is his preface, which survives in the *Anthology*'s fourth Book along with the prefaces of his successors in the garland-weaving trade (another indication of the *Anthology*'s complicated back story and slightly clumsy composition). These successors include Philip, who compiled a follow-up *Garland* of more recent poets in the middle of the first century CE – this one *was* arranged alphabetically, more or less, with no differentiation into thematic categories at all; and Agathias, a Christian anthologist of the sixth century, who pads the preface of his *Cycle* with praise of the Emperor Justinian. Many of the poems selected by Agathias and later included in the *Anthology* are recognizable by the Byzantine official titles given to their authors.[13] Agathias followed Meleager in his organizational scheme, but on a slightly larger scale – seven categories, each filling a book. These categories included several that play with inscriptionality: imaginary dedications, captions for works of art (such as Myron's *Cow*), and epitaphs. But Agathias also included reflections on Fortune, humorous invective, love-poems, and sympotic verse (132–3):

> ...the joys of Bacchus, and tipsy dances, and wine, and the mixing-bowl, and lavish banquets.

We find Agathias' categories carried across into the structure of the *Anthology* as we have it, showing that its compiler leaned on him heavily.

There were other proto-anthologies too, notably the *Anthologion* of Diogenianus, probably compiled in the mid-second century CE.

---

[12] Cameron 1993: 20–6.
[13] Ibid.: 16–17, 37.

None of them survives today. Cameron argues that even Constantine Cephalas, the tenth-century compiler of the *Greek Anthology*, did not have access to complete copies of the *Garlands*; he made do by juggling two different versions of each, all of them more or less abridged. His copy of Agathias, on the other hand, was very good.[14] Cephalas also had access to at least one collection on a specialist topic: the *Mousa Paidikē* ('Boyish Muse'), a repository of homoerotic epigrams that had grown up around the collected poems of the second-century poet Strato of Sardis. The *Mousa Paidikē* became the *Anthology*'s twelfth Book.

Cephalas modelled the organization of his *Anthology* on the example of Agathias, scaling it up even further. Book Five, for instance, consists of heterosexual erotic epigrams; Book Seven, funerary. The massive ninth Book is filled with 'epideictic' epigrams (827 in all), a vague and permeable category of epigrams displaying the features of declamatory rhetoric.[15] Even the 258 poems of the *Mousa Paidikē* make it far larger than any genuinely ancient poetry book.

There are several exceptions to the general principle of arrangement, especially early on. Book One flags up the compiler's pious credentials by collecting inscriptional epigrams from Byzantine churches. Book Two is a weird hexameter poem by an Egyptian tourist, Christodorus of Thebes, cataloguing the statues in a famous gymnasium at Constantinople. A disproportionately short third Book reports nineteen epigrams inscribed on a monument at Cyzicus, erected by the Hellenistic dynasts Attalus and Eumenes in memory of their mother. All of this early material may well have been tacked onto Cephalas' original design by the copyists who produced the Palatine manuscript.[16] The fourth Book, as we have seen, collects the verse prefaces of Cephalas' predecessors. The interminable eighth Book is by another mother's boy, Saint Gregory the Theologian (fourth century CE). At the *Anthology*'s far end, a fifteenth Book admits defeat and presents 'Assorted Poems' that the compiler had failed to fit into his previous categories, including additional Christian verses and the so-called *tekhnopaignia* – epigrams, mostly Hellenistic, in the shape of the objects they describe (an axe, an altar, a shepherd's pipe). We will see an example of such a poem in Chapter 4.

---

[14] Ibid.: 44–8.
[15] For further discussion of the term 'epideictic', see Ch. 2.
[16] Bing and Bruss 2007b: 21.

There is occasional subdivision within some individual Books. The run of epigrams on Myron's *Cow* is one instance. Another is *AP* 11.65–225, a series of satirical or 'skoptic' poems divided up by subheadings into small categories. Cephalas must have taken these subheadings from his source for this part of Book Eleven – conceivably a version of a book by the main skoptic poet, Lucillius, who has poems in each of the categories. Book Eleven also has its own, separate preface, the origin of which remains unclear. It is not for nothing that the *Anthology* has recently been called a 'labyrinth'.[17]

These quirks reflect the complex and messy sources available to Cephalas in compiling the *Anthology*. What happened to the work thereafter is almost as confusing for the uninitiated reader. Several times now we have used the abbreviation '*AP*'; this stands for *Anthologia Palatina*, the Palatine Anthology. This fairly reliable parchment manuscript version of Cephalas' tenth-century original was probably produced during the anthologist's own lifetime by two of his pupils.[18] It is named for the Palatine Library in Heidelberg, where it was found in 1606 by the great humanist scholar Claude de Saumaise, more widely known by his Latinized form Salmasius. The single surviving exemplar of Cephalas' text, it had not been read for centuries. Prior to its rediscovery, the only known 'Greek Anthology' was a fourteenth-century abridgement and rearrangement of Cephalas' text in seven books by a Byzantine monk, Maximus Planudes. Many of Planudes' editorial decisions were morally motivated: the *Mousa Paidikē* was an obvious case for excision. This was the 'Anthology' the Renaissance knew; and it was one of the first classical Greek texts to be published in print.[19]

Nowhere in his Anthology (now known as the *Anthologia Planudeana* or '*APl*') had Planudes made it clear that his text was merely a bowdlerized version of a larger work – 'smaller and vastly inferior'.[20] The rediscovery of the Palatine Anthology thus came as a complete surprise. Thousands of poems we had never even known we had lost suddenly came back from the dead. No-one had even heard of Cephalas before, and Planudes was suddenly revealed as a hack by Saumaise's

---

[17] Bing and Bruss 2007a: ix; and cf. Bing and Bruss 2007b: 20; Gutzwiller 1998: ix.

[18] Bing and Bruss 2007b: 20–1.

[19] 'Printed versions of [the *Anthology*] have been available in the West virtually since the invention of the printing press' (Bing and Bruss 2007b: 22). The first (1494) was by John Lascaris, who also produced *editiones principes* of (among others) Callimachus, Apollonius of Rhodes, and Lucian.

[20] Cameron 1993: 17.

characteristically astute identification of exactly what it was he had found. However, knowledge of the Palatine Anthology was slow to spread. Saumaise's own plans for publication went nowhere, and the manuscript migrated through various major European libraries.

Astonishingly, the first complete edition of the Palatine text did not appear until the very end of the eighteenth century – more or less two hundred years after Saumaise's discovery. A selection came out first, Brunck's *Analecta Veterum Poetarum Graecorum* ('Selection of Ancient Greek Poets', 1772–6), arranged by author; and finally a full scholarly edition in several volumes, by Jacobs (1794–8). Even Jacobs' first edition took liberties with the manuscript text: he followed Brunck in presenting the poems by author, arranging these in no discernable order. Two decades on, he relented and offered a revised edition that faithfully presented Cephalas' Agathian structure.

Just as astonishing is that, in the years and decades after Brunck and Jacobs, some publishers preferred to stick with the familiar text of the obsolete Planudean Anthology.[21] Its proportions were manageable, the plates were to hand, and it was free of sexually controversial content. Addressing the working classes, an eminent Victorian critic wrote cagily that 'there are not a few epigrams suppressed by [Planudes] which have since come to light, and which had better never have been published or never written'.[22] Even to describe their contents would be morally dangerous to society.

The Greek Anthology as we have it today consists of the fifteen Books of the Palatine Anthology, followed by a 'Planudean Appendix' of 388 poems occurring in Planudes but not in the Palatine manuscript. The Appendix is also known as Book Sixteen. That its poems survive by chance in Planudes' radical abridgement, but *not* in the faithful and relatively complete Palatine Anthology, hints at the scale of what we may have lost to attrition in even the (probably) relatively few years between Cephalas' original and the copying of the Palatine manuscript. Many of the epigrams of the Appendix are on works of art; these may derive from an entire lost Book of Cephalas' *Anthology*.

---

[21] A lavish illustrated edition by J. de Bosch and D. J. van Lennep, completed in 1822, reproduces a 1566 text of Planudes by Henricus Stephanus (Henri Estienne); the Tauschnitz *Anthology* of 1829 must spell out in its title that it is *ad Palatini codicis fidem edita*, 'faithful to the Palatine manuscript'.

[22] Neaves 1874: 4–5.

## 'The joys of Bacchus': Greek epigram in performance

What were all these epigrams *for*? We saw that three of Agathias'
categories of poems had inscriptional origins, on tombs, statues, and
monuments. Four did not, and together they supply a clue to an
important context for epigram in the Hellenistic and Roman periods.
Fortune is fickle, these poems tell us: we should live for today, see the
funny side, and fall in love; and we should drink together to celebrate
our good fortune. Three of these categories – protreptic (advisory),
erotic, and skoptic – come together in a masculine domain defined
by the fourth: the symposium, a traditional after-dinner drinking
party with entertainments of the kind we saw Charicles attend in our
Prologue. Elegy, the characteristic metre of the epigram, was also by
now the name of a characteristic type of poetic song, written in that
metre and intended for performance in a sympotic context. Elegies
were generally longer compositions, with themes and concerns unlike
those of epigram, but we find suggestive parallels to Agathias' non-
inscriptional categories in elegiac remnants such as the Theognidea.[23]
The symposium is also what garlands – and *Garlands*? – are made for.
In the Greek world after Alexander, the normative social institutions
of the symposium and gymnasium formed a classicizing axis along
which Greek male identity was constructed, tested, and affirmed. The
gymnasium formed the body beautiful on canonical lines, and brought
it into contact with the community of its peers; the symposium
broadened the mind and forged the personal connections of the
private citizen.[24]

Types of Greek epigram with non-inscriptional topics map very
neatly onto sympotic activities and concerns – *too* neatly, a sceptical
critic might argue.[25] The *Mousa Paidikē* is an obvious case in point.
Praise of pretty boys is always at home in the symposium, whether
incised as slogans on red-figure amphorae (the '*kalos*-names' so useful
in assigning dates to pots and painters), called out drunkenly as the
wine dregs are thrown in the messy game of *kottabos*, or – we might
think – inspiring the composition of witty short poems. Poems on

[23] For a discussion of archaic elegy and its possible relation to Hellenistic sympotic epigram
by an expert on the Theognidea, see Bowie 2007.
[24] For useful discussion of the complementary roles of athletics and literary culture in identity
formation, see e.g. Cribiore 2001; Gleason 1995; Newby 2005; Nisbet 2003b. Whitmarsh 2005:
29–32 concisely explains the importance of the trained body to sophistic self-presentation.
[25] Cameron 1995 argues vigorously for composition at symposia; for useful cautions, see now
Bing and Bruss 2007b: 12–14.

the vicissitudes of life, cutting pretension down to size, or ridiculing unsociable behaviour and attitudes are equally at home in this context. These topics remind the symposiasts of the values they share, and of the importance of coming together to celebrate them. Life is too short not to:

> Drink now and love, Damocrates! For we shan't be drinking for ever, and we won't always be keeping company with boys. So let us wrap our heads in garlands and sprinkle them with myrrh, before others bring the same things as offerings to our tombs. For now, let my bones drink wine for the most part – and when they are dead, let Deucalion's flood wash them away.

> The astrologers tell me I am short-lived. I *am*; but, Seleucus, I don't care. We all go down to Hades by one route; and if mine is quicker, I shall lay eyes on Minos sooner. Let us drink! For it's true what they say: wine is a horse fit for the road, while pedestrians [i.e. non-drinkers] must take the footpath to Hades.[26]

Book Eleven of the *Anthology* shows us how these types of implicitly symposiac poems come together with explicit ones and cross-fertilize. Its prose preface, perhaps dating from the Second Sophistic, asserts that sympotic and skoptic poems naturally fit together:[27]

> The sympotic type is made up of skoptic jests and cautionary maxims from the ancients, who were forever improvising at one another over drinks. Therefore, in order that you may enjoy your share of these as well, I have organized the following selection.

This is not *exactly* evidence – or at least, it is not a document. As a grand and confident generalization it reassures a nostalgic Greek readership (or a readership identifying as Greek) that their current cultural practices are seamlessly continuous with those of an ideal classical past. The claim about 'the ancients' is probably meant to suggest classical Athens: to the Second Sophistic this was the only past worth having. If so, it is a misrepresentation of what we know of classical practice (and presumably of what *they* knew as well) – that there was no literary or sympotic epigram as such in classical Athens.[28]

---

[26] *AP* 11.19 (Strato), 23 (Antipater (of Sidon?)).

[27] For an excellent introduction to the 'Second Sophistic' – broadly, Greek culture in the Roman world of the early centuries CE – see now Whitmarsh 2005, with extensive bibliography.

[28] One could add caveats. Short quotations from elegy could have been seen as epigram-like by a later age projecting its own categories back into the past; and at Pl. *Phdr.* 264c–d Socrates illustrates a point in his argument by quoting from memory a funerary epigram for the legendary King Midas. This epigram is represented as circulating orally – 'some say' that it is inscribed on Midas' grave, perhaps with the implication that others disagree, and Socrates has no way of determining whether it is genuine or not. Of course, Plato is not the same thing as

The author of the preface is caught red-handed trying to retrofit epigram into the canon. This does not make the preface useless. Its message is probably what Greeks under Rome *wanted* to believe – a desire that led to numerous ancient fakes of epigrams by 'Plato', and indirectly (much later) to the ersatz epigrams of Becker's *Charicles*. It seems reasonable to suppose that epigram was a common feature at later Greek symposia; otherwise, there would be no need to look to the revered past to justify its inclusion.

Studying Callimachus and his circle, Alan Cameron has argued vigorously that epigram was already a sympotic form at court in the Hellenistic period.[29] Poets improvised rough versions of poems as their contributions to the after-dinner entertainment, and later worked the better ones up for publication. This is an intuitively attractive model for epigram production within Alexandria's metropolitan and consciously Hellenic elite, and goes a long way towards explaining why the new genre took off. Epigram's defining technique of variation on a theme (seen to eventually exhausting effect in the poems on Myron's *Cow*) was an ideal fit with the symposiac dynamic of 'capping', in which participants tried to match and outdo each others' contributions to the entertainment. Once the genre became associated with the symposium, its range of themes naturally expanded and refocussed to address the values and activities of its new performative context – from tombs and statues to wine and pretty boys.

We will see that Catullus represents the Latin epigrams of the Neoterics as operating in exactly the same way as those of the highbrow Hellenistic symposiasts. In the world conjured up by the Catullan corpus, suave young party animals jot down brilliant improvisations in reusable *tabellae* – books of wax tablets – and later work them up for publication in smartly packaged literary collections. Epigram enters their repertoire as part of a wider pattern of self-fashioning against the deliciously risqué models of the Alexandrian elite, seen through the filter of late Hellenistic mediators such as Meleager. Whatever his actual practice may be, Catullus talks the talk of the smart Callimachean.[30]

---

the performance of epigrams as sympotic entertainment – and Plato is in any case poor evidence for actual social practice. For a fascinating and bold discussion of the Midas epigram, see Munn 2006: 70.

[29] Cameron 1995: 71–103.

[30] Catullus the scholar-poet and Catullus the edgy urban contender sit uneasily together as personae. The tension between them may be a designed literary effect: see Nisbet 2007a: 548.

However, the structure of ancient Greek books of epigram may also reflect use at symposia beyond the charmed circle of the Ptolemies. 'Capping' was collaborative as well as competitive: each contribution was meant to respond to the one that preceded it. Ordinary symposiasts knew that they were not Callimachus; prior reading of epigram books arranged by category could have helped them recall to mind suitable poems that matched the theme of the moment. Fragmentary copies of books of epigram on papyrus from the rubbish dumps of the Greco-Roman city of Oxyrhynchus in Egypt in the first few centuries CE are comparatively low end in their production values, perhaps suggesting that epigram (and particularly skoptic epigram) was becoming accessible to a wider demographic than was true for more traditional literary genres.[31]

Greek epigram in this more inclusive Greco-Roman milieu was certainly not highbrow – Plutarch's *Table-Talk*, a compendium of elite sympotic lore, disdains to acknowledge its existence – but this will have made it all the more attractive to many of its consumers. Their idea of a good symposium excluded high-end intellectuals as dull and pretentious. This parody of a dinner-invitation goes to a guest with a Roman name:

You know the rule that governs my little dinner. Today, Aulus, I invite you under new precepts for the symposium. No lyric poets at my table – and no starting (or putting up with) literary criticism.[32]

## Greek epigram now

The discovery of epigrams and related material on papyri from Oxyrhynchus set the stage for exciting developments in modern epigram studies. Over the twentieth century, a succession of minor finds suggestively mapped out the uses of Greek epigram in the life of a provincial city.[33] In one large fragment of the first century CE (P.Oxy.

---

[31] Ibid.: 14–35. For a lively introduction to Oxyrhynchus and its papyri, see Parsons 2007; for specialist discussion, see Bowman et al. 2007. This publishes a centennial exhibition, some exhibits from which may still be viewed online at http://www.papyrology.ox.ac.uk/POxy/VExhibition/exhib_welcome.html (accessed 3 November 2009).

[32] *AP* 11.10 (Lucillius); cf. 11.20 (Antipater of Thessalonica).

[33] For a fuller discussion of the papyrus evidence on epigram, including material from other sites, see Gutzwiller 1998: 20–36; more briefly on Hellenistic anthology-making, see Stephens

LIV 3724), an ancient editor lists the first two or three words of nearly
two hundred epigrams; many of them (but probably not all) are by
the important literary theorist Philodemus of Gadara, a houseguest
of L. Calpurnius Piso Caesoninus in the Bay of Naples a century
earlier, whose poems can be read in a good modern edition.[34] These
'incipits' (beginnings, from the Latin *incipit*, 'it begins') are a common
way of identifying verse literature in antiquity – Homer's epic of war
is as likely to be cited under 'Sing, Goddess, the wrath' as by its title,
*Iliad*. The scholars and booksellers of Oxyrhynchus are sifting and
cataloguing on a large scale. There are occasional ticks in the margin;
whatever the project is (a themed anthology? a collected edition?),
individual poems are being found, identified, and checked. Each tiny
poem is treated as a self-sufficient literary work.

At a more modest level, any literate participant in this culture could
become their own literary garland-maker, sourcing their materials as
and when. One small fragment (P.Oxy. LXVI 4501) carries a complete
epigram, the start of another, and an epigram-sized gap in between,
ready to be filled in from a separate source that the compiler never
managed to acquire (epigram was a 'lossy' genre from the start).
This points to a textual economy of circulation and exchange, and
reminds us that we should see epigram against a wider pattern of
the social uses of literature in Greco-Roman Egypt. Because of its
climate, Egypt is the only imperial province from which such material
survives; it also happened to be the only commercial source of papyrus
in antiquity, but there is no reason to think that its literary culture was
fundamentally different to that of other parts of the empire. Friends
made copies and recommended connections, as in the famous circular
letter from Oxyrhynchus, P.Oxy. XVIII 2912:[35]

I pray that you are in good health, my lord brother... Make copies of Books 6 and 7
of Hypsicrates' *Characters Mocked in Comedy* and send them to me. For Harpocration
says that these volumes are among Polion's books. But it's a fair bet that other people
have them too. He also has epitomes in prose of Thersagoras' *The Myths of Tragedy*...

The consumers of these texts are also keen amateur producers, in a
world without many professional ones; books become a convenient

---

and Obbink 2004: 12–13. Krevans 2007: 132–3 concisely attests the diversity and energy of
ancient collecting practice.

[34] Sider 1997, with a valuable introduction, pointing out among other things that this is the
'Piso' of Cicero's *In Pisonem*.

[35] Recently re-edited by Hatzilambrou 2007.

pretext for social exchange and networking. Strikingly, though, most of the books they are seeking are not canon classics: they are digests and dictionaries. These efficient secondary texts chunk and concentrate *paideia* for busy, real-world readers. As the instantly portable *ne plus ultra* of digested culture, the single epigram epitomizes in microcosm this world of the literary quick fix.

A more recent papyrus discovery is even now fleshing out our understanding of epigram's classic macrocosm – the published book of many epigrams by a single hand, arranged by category. The 'Milan Posidippus' (P. Mil. Vogl. VIII 309) is a nearly complete poetry book of 112 poems, almost certainly all composed by the important Hellenistic author Posidippus of Pella.[36] Recovered from the papier-mâché casing ('cartonnage') of a late second-century-BCE mummy, and published in 2001, the book divides its poems into a series of headed categories. This discovery usefully confirms an already fairly safe working hypothesis of earlier epigram-scholarship: Hellenistic epigrammatists did indeed arrange by category.

More important and exciting is the *range* of categories presented by Posidippus. Their diversity and originality suggest a new understanding of how Hellenistic epigrammatists worked. A decade ago, our picture of the genre in this period was comfortably stable. Much like Caesar's Gaul in *Asterix*, Hellenistic epigram was divided into four parts: erotic, sympotic, dedicatory, and funerary types. These were Meleager's categories, of course, and the early scholarship did not speculate beyond them; by unspoken consent, these were the main and perhaps the *only* types of Hellenistic epigrams.[37] But the Milan Posidippus interleaves traditional dedicatory and funerary categories with unheard-of types. There are epigrams 'upon' bronze statues, but also on tiny gemstones, pushing the fiction of inscriptionality to breaking point; on victories in horse and chariot races, a new subset of dedicatory poem; on people lost at sea in shipwrecks (fictional epitaphs for empty tombs). Other categories include omens related to birds, and miraculous cures from diseases. Meleager's retrospective selection now appears thin and restrictive.

The Milan papyrus is also beginning to reveal the organizational and thematic subtleties of an original Hellenistic epigram book. The poems interrelate, within and across their categories: names recur, in

---

[36] For token and impressionistic dissent, see Lloyd-Jones 2001.

[37] E.g. Tarán 1979: 3 on her aim of studying examples from 'all four classes of Hellenistic epigrams'.

scenarios that seem to connect into stories; the last word of the final poem in one category seems to suggest the theme of the next. Many poems, such as the impossible inscriptions of the gemstones category, seem in combination to speak figuratively of the epigrammatist's art as a literary miniaturist.[38]

These recent discoveries on papyrus have inspired a new wave of critical thought about epigram among Hellenists; the contributions to recent landmark collections reflect the quality and diversity of the work currently being done.[39] Simultaneously, innovative work by leading Latinists is extricating the scholarship on Martial from its former methodological stasis. Older twentieth-century views on the solitary major Latin epigrammatist had typically been disdainful. Martial was 'a nasty little man', a servile flatterer of despots, only worth reading as a source of picaresque urban colour.[40] His reporting of street-level incident made him appear ideal for padding out school sourcebooks on daily life in ancient Rome, and topographers of the *Urbs* could sieve the corpus for likely-sounding archaeological nuggets; but he was hardly proper literature. Much of this work reflected the sluggish state of play in studies of Roman satire prior to the late 1980s.[41] Martial's rehabilitation began with his identification by the late J. P. Sullivan as an 'Unexpected Classic'; since then, important studies have begun to reveal his sophistication as a literary author and an innovator within his genre, particularly at larger structural levels.[42]

The scope for original research is now wider than ever before. The later Latin epigrammatists of the fourth century await a Sullivan of their own; but the most famous of them, Ausonius, is vigorously defended by recent publications, and post-classical poets of even later centuries are beginning to attract attention. As the romantic cult of originality loses its historic hold over the academy, the skills of these late poets as receivers and transformers of material from the canon are increasingly appreciated.[43] (Perhaps the *Anthology*'s Christian poets,

---

[38] Gutzwiller 2004 offers some striking initial suggestions along these lines.

[39] I have in mind Gutzwiller 2005c and especially Bing and Bruss 2007a.

[40] For 'nasty little Martial', see Highet 1954: 19.

[41] On Martial and the sourcebooks, see Nisbet 2006: 160. The turning point in Anglophone studies of Latin satire is Braund 1989.

[42] For Martial recuperated as a classic, see Sullivan 1991. Examples of recent studies include major articles by Fowler (1995) and Lorenz (2004) and the recent monograph by Fitzgerald (2007).

[43] On Ausonius, see Kay 2001, aiming at quite a wide readership, and the very serious English edition and Oxford Classical Text by Green (1991 and 1999); and cf. provocatively Nugent 1990 on Ausonius and the 'post-modern' poetics of Late Antique epigram. Kay 2006

so breezily dismissed earlier in this very introduction, will be next in line for critical reappraisal.) Inscriptional epigram remains shockingly under-exploited, in part because of difficulties of access that are gradually being solved. Its dissemination is already enabling insights that leap across the boundaries of genre to energize the study of other ancient verse forms, a phenomenon also seen with the publication of the Milan papyrus.[44] The recent scholarship on the genealogy and reception history of the *Anthology* is outstanding, but is surely not the last word on those inexhaustible subjects; epigram's place in the classical tradition has some takers, but its uses in reception make for an exciting story that is only now beginning to be written.[45]

Like modern-day Meleagers we pick and choose, making of epigram what we will. This short book is a case in point, and we hope that it will provoke independent exploration of ancient epigram in all its diversity, in the *Anthology* and beyond.

directs attention to the anonymous sixth-century poet of the booklike sequence 78–188 in the miscellany *Anthologia Latina*, placing him in Vandal Carthage; this makes him a contemporary and neighbour of Luxorius, the named poet of *AL* 287–375.

[44] For information on modern collections of inscribed epigram, see Bing and Bruss 2007b: 17–19. Carrying over insights from the Milan roll to Latin lyric, elegy, and epic, see Thomas 2004, and cf. Dinter 2005. On literary response to inscriptional epigram, see e.g. Ramsby 2007 on Roman elegy.

[45] Epigram in the classical tradition can be followed up through Sullivan 1991 and Haynes 2007, both with exhaustive referencing. The closing chapter of the present book develops *an* approach to the study of epigram in reception.

# I THE INSCRIPTIONAL BEGINNINGS OF LITERARY EPIGRAM

O stranger! (we pray thee), tell the Lacedaemonians that we are lying here, having *obeyed* their words.[1]

## Inscribed epigram: voices in a landscape

As was seen in the Introduction, the generic identity of epigram is governed by two senses of the Greek preposition *epi*: an epigram may be physically inscribed 'on' an object, or 'on the subject of' an object (or something else: a person, an event). This chapter is concerned with epigrams physically inscribed on a stone or other object. In spite of the fact that inscribed epigram comes first chronologically (beginning as early as the eighth century BCE), includes some of the most famous lines in Greek literature (such as those above), and numbers famous names such as Simonides among its exponents, it can sometimes be treated as the poor relation of literary epigram, which had its heyday in the Hellenistic period (see Chapter 2). There is a perception that epigram comes into its own once it has 'escaped', as it were, from its stone or other physical medium, and is thus at liberty to use its words to create a virtual object in the reader's mind (or not, as the poet chooses).

There are a number of reasons for this relative neglect. Inscriptional epigrams are for the most part less accessible to modern readers, found in untranslated corpora such as Hansen's two-volume *Carmina Epigraphica Graeca*, and many of them are fragmentary. Also, because the vast majority of them perform one of two basic functions ('funerary', commemorating one or more dead persons, or 'dedicatory', identifying an object as an offering to a god), they

---

[1] 'Simonides' 22b *FGE*, trans. John Ruskin. The Spartans' epitaph at Thermopylae had a powerful grip on Ruskin's imagination; he refers to it repeatedly and, in one much-quoted passage, describes it as 'the noblest group of words ever, so far as I know, uttered by simple man concerning his practice': Ruskin 1860: 172. The emphasis on the word 'obeyed' is Ruskin's.

are inevitably repetitious and to some extent formulaic. On the other hand, one of the consequences of this dependence on formulae is that even the smallest variations may be significant, and one of the most interesting qualities of inscribed epigram is precisely its place on a physical surface and (usually) within a landscape. While recent years have seen a marked increase in scholarly attention to inscribed epigram, there is much work still to be done.[2]

Epigrams form only a tiny proportion of the mass of inscribed text that characterized the townscape of a city such as Athens in the time of the democracy;[3] however, whereas non-verse inscriptions, such as decrees or tribute lists, are mostly characterized by impersonal recording of what has happened or been decided, inscribed epigrams regularly emphasize the creation of a voice, or voices, in the landscape: they vaunt their ability to make stones speak.[4] They do this by devices such as first-person speech, deictic words (words that point to the object: 'this is...'), and second-person address to the reader. This conjuring of the voice is particularly poignant in the case of funerary epigrams, which is probably why they have been the focus of much scholarship on inscribed epigram.[5]

The first two devices are well illustrated in a very simple epitaph of the early fifth century BCE, from the plain of Marathon (*CEG* 72 = IG I³ 1260), consisting of a single hexameter line:

σε̂μα τόδ' εἰμὶ Κρίτ|ο Τελέφο Ἀφι|[δναίο].[6]

[that is, σῆμα τόδ' εἰμὶ Κρίτου Τελέφου Ἀφιδναίου].

---

[2] Andrei Petrovic puts it more strongly: 'In spite of the fact that the relevant epigrams are now easily accessible due to the appearance of...*CEG*...it would, perhaps, still be fair to say that epigram's pre-Hellenistic history is today not much better known than when Richard Reitzenstein wrote *Epigramm und Skolion* in 1893' (Petrovic 2007a: 67–8). Baumbach, Petrovic, and Petrovic (in press) is eagerly awaited at the time of writing.

[3] Eight per cent in the fifth century BCE and four per cent in the fourth, according to Bing and Bruss 2007b: 3.

[4] For a detailed survey of the different voices in which inscribed epigrams speak, their different addressees, and the conventions they observe, see Tueller 2008: 12–56.

[5] See especially Bruss 2005, and now also Tsagalis 2008, focusing on fourth-century funerary epigrams and in particular on their 'gnomic' (proverbial) quality.

[6] I follow Hansen's transcriptional conventions in *CEG*, adding diacritics but retaining letter-forms that approximate to those of the original; for convenience, I also provide a version in the more familiar Ionic alphabet of inscriptions cited in the main text (not in footnotes). In transcriptions, square brackets [] surround letters lost from the original and supplied by modern editors, and curly brackets {} surround letters that are present in the original but that modern editors believe to have been inscribed in error.

I am this grave-marker [*sêma*] here of Critus, [son] of Telephus, of [the deme] Aphidnae.[7]

The words cause the monument not merely to speak, but to display self-consciousness and a sense of particularity ('I am *this* grave-marker...'): the inscription tells us that the role of the stone is to point to the invisible deceased,[8] and the specific identity that the epigram gives to the stone ensures that the deceased man has a continuing and particularized presence in the world of the living.

A sixth-century Athenian epitaph (*CEG* 28 = IG I³ 1204; this time an elegiac couplet – that is, a hexameter followed by a pentameter, the metrical form that will become standard for epitaphs in the fifth century and set the norm for later epigram) illustrates the third device, where the stone addresses the passer-by directly, here in a peremptory tone:

> ἄνθροπε hοστείχε[ι]ς καθ' ὁδὸν φρασὶν ἄλα μενοινῶν,
> στêθι καὶ οἴκτιρον σêμα Θράσονος ἰδόν.

> [that is, ἄνθρωπε ὃς στείχεις καθ' ὁδὸν φρασὶν ἄλλα μενοινῶν,
> στῆθι καὶ οἴκτιρον σῆμα Θράσωνος ἰδών.]

> You there, who are walking along the road with other things on your mind,
> Stand still, and pity, as you see the marker of Thrason.

The words on the stone (whose speaker is, in this case, unspecified: the marker, or Thrason himself?) both enact its function and prescribe how that function is to be performed.[9] They demand the attention of the

---

[7] Following the text of *CEG*, with Bruss 2005: 11 n. 53; Κρίτου Τελέφου is unusual for 'Critus son of Telephus' (we would expect e.g. Κρίτου τοῦ Τελέφου); it has been suggested that the adjective κριτὸν should be read: 'I am this chosen marker for Telephus of Aphidnae' (Daux 1975: 149). Svenbro 1993: 32 translates σῆμα τόδ' εἰμὶ (the words I have rendered literally 'I am this grave-marker') as 'Here I am, the tomb'.

[8] The word *sêma* (whose general meaning is 'sign', hence the English words semantics and semiotics) is frequently used in reference to burial places, and can be translated 'tomb'; I use 'grave-marker' in order to keep in mind the implication of *pointing* to something else, and the connection with the verb *sêmainô* – 'show by signs', 'point out', 'indicate'.

[9] In early funerary epigrams the voice is usually either that of the monument ('I am the marker of X', as in Kritos' epitaph) or an unlocated voice ('this is the marker of X', as in Thrason's). Less commonly it is the dead person her/himself, as in *CEG* 80 = IG I³ 1503 (Aegina, early to mid-fifth century): χαίρετε οἱ παριόντες· ἐγὼ δὲ Ἀντιστάτες hυὸς Ἀτάρβο / κεῖμαι τêιδε θανὸν πατρίδα γêν προλιπόν ('I wish you well, passers-by: but I, Antistates, son of Atarbos, lie here having died and left my native land behind'); or, more elaborately (with the voice of the dead man 'quoting' the voice of the stone), *CEG* 108 = IG XII, 9 285 (found at Eretria in Euboea, mid-fifth century): χαίρετε τοὶ παριόντες· ἐγὼ δὲ θανὸν κατάκειμαι. / δεῦρο ἰὸν ἀνάνεμαι, ἀνὲρ τίς τêδε τέθαπται· / ξêνος ἀπ' Αἰγίνες, Μνεσίθεος δ' ὄνυμα· / καί μοι μνêμ' ἐπέθεκε

passer-by (however preoccupied with other thoughts); paradoxically, of course, because the demand will only be 'heard' by someone who has already stopped to read it, but we can see a correspondence with the role of the physical writing itself in drawing attention to the stone and arousing curiosity.[10] It goes on to instruct the reader as to where the marker 'points', namely to the deceased Thrason, and as to the behaviour towards him that custom demands, namely the expression of pity. Thus, even a very simple inscription can provide a kind of script for performance spatially focussed on the grave-marker, and define the space around the tomb as a place for enduring commemoration of the deceased, in action as well as words.

A dedicatory epigram from the base of a bronze statuette (*CEG* 286 = IG I³ 1204, early fifth century BCE) similarly dramatizes the encounter between object and reader:

πᾶσιν ἴσ' ἀνθρόποις hυποκρίνομαι hόστις ἐ[ρ]οτᾶι
hός μ' ἀνέθεκ' ἀνδρόν· Ἀντιφάνες δεκάτεν.

[that is, πᾶσιν ἴσ' ἀνθρώποις ὑποκρίνομαι ὅστις ἐρωτᾷ
ὅς μ' ἀνέθηκ' ἀνδρῶν· Ἀντιφάνης δεκάτην.]

To all people I give the same answer, when someone asks me
What man dedicated me: 'Antiphanes, as a tithe'.

Each encounter between this statuette and a reader is a question-and-answer session, in which Antiphanes' act of piety is rehearsed over and over again. In a discussion of this inscription, Jesper Svenbro draws attention to the cultural associations of the verb *hupokrinomai*, which I have translated above as 'I give...answer'. This verb was also used of providing interpretations of enigmatic phenomena, such as omens, as well as being the verb that came to be used for acting in a play, the profession of the *hupokritês*, 'actor' – possibly, as George Thomson suggested, because the actor began as someone who stepped forward

φίλε μέτερ Τιμαρέτε / τύμοι ἐπ' ἀκροτάτοι στέλεν ἀκάματον, / hάτις ἐρεῖ παριôσι διαμερὲς ἄματα παντα· / Τιμαρέτε μ' ἔσστεσε φίλοι ἐπὶ παιδὶ θανόντι ('I wish you well, passers-by: but I died, and lie here. Come here, and read what man is buried here: a foreigner, from Aegina, and my name is Mnesitheos. My mother, Timarete, placed a memorial over me, on the top of my tomb, a tireless stele that unceasingly for all time will say to passers-by, "Timarete set me up over her dear son when he died."') On the range of voice possibilities, see further Sourvinou-Inwood 1995: 279–83; also 180–216 on the significance of *khaire(te)* 'I wish you well' (211–15 on Mnesitheos' inscription).

[10] 'The communication of the σῆμα is thus rooted in visual contact... The verbal and visual message of the grave complex is imagined as initiating physical and psychological change in the reader' (Derderian 2001: 73).

from a chorus to explain (interpret) for the audience the mythological story on which the performance was based, and later came to provide this 'interpretation' by impersonating characters in that story. Thus the statuette with its inscription is a speaking object: an enigma that interprets itself; or a self-contained performance.[11]

We may compare this with an even earlier dedication, the famous Mantiklos statuette (*CEG* 326). This bronze figure of a young man, from Boeotia and dating from the early seventh century BCE, bears the following inscription:

> Μάντικλός μ' ἀνέθεκε ϝεκαβόλοι ἀργυροτόξσοι
> τᾶς {δ}δεκάτας· τὺ δέ, Φοῖβε, δίδοι χαρίϝετταν ἀμοιβ[άν].

[that is, standardizing the letter-forms but retaining the dialect of the original:
> Μάντικλός μ' ἀνέθηκε ϝεκαβόλῳ ἀργυροτόξῳ
> τᾶς δεκάτας: τὺ δέ, Φοῖβε, δίδοι χαρίϝετταν ἀμοιβάν.]

Mantiklos dedicated me to the far-shooting god of the silver bow
As a tithe: and you, Phoebus, grant a pleasing reward.

Every reader of the epigram recreates Mantiklos' act of dedication and repeats his prayer to the god for a 'pleasing reward'.[12] Inscribed epigrams such as these, which draw the reader into a performance, anticipate the elaborate and playful dialogues developed by authors of Hellenistic literary epigram, which we will encounter in the next chapter.

## Hearing voices: readers of inscribed epigrams

It has been assumed so far that epigrams were inscribed on stones and other objects in ancient Greece with the intention, and in the expectation, that they would be read, probably aloud,[13] and thus give a

---

[11] Svenbro 1993: 171–4, quoting Thomson 1941: 183. I am less convinced by Svenbro's further suggestion that, by making the performance self-contained, the use of the verb *hupokrinomai* here specifically presupposes a scenario of *silent* reading.

[12] See Day 1994: 39–43 and 56; Day 2000: 42–54. On the Mantiklos inscription see also e.g. B. Powell 1991: 167–9; Henrichs 2003: 48. For an inscription that draws the reader into a more strenuous and solemn performance, see Day 2007: 39–40 on the Ambracia cenotaph.

[13] On reading aloud as the norm, see e.g. Knox 1968, Svenbro 1993: 18, Day 2007: 32. Gavrilov 1997 presents evidence that silent reading was much less unusual in antiquity than has often been assumed, and makes the important point that, in order to read aloud effectively from any text (and *a fortiori* from an ancient inscribed text lacking punctuation or word divisions), it is necessary to acquire the technique of scanning ahead, in effect of reading silently.

lasting presence in the world to people and events that might otherwise be forgotten.[14] In the case of monuments for the dead, an inscription turns a grave-marker (Greek σῆμα, *sêma*) into a memorial (μνῆμα, *mnêma*).[15] The assumption seems natural, but is not inevitable; there are examples of inscriptions that clearly were *not* meant to be read, at least not by human eyes;[16] and it has been argued that classical city-states created public inscribed texts (laws, decrees, and the like) primarily for symbolic, rather than practical, purposes.[17] There is also, of course, the question of what proportion of passers-by had the literacy (and leisure) required in order to obey a grave monument's demand to be read, the answer to which is the subject of much debate, and certainly varied a great deal from place to place and from time to time.[18] Recent scholarship has, however, emphasized the importance of the *implied* reader in inscribed epigram, arguing in effect that inscriptions demand so insistently to be read that it is culturally paradoxical to suppose that they were not.

One particularly influential study, by Jesper Svenbro (1993), takes as its starting point a single famous monument: the Phrasikleia kore. This statue of a girl, from the mid-sixth century BCE, was excavated in Attica, in what was the ancient rural deme of Myrrhinous, in 1972.[19] The girl to whom the statue was dedicated came from an aristocratic family (Svenbro suggests that she may have belonged to the family of the Alcmeonidae, which later produced Pericles); and the figure

---

[14] For a radically sceptical view of the extent to which inscribed epigrams actually *were* read, see Bing 2002. Bing points out that ancient texts contain surprisingly few descriptions of inscribed texts being read, and argues that modern scholars assume they were read (a) because, as has been seen, the epigrams frequently anticipate their encounter with a reader (an anticipation that need not correspond to reality) and (b) because, as habitual readers themselves, scholars cannot imagine that passers-by would *not* have been moved by curiosity to read inscriptions. As we will see, the expectation voiced in the inscriptions themselves, and the clear assumption of ancient writers from Herodotus onward that inscribed epigrams are significant and interesting, weighs heavily on the other side. Bing's argument depends on strained or one-sided interpretation of the evidence. For inscribed epigram as a form of writing that invites and presupposes the act of reading (both of which, it must be admitted, are perfectly compatible with *not* being read in practice), see Day 2007: 32 with n. 16. On the influence of inscriptional epigram on later literary epigram (which obviously presupposes at least *some* reading), see Fantuzzi 2004b: 283–91 and Bettenworth 2007; also Meyer 2007 on the relationship between epigram and reader in the Hellenistic period.

[15] On *sêma* and *mnêma*, see further Sourvinou-Inwood 1995: 140–9 and Bruss 2005: 23–34.

[16] See Bodel 2001: 19–24 for a brief account of such 'symbolic epigraphy'.

[17] For a balanced and accessible overview, with suggestions for further reading, see Sickinger 2007.

[18] The literature is extensive; see e.g. Harris 1989, Thomas 1992.

[19] See Svenbro 1993, especially 8–25; and, for further interpretation of the statue, as well as its inscription, Hurwit 2007.

appears to have been buried not long after being erected, perhaps to protect it from being damaged by enemies. Its base, which was already known before the excavation of the statue itself, is signed by the sculptor ('Aristion of Paros made me') and bears the following epigram (*CEG* 24 = IG I³ 1261):

σῆμα Φρασικλείας. κόρε κεκλέσομαι αἰεί,
ἀντὶ γάμο παρὰ θεὸν τοῦτο λαχôσ' ὄνομα.

[that is, σῆμα Φρασικλείας. κούρη κεκλήσομαι αἰεί,
ἀντὶ γάμου παρὰ θεῶν τοῦτο λαχοῦσ' ὄνομα.]

*sêma Phrasikleias. kourê keklêsomai aiei,
anti gamou para theôn touto lakhous' onoma.*

Grave-marker of Phrasikleia. I shall be called a girl [*korê*] always,
Instead of marriage receiving this name from the gods.[20]

As Svenbro demonstrates, Phrasikleia's name is loaded with significance: a fact which the author of her epitaph has exploited to the full. The second element, derived from *kleos* ('fame', 'glory'), is what encourages Svenbro to identify her as an Alcmeonid, since *kleos* is recurrent in Alcmeonid names: Megacles and Cleisthenes as well as Pericles.[21] Of course, *kleos* in a woman's name has different connotations than in a man's name, suggesting good repute, especially for chastity, rather than renown for bravery in battle. The first element, *Phrasi-*, can be interpreted in several ways. It matches one form of the dative of *phrenes* ('mind', 'thoughts') – φρασί(ν), a word we have encountered in *CEG* 28 above – giving 'she who is famous for her thoughts/good sense' (compare Penelope's epithet *periphrôn*, 'very thoughtful', in the *Odyssey*). On the other hand, it may also be derived either from the active verb *phrazô* ('I indicate', 'I point out'), giving something like 'she who indicates *kleos*', or from the middle voice of the same verb, *phrazomai* ('I indicate to myself'), hence 'I take thought for/am mindful of', giving 'she who is mindful of *kleos*'. By analogy with other Attic girls' names in which the suffix *-kleia* is combined with an initial

---

[20] I follow Hansen in *CEG* in punctuating after 'Phrasikleia': on this reading, the first two words simply mark the *sêma*; then the feminine nominative *kourê* introduces the speaking 'voice' of Phrasikleia. Svenbro prefers to read the epigram as a single continuous sentence: 'I, Phrasikleia's *sêma*, shall always be called...'. On the complexities of the relationship between the poem's neuter subject (the *sêma*) and its feminine subject (Phrasikleia), see further Tueller 2008: 160–1, with references to other scholars' views.

[21] Svenbro 1993: 13.

verbal element (Dexikleia, Mnesikleia, Sosikleia), Svenbro argues that the verbal derivation of *Phrasi-*, from *phrazô/phrazomai*, is likely to be uppermost; so the primary significance of her name is, in his formulation, a combination of 'she who draws attention to *kleos*' and 'she who pays attention to *kleos*'.[22] He notes further that the verb *phrazô* is used in particular of articulating or drawing attention to something *silently*, without speaking.[23] *Kleos*, by contrast, is an inherently vocal phenomenon, something which is spoken aloud, sung, or heard.[24]

Thus the first two words of Phrasikleia's epigram exploit a tension inherent in her name to reveal her as someone particularly appropriate for, and deserving of, commemoration by a funerary epigram: she is someone who *silently* draws attention to her *spoken* good repute. It is also by her modest silence – a virtue in life, now perpetuated by death and by representation in stone – that she takes heed of, and preserves, her good repute. Phrasikleia herself is silent, even as she speaks to us;[25] it is up to the viewer to furnish her with her *kleos* by reading the epigram aloud. The point is reinforced by the alliteration of *-k-* in the following words, *kourê keklêsomai* ('I shall be called a girl'): in reading this, the viewer announces once again the virginal status that constitutes Phrasikleia's *kleos*, and that is the (only) compensation the gods have given her for the fulfilment in marriage that she never achieved. Just as Achilles in the *Iliad* is offered *kleos* in place of his safe return from Troy (9.413), so Phrasikleia will receive the good repute that her name signals in place of her marriage; and *keklêsomai aiei* ('I shall *always* be called...') underlines the role of the reader in ensuring that her *kleos*, like Achilles', will be *aphthiton* ('unperishing').[26]

The iconography of the statue echoes the message of the poem. The girl holds in her left hand a closed lotus bud, and wears a crown in

[22] Ibid: 14.

[23] Ibid: 15–16, citing, among other examples, Clytemnestra's instruction to Cassandra at Aesc. *Ag.* 1061: 'instead of speaking, make signs [*phraze*] with your foreign hand'.

[24] Cf. e.g. Hom. *Il.* 2.486, 9.189; Hom. *Od.* 8.73. Hence the paradox in the notorious pronouncement of Thucydides' Pericles in his funeral speech, that the best reputation (*doxa*) for women is to have the least fame (*kleos*), i.e. to be least spoken of, among men.

[25] See Day 1989: 26: 'Readers play the role of Phrasikleia, brought to life in the kore that seems to utter her own lament and eulogy.' Derderian 2001: 80 points out that, while the prose attribution inscription ('Aristion of Paros made me') indicates the speech of the monument, the epigram itself hovers between suggesting the speech of the monument and the speech of the dead Phrasikleia herself: it 'could either reflect the speech of the kore-statue mounted at the site, Phrasikleia as a continual kore in death, or a joint entity in which the speaking kore-statue is viewed as the embodiment of the dead Phrasikleia'.

[26] Svenbro 1993: 23 n. 69. On the deep roots of the notion of *kleos aphthiton*, possibly going back to a pre-Greek Indo-European poetic tradition, see Katz 2005: 25–6 (with references to earlier literature).

which lotus buds alternate with opening flowers: Phrasikleia has died on the verge of the full maturity represented by marriage, but without attaining it.[27] There is a clear accumulation of correspondence between Phrasikleia's death on the verge of marriage, her silent testimony to her spoken reputation, and the silent witness of the written text, which requires the reader's voice to actualize it in speech.[28]

Apart from internal evidence suggesting that inscribed epigrams *demanded* to be read, our first evidence that they were indeed read consists in their being quoted by ancient authors in the context of larger texts, such as the histories of Herodotus and Thucydides. We will now examine the testimony of these early readers and collectors of epigram.

### The first epigraphers: epigrams in history and history in epigrams

I have already observed that inscribed epigram is less accessible today than literary epigram, and the same was true in antiquity: inscriptions were scattered over the Greek world, and tended in the course of time to be damaged, buried, or obscured through incorporation into later structures. It was therefore an important development when inscribed epigrams started to be incorporated into literary texts, thus assisting their dissemination and their survival. It seems likely that the historians' practice of citing epigrams to support or illustrate historical points provided the catalyst for the creation of collections of inscribed epigrams as objects of interest in their own right; this opened the way (if it was not open already) for the 'forgery' of inscribed epigrams – to serve, for example, the interests of historical or rhetorical controversy

---

[27] On the Phrasikleia *korē*'s iconography, see further Sourvinou-Inwood 1995: 249–50; and on the treament of the theme of death before marriage in ancient epitaphs, see Lattimore 1962: 192–4.

[28] See Hurwit 2007: 266–7, and Svenbro 1993: 19–25, pursuing the symbolism further: Svenbro sees Phrasikleia as an analogue of the goddess Hestia, another *kourē* granted eternal virginity in place of marriage (*Homeric Hymn to Aphrodite* 29), and the lotus-flower, said to open at sunrise and close at sunset, as a symbol of the hearth-fire that Phrasikleia kept alight. In its thematic connections between poem and iconography, and its evocation of the boundary between speech and silence, the Phrasikleia monument anticipates the later tradition of ecphrastic epigram (poems describing [often imaginary] works of visual art, such as those on Myron's *Cow* already encountered in the Introduction), in which the opposition of voice and voicelessness is an important theme: see Männlein-Robert 2007.

– and thus in turn for the composition of epigrams as an autonomous literary activity.

As has been seen, inscribed epigrams are rooted in a landscape, and part of their function is to direct and control the reader's attention to a monument or object. Thus to remove them from this landscape and incorporate them into a text is to deprive them of part of their frame of reference. The author quoting them then has the opportunity to provide them with a new context. Once epigrams started to be composed with literary dissemination in view, and the idea of a preceding inscribed epigram became at most conventional, it became one of the functions of the epigram itself to define its context and frame of reference: as we will see in the next chapter, the creation of virtual landscapes and scenarios is one of the joys of the Hellenistic literary epigram.

Herodotus reports eight inscribed epigrams in total. The first is a poem that accompanied the dedication by Mandrocles of Samos (the builder for King Darius of Persia of a bridge across the Bosporus to facilitate the invasion of Scythia) of a picture, illustrating his achievement, that he placed in the temple of Hera (4.88 = 'Simonides' 4 *FGE*).[29] This is followed by a group of three dedicatory inscriptions that Herodotus says he has seen, written in what he calls 'Cadmean letters', on three tripods in the temple of Apollo Ismenios in Thebes (5.59–61). He adduces them here in support of a theory of his about the origins of the Greek alphabet. Herodotus rightly believes the alphabet to have been borrowed from the Phoenicians, but takes this borrowing back to an impossibly early date, associating it with Cadmus, the mythological King of Thebes (and ancestor of Oedipus), who is said in some stories to have come from Phoenicia to Greece. Two of the dedications as quoted by Herodotus clearly purport to have been made by mythical heroes (Amphitryon and Laodamas), and Herodotus interprets the third – a dedication to Apollo by a certain Skaios, who has won a boxing match – as belonging to the same period of the (mythic) past. It is clearly the case that the tripods either did not exist or were forgeries. A further problem is that Herodotus claims, as one of the details of his argument (5.59), to have detected a notable

[29] As will be seen shortly, the use of the name 'Simonides' in inverted commas here (corresponding to one of the headings in *FGE*) reflects a habit, both in antiquity and among modern scholars, of collecting early epigrams, particularly those on historical subjects, under the name of Simonides (of Ceos, lived *c*.557/6–468/7 BCE). As I will show, however, in discussion of the *Sylloge Simonidea* below, pp. 45–7, how many of these epigrams can in fact plausibly be attributed to Simonides is a matter of vigorous ongoing scholarly debate.

resemblance between this 'Cadmean' script and the Ionian alphabet, a claim that is very hard to make sense of given what we know about early Boeotian script.[30] Scholars have approached this problem in various ways;[31] what we can clearly conclude is that epigram's transition from inscriptional to literary contexts is already accompanied here by a certain fluidity in the relationship between poems and actual events (though this fluidity doubtless existed earlier). Epigrams can readily be adapted, selected, presented out of context, or even invented, to prove a point.

The next Herodotean epigram, from a dedication on the Athenian Acropolis,[32] commemorates a victory of the Athenians over Boeotian and Euboean enemies in 507/6 BCE. As quoted by Herodotus, it runs as follows (5.77, cf. 'Simonides' 3 *FGE*, IG I³ 501 A + B, on which see below, p. 33; *AP* 6.343; M.-L. 15):

> ἔθνεα Βοιωτῶν καὶ Χαλκιδέων δαμάσαντες
> παῖδες Ἀθηναίων ἔργμασιν ἐν πολέμου
> δεσμῷ ἐν ἀχνυοέντι[33] σιδηρέῳ ἔσβεσαν ὕβριν·
> τῶν ἵππους δεκάτην Παλλάδι τάσδ' ἔθεσαν.

When they had overcome the peoples of Boeotia and Chalcis,[34]
The children of Athens, in the work of war,
Quenched their hubris with painful chains of iron:
From this, they dedicated these horses, to Pallas, as a tithe.

The monument commemorates an occasion when Athens, not long since liberated from the regime of the Peisistratid 'tyrants', faced an existential threat: simultaneous invasions by enemies from the Peloponnese, Boeotia, and Euboea. Herodotus describes how the

---

[30] West 1985: 292–3.

[31] Ibid.: 294–5 speaks of 'wishful thinking' and 'ingenious but ill-founded speculation' on Herodotus' part; she casts doubt on his claim of autopsy, and hints, without quite saying so, that we may be dealing with a pure invention on his part. Day, on the other hand, suggests a more innocent explanation: '[p]erhaps early in the sixth century, the local authorities inscribed them [i.e. the tripods], probably as labels to explain an oral tradition' (Day 1994: 40). Powell, whose book provides a useful account of what we know about the real origins of the Greek alphabet, simply describes the inscriptions as 'forgeries' (B. Powell 1991: 6 n. 7).

[32] The exact location has long been considered problematic, because of an apparent discrepancy between Herodotus' description and that of Pausanias (1.28.2); see e.g. M.-L., p. 29, and West 1985: 284–5. Petrovic 2007b: 213 argues that this concern is based on a misunderstanding of Pausanias' text, and that the two accounts are in fact consistent.

[33] The text here is problematic. The word does not survive on either of the two stones; the manuscript traditions offer ἀχνυ(ν)θέντι or ἀχλυοέντι. I follow Page (*FGE*) in adopting Hecker's emendation ἀχνυοέντι. See most recently Petrovic 2007b: 214–15 and Kaczko 2009: 113 n. 69.

[34] Chalcis was an important city-state on the island of Euboea.

Peloponnesian threat faded as a result of internal divisions, while the Athenians went on to defeat first the Boeotians and then the Euboeans on the same day, taking many prisoners. The prisoners were held in chains until ransomed (Herodotus 5.74–7). Once the ransom moneys had been paid, the Athenians marked both the acuteness of the threat and the completeness of their revenge by dedicating a striking monument on the Acropolis, consisting of the chains in which the prisoners had been held, a bronze chariot dedicated to Athena as a tithe of the ransom, and a dedicatory epigram.

The epigram is unusual because, for once, we are able to compare the text as reported by Herodotus with the text as it appeared on the actual stone – or rather stones, because fragments have been found of not one but two monument bases from the Acropolis, both inscribed with badly damaged, but still clearly identifiable, remnants of this epigram (IG I³ 501 A and B).[35] As it turns out, these stones tell a rather interesting story. From the letter-forms used on them, one can be dated to the late sixth century, and is thus likely to be the original, while the other belongs to the middle of the fifth century. The obvious inference is that the original monument was destroyed when the Persians sacked Athens but was then replaced sometime in the fifth century (Herodotus comments that, in his day, the actual chains were still there, but hung on walls 'scorched with fire by the Mede' [5.77.4][36]). The fragments of the fifth-century base match Herodotus' text; those of the older base, on the other hand, reveal a significant difference. They make it clear that the first and third lines were originally the other way round:[37]

δεσμῷ ἐν ἀχνυοέντι σιδηρέῳ ἔσβεσαν ὕβριν
παῖδες Ἀθηναίων ἔργμασιν ἐν πολέμου
ἔθνεα Βοιωτῶν καὶ Χαλκιδέων δαμάσαντες·
τῶν ἵππους δεκάτην Παλλάδι τάσδ' ἔθεσαν.

---

[35] On the few but interesting cases where we are able to compare inscribed and manuscript versions of the same epigram, see Kaczko 2009 (112–14 on this epigram in particular).

[36] Presumably Herodotus had seen this for himself. The truth status of Herodotus' claims to autopsy, that is, to be a first-hand witness to scenes that he describes, is notoriously controversial, but it seems fairly certain that, wherever else he did not visit, he did go to Athens – and is thus very likely to have examined monuments on the Acropolis. See further West 1985: 284.

[37] *Pace* Erbse 1998: 225, who suggests that Simonides originally wrote the epigram in the form in which it appears on the later stone; that the Athenians themselves, in the heat of their indignation, reordered the lines for a more pointed effect; and that the 'correct' order, having become known after Simonides' death, was therefore used on the new monument. The hypothesis seems unnecessarily elaborate, and is, as Erbse acknowledges, undemonstrable.

With painful chains of iron they quenched hubris,
The children of Athens, in the work of war,
When they had overcome the peoples of Boeotia and Chalcis:
From whom they dedicated these horses, to Pallas, as a tithe.

In a sense, the change of order makes no difference to the meaning of
the epigram: the information conveyed is the same either way. It could
be seen simply as illustrating the pliability of epigram as a genre, the
way these small poems lend themselves to being manipulated and
playfully adapted – a quality that we will see exploited to the full in
the Hellenistic period. In another sense, however, it makes a crucial
difference both to the emphasis of the poem and to the inscription's
relationship with the reader, and with its physical setting.

In the Greek of the original version, the first line is framed by
the words 'chains...hubris'. The first word points to the unusual
neighbouring presence of the chains themselves: a reminder of the
physical reality both of the threat to the city and of the retribution
visited by Athens on her enemies. The tone is righteously indignant,
and moralizing: the punishment of this particular act of hubris stands
for the punishment to be expected by hubris in general, and the defeat
of these enemies is cast as the defeat of a sinister abstract force.[38]

In the revised version, on the other hand, the 'headline' of the
inscription has changed: the chains (transformed by fire, no longer
having any immediate significance for a fifth-century reader and
perhaps no longer adjacent to the monument in any case) lose their
prominence, and the primary point is no longer indignation at the
violent presumption of the invaders. The reordering reinterprets the
monument as an enduring symbol of the Athenians' natural propensity
to triumph over their enemies.[39] The question presumed to be in the
reader's mind is not 'what is the significance of these chains?' but
rather 'which enemies did we defeat this time?', and the epigram gives
the answer: the Boeotians and Euboeans.[40] The verses now move along

---

[38] In view of the frequency of the motif of binding Titans and other gigantic opponents of the
Olympian gods in the *Theogony*, it is tempting to see this epigram as casting Athens' victory over
these invaders as a kind of Titanomachy, one of the emblematic victories of order over chaos
(see e.g. Hes. *Th.* 664–722 (esp. 718–9 δεσμοῖσιν ἐν ἀργαλέοισιν ἔδησαν...ὑπερθύμους περ ἐόντας,
'they bound them in hurtful chains...high-spirited though they were').

[39] I believe that the renewed and revised significance given to the inscription by this reordering
is independent of the question whether the rededication was associated with some particular
historical event, e.g. the Athenian victory over a Boeotian army at Oinophyta in 457/6 (Thuc.
1.108.3); on this and other theories, see Petrovic 2007b: 213–14.

[40] Similarly Kaczko 2009: 114: 'It is likely that...the sequence of the lines was altered because
now the focus was on the supremacy gained by the Athenians upon some of their major Greek
enemies'.

a trajectory from the concrete to the abstract, and from the particular to the universal: instead of some chains leading to a ransom leading to a statue, the reader is made to think of (yet another) Athenian victory leading, naturally, to an appropriately grand and pious dedication to Athena: business as usual, and as it must go on. This inscription thus provides a striking example of the adaptability of epigram and its capacity, even in its inscribed form, to be reused to fit new occasions and new contexts.

Herodotus' final series of epigrams is by far the most famous: the dedications at the battlefield of Thermopylae. After his account of the battle, Herodotus presents a series of different kinds of memorials to those who fought there. First there is the stone lion commemorating Leonidas (7.225), an iconographic representation both of his courage and of his name (*leôn* being the Greek for 'lion').[41] Then there is the oral tradition (its orality underlined by the words *legetai...phasi...phasi*, 'it is said...they say...they say') concerning the wit and bravery of the Spartan Dienekes: when it was reported that the enemy were so numerous that their arrows would block out the sun, he replied that this was good news, since the battle would be fought in the shade (7.226); Dienekes left this and other similar sayings as his 'memorials' (*mnêmosyna*). Finally, there are the written words (again, Herodotus emphasizes the medium, here by repeated use of the verb *epigraphô* and the noun *epigramma*) of the inscribed epigrams (7.228; 'Simonides' 22a *FGE* = *AP* 7.248, 22b *FGE* = *AP* 7.249, and 6 *FGE* = *AP* 7.677):

Θαφθεῖσι δέ σφι αὐτοῦ ταύτῃ τῇ περ ἔπεσον καὶ τοῖσι πρότερον τελευτήσασι ἢ <τοὺς> ὑπὸ Λεωνίδεω ἀποπεμφθέντας οἴχεσθαι ἐπιγέγραπται γράμματα λέγοντα τάδε·

Μυριάσιν ποτὲ τᾷδε τριακοσίαις ἐμάχοντο
ἐκ Πελοποννάσου χιλιάδες τέτορες.

Ταῦτα μὲν δὴ τοῖσι πᾶσι ἐπιγέγραπται, τοῖσι δὲ Σπαρτιήτῃσι ἰδίῃ·

---

[41] Lions often appeared on collective monuments for the war dead (Fantuzzi and Hunter 2004: 328 n. 152), so the association of this one with Leonidas in particular may simply be Herodotus' interpretation, or that of his informant. On the significance of lions on grave monuments see Sourvinou-Inwood 1995: 256–8 and 271–5 (though Herodotus' words do not, of course, imply that the lion marked Leonidas' actual grave: see Connor 1979: 25 n. 19).

Ὦ ξεῖν', ἀγγέλλειν Λακεδαιμονίοις ὅτι τῇδε
κείμεθα, τοῖς κείνων ῥήμασι πειθόμενοι.[42]

Λακεδαιμονίοισι μὲν δὴ τοῦτο, τῷ δὲ μάντι τόδε·

Μνῆμα τόδε κλεινοῖο Μεγιστία, ὅν ποτε Μῆδοι
Σπερχειὸν ποταμὸν κτεῖναν ἀμειψάμενοι,
μάντιος, ὃς τότε Κῆρας ἐπερχομένας σάφα εἰδὼς
οὐκ ἔτλη Σπάρτης ἡγεμόνα προλιπεῖν.

Ἐπιγράμμασι μέν νυν καὶ στήλῃσι, ἔξω ἢ τὸ τοῦ μάντιος ἐπίγραμμα, Ἀμφικτύονές εἰσί
σφεας οἱ ἐπικοσμήσαντες· τὸ δὲ τοῦ μάντιος Μεγιστίεω Σιμωνίδης ὁ Λεωπρέπεός ἐστι
κατὰ ξεινίην ὁ ἐπιγράψας.

For these men, who were buried in the place where they fell, and for those who died
before the departure of the men sent away by Leonidas, letters have been inscribed that
say the following:

> Here once against three hundred tens of thousands fought
> Four thousands from the Peloponnese.

That has been inscribed for all of them, but for the Spartans in particular:

> Stranger, report to the Lacedaemonians that here
> We lie, obedient to their words.

That is for the Lacedaemonians, but for the seer [Megistias, who foresaw the destruction
of the Greek army but declined Leonidas' invitation to leave it: 7.221] there is the
following:

> This is the monument of famed Megistias, whom once the Medes
> Killed, when they crossed the River Spercheios,
> The seer, who, knowing well the death-spirits [Kêres] were then
> approaching,
> Could not bear to abandon Sparta's chief.

In the case of the inscriptions and the stones, with the exception of the seer's inscription,
it was the Amphictyons [i.e. the members of the Amphictyonic Council that oversaw

---

[42] This is the text quoted by Herodotus. An alternative line-ending, πειθόμενοι νομίμοις
('obeying [their] laws'), transmitted by the orator Lycurgus (fourth century BCE) and by several
other ancient writers who quote these famous lines, is reflected in many modern translations.
Page (*FGE* pp. 233–4) argues for Lycurgus' text on the grounds that it makes better sense and
appears to have been the version familiar in antiquity (cf. e.g. *legibus obsequimur* in Cicero's
translation of the lines at *Tusculans* 1.101); Petrovic 2007b: 249 defends Herodotus' text as the
*lectio difficilior* (more difficult reading).

the sanctuary at Delphi] who gave them these honours; the inscription for the seer Megistias was inscribed by Simonides son of Leoprepes, because they were friends.

This passage is of great interest for many more reasons than that it contains, in the inscription for the Spartan dead, two of the most quoted lines in all of Greek poetry. First, there is the frame within which Herodotus presents these three poems. As has been seen, they form the climax of a triad of memorials to the battle: first the iconic statue, then the orally transmitted story, and finally the inscribed words, a lasting voice capable of telling the visitor to the battlefield directly and authoritatively about what happened there. In fact, however, the words do not 'speak for themselves' but require interpretation and organization by the historian. As presented by Herodotus, they, too, form a neat triad: a general epitaph for the fallen; a special, and specially appropriate, epitaph for the most notable group among the fallen, the Spartans (whose leader, Leonidas, has already been commemorated); and finally an epitaph for a significant individual, who displayed Achillean heroism in his clear-sighted choice of honourable death over obscurity.[43] On closer examination of the poems themselves, however, it immediately becomes clear that they form no such neat pattern. The first poem is plainly not an epitaph but a memorial of the battle, and its reference to 'four thousand from the Peloponnese' commemorates neither *all* those who fell (among whom were Boeotians as well as Peloponnesians) nor *only* those who fell, but rather the entire Peloponnesian contingent, including those whom Leonidas sent away before the final stand. The famous second poem, by contrast, is indeed an epitaph, albeit an epitaph of a rather unusual kind: the dead are barely identified, while the manner of their death (beyond the theme of 'obedience'), the identity of their enemy, and the outcome of the battle are not mentioned at all. The epitaph for Megistias is important above all because of the context Herodotus provides for it in linking it with the name of a poet, and one of the most famous poets of his time, Simonides of Ceos (*c.*555–466 BCE). The particular significance of this will become apparent shortly.

The questions of exactly what monuments were to be found at the battlefield of Thermopylae, what inscriptions they bore, and how

---

[43] See West 1985: 288, who points out (n. 44) that the fortune of Megistias, who sends his son to safety but dies gloriously himself, neatly inverts that of the Homeric seer Merops (Hom. *Il.* 2.831–4 = 11.329–32), who tried unsuccessfully to persuade his sons not to go to their deaths at Troy.

Herodotus acquired his information about them continue to be very vexed. 'Simonides' 23 *FGE* (reported by the geographer Strabo in the first century CE as appearing on 'the first of the five stelae' at Thermopylae, Strabo 9.4.2) is an epitaph for Locrians who died at Thermopylae, though they were not present at the last stand; Philiadas 1 *FGE* commemorates the Thespians, who were; but its connection, if any, with the original dedications is highly uncertain. Scholars have given varied explanations for Herodotus' misleading description of the series of poems he presents. Page comments that 'Herodotus has not stopped to think what he is saying', and attributes the historian's failure to notice the absence of the Thespians from the first poem to the bias of his Spartan sources: 'Herodotus has naively repeated what he was told, not noticing that this inscription is not what he says it is, an epitaph; or that, if it were an epitaph, it could not include, as he says it does, the Thespian dead'.[44] Petrovic, on the other hand, believes he can salvage Herodotus' veracity.[45] He argues that Herodotus does not explicitly call the first poem an epitaph, and that, in the clause 'that has been inscribed for all of them', 'all' should be taken to mean 'all the Peloponnesians', by contrast with the Spartan *homoioi* who are mentioned next; he attributes the disappearance of the Thespians to Spartan influence on the Amphictyons who commissioned the monuments. This interpretation does a certain amount of violence to the text. The passage quoted follows directly on Herodotus' report as to which of the Lacedaemonians *and the Thespians* displayed greatest valour in the combat; the form of words 'for these men, who were buried...letters have been inscribed' (*thaphtheisi sphi...grammata epigegraptai*, more literally 'on/for them having-been-buried...letters have been written') strongly suggests an inscription for a grave; and, if 'all' means 'all the Peloponnesians', this is something that can only become apparent to the reader or hearer in retrospect, having reached the contrasting reference to the *Spartiatai*.

Much more plausible than Page's naïve Herodotus (scholars have become much less inclined to regard Herodotus as a naïve author since *FGE* was published in 1981) or Petrovic's riddling Herodotus is the Herodotus we encounter in Stephanie West's article of 1985: an author who is willing to manipulate epigraphic (and other) material

---

[44] *FGE* pp. 232–3.
[45] Petrovic 2007b: 238–41.

for artistic effect, and who is extremely adept in doing so.[46] But where West's focus as a scholar of ancient historiography is on Herodotus' unscrupulousness (by modern standards) as an epigrapher, from our perspective as we trace the history of epigram, it is possible to see his procedure in a rather different light. Herodotus collects epigrams (whether at first or second hand), selects from them, and arranges them in such a way that they interact with each other and function collectively as an artistic composition greater than the sum of its parts. They invest the dead of Thermopylae with an appropriate heroic grandeur and noble simplicity, while underlining the key themes of impossible odds, collective obedience to authority, and individual self-sacrifice. On a much smaller scale, we may see Herodotus as foreshadowing, and providing an example to, authors of the Hellenistic period and after who collected epigrams and arranged them in poetic 'garlands'.[47]

Herodotus is not the only classical Greek author to record and discuss epigrams. Thucydides, ever more sparing than Herodotus, quotes only three.[48] The first is an inscription that, Thucydides tells us, the Spartan commander Pausanias placed on a dedication at Delphi, thus adding to the Spartan government's suspicions of him by appearing to claim sole credit for victory at Plataea (1.132.2 = 'Simonides' 17a *FGE*). The second, a dedication by the younger Peisistratus (son of Hippias and grandson of the tyrant Peisistratus) commemorating his tenure of the office of archon, is also preserved on stone (6.54.7 = 'Simonides' 27b *FGE* = IG I³ 948 = *CEG* 305 = M.-L. 11); oddities in the letter-forms of the inscription have led to a long-running controversy about its date.[49] Another interesting point is that Thucydides reports this

---

[46] West 1985: 288: '[Page's] view does less than justice to the talent which transmuted a jumble of oral tradition into an episode which, in its appeal to our imagination, rivals Roncevaux and the battle in the West where Arthur fell'. Petrovic 2007a: 57 likewise thinks in terms of a rhetorical strategy on Herodotus' part, but suggests that the mismatch between the poems and their frame, and in particular the unusual failure of Megistias' epitaph to mention his origin (as an Acarnanian, and thus one of those *not* from the Peloponnese who fell at Thermopylae), has the effect of prompting the 'careful reader' to think critically about the roles of different Greek states in the battle and about the reliability of official versions. Clearly it is possible for the passage to be read on a number of levels.

[47] On Herodotus as a creator of 'mini-collections', anticipating Hellenistic practice, see Petrovic 2007a: 56.

[48] See Petrovic 2007a: 53–5 on Thucydides' use of epigrams.

[49] Peisistratus' father, the tyrant Hippias, was expelled from Athens in 511/10 BCE, and there is independent evidence (namely the letters ...στρατ... in an archon list, SEG 10: 352 line 6, see also SEG 21: 96) that Peisistratus may have been archon in 522/1. Some experts argue, however, that the letter-forms are not consistent with such an early date, and would place the inscription

epigram as being written 'in dim letters' (ἀμυδροῖς γράμμασι), whereas modern epigraphists have found the inscribed stone to be very legible. The standard explanation is that the letters were originally painted as well as engraved, and that what struck Thucydides was that the paint had faded;[50] in any case, assuming that the stone Thucydides saw was the same as the one that survives, his remark provides a small piece of evidence that at least one ancient reader had quite high expectations of the legibility of inscribed epigram. Finally, there is an epitaph for another member of the Peisistratid dynasty, the younger Peisistratus' sister Arkhedike (6.59.2 = 'Simonides' 26a *FGE*):

> ἀνδρὸς ἀριστεύσαντος ἐν Ἑλλάδι τῶν ἐφ' ἑαυτοῦ
> Ἱππίου Ἀρχεδίκην ἥδε κέκευθε κόνις,
> ἣ πατρός τε καὶ ἀνδρὸς ἀδελφῶν τ' οὖσα τυράννων
> παίδων τ' οὐκ ἤρθη νοῦν ἐς ἀτασθαλίην.

> Of a man at the forefront of men in Greece of his generation,
>   Of Hippias, this dust conceals the daughter, Arkhedike,
> Who, though her father, husband, and brothers were tyrants,
>   And her sons too, was never roused in mind to wickedness.

This epitaph, the second epigram to be attributed by an ancient source to Simonides,[51] is unusual in that it does not name Arkhedike's husband (identified by Thucydides as Aiantides, son of the tyrant of Lampsacus, Hippoklos), a fact presumably explained by its composer's desire to focus attention on the extraordinary prestige of her father Hippias.[52]

---

in the fifth century. If this is correct, it provides remarkable (some would say unbelievable) evidence that the younger Peisistratus continued to enjoy high esteem at Athens after his family's fall from power. M.-L. support an earlier date; Page (*FGE* p. 240) reserves judgement but seems to find the arguments for a later date convincing. See Arnush 1995, especially 144–50 (suggesting a late dedication commemorating an earlier archonship), and most recently Petrovic 2007b: 260–4 (cautiously suggesting that public office for Peisistratus after 510 is at least 'not unthinkable').

[50] See e.g. Hansen in *CEG*, Page in *FGE* p. 240, Petrovic 2007b: 265–6 (reporting other theories as well).

[51] By Aristotle, *Rh.* 1367b20. 'The evidence [i.e. Aristotle's] is of little or any value' (Page, *FGE* p. 239); *contra*, Petrovic 2007b: 259, but Petrovic's argument that we cannot prove that collections containing epigrams falsely ascribed to Simonides were circulating in the time of Aristotle seems to me topsy-turvy: we equally cannot prove that any such collections always got their ascriptions right, and have no *prima facie* reason to assume so. See further on the '*Sylloge Simonidea*' below, pp. 45–7.

[52] For further discussion see Lavelle 1986; Petrovic 2007b: 251–2. It may also be worth mentioning the principle noted by Fantuzzi that, in epitaphs for women, even elite women such as Arkhedike, epigrammatists avoid giving an excessive amount of family information (Fantuzzi 2004b: 292, with n. 26, referring to Theophr. *Char.* 13.10, where putting too much information about a deceased woman's family on her tomb is a character trait of the *periergos*, the man who

Fourth-century writers followed Herodotus' and Thucydides' lead in reporting inscribed epigrams, and orators exploited them resourcefully for political and ideological ends.[53] Thus, in the final struggle between Demosthenes and Aeschines in 330 BCE, which ended the latter's political career, one of Aeschines' arguments was that even the greatest leaders in 'the good old days' did not expect or receive such extravagant honours as the crown that has been voted to Demosthenes. To prove this, he quotes an epigram inscribed across three stelae by the generals of the Athenian force that expelled the Persians from the Thracian town of Eion, back in 475 BCE. His point is that it does not even record the names of the generals, but instead awards glory to the people of Athenians collectively. The inscriptions have not survived, but it has been argued persuasively that Aeschines manipulates the original order of the three segments of the poem in order to make his point more powerfully.[54]

Reordering of lines is again at issue in another famous, and fascinating, citation of an epigram by a fourth-century writer. The epigram points forward to the next chapter because, while it presents itself as

overdoes it: see Diggle 2004: 330–1). See also Obbink 2004: 294–5, discussing later epigrams (by Posidippus) for which this one may provide a model.

[53] Petrovic 2007a: 58–9 notes the contrast between earlier orators, who do not quote epigrams, and later orators, who do (his opposition between 'fifth century' and 'fourth century' is misleading, since the careers of Lysias and Isocrates began in the fifth century but fell mostly in the earlier part of the fourth). This may be not so much a trend, as he suggests, as a reminder that the two bodies of work are not comparable. Demosthenes and Aeschines were not just rhetoricians but *rhêtores*, i.e. politicians active in the assembly, and their surviving political speeches are records (whether accurate or not) of actual performances on the public stage. Of the 'earlier' orators mentioned by Petrovic, Antiphon was indeed a *rhêtôr* but his political speeches have not been preserved; Lysias was a metic, and thus not a direct participant in Athenian politics; and Isocrates was a writer of political speeches in various fictive forms but did not perform in live debates. It is therefore perfectly possible that political orators of the early fourth (and indeed fifth) century *were* in the habit of quoting inscribed epigram: we simply lack evidence one way or the other.

[54] Aeschin. 3 *In Ctes.* 184 = 'Simonides' 40b, c, a *FGE* (in that order). On the question of order, see Page in *FGE* pp. 255–7; Petrovic 2007a: 59 n. 42. Other examples of epigram in fourth-century oratory are Lycurg. *Leoc.* 109 = 'Simonides' 21 and 22b *FGE*, an epitaph for the Athenian dead of Marathon and the famous epitaph for the Spartans at Thermopylae; [Dem.] 7 *On the Halonnesus* 40 = Anonymus 109 *FGE*, dedication of an altar as a boundary marker in Thrace; Aeschin. 3 *In Ctes.* 190 = Anonymus 114 *FGE*, SEG 28: 45.73–6, honorific inscription in the Metroon honouring supporters of democracy against the Thirty in the civil strife of 404/3 (the 'heroes of Phyle'); Dem. 18 *De cor.* 289 = Anonymus 126 *FGE*, epitaph for the dead of the battle of Chaeronea in 338 BCE (but, of the ten lines transmitted in Demosthenes' text, it is probable that only one – the one actually quoted by Demosthenes – is original: see Yunis 2001: 270–1). Two inscribed epigrams, an epitaph and a dedication to Asclepius, may conceivably have been composed by Aeschines himself: *CEG* 519, SEG 16:193 and *CEG* 776 = IG IV², 1 255 = *AP* 6.330.

inscriptional, it is very likely that it never was, actually, inscribed; thus it is an early example of purely 'literary' epigram. In spite of this, as will become clear, it tells an interesting story about early attitudes to inscribed epigram. In Plato's dialogue that bears his name, Socrates' friend Phaedrus, who is a fan of the orator Lysias, reads out a playful speech that Lysias has composed, arguing that a boy is best advised to choose an admirer who is not under the influence of Love. Socrates, less than impressed by Lysias' composition, is induced to improvise his own speech on the same theme. After this he proposes to leave, but reports that he has received a warning from his 'divine sign': since Love is a god, it cannot be right to speak ill of him. Socrates must therefore retract, and he delivers a visionary speech in which Love is revealed as a divine madness capable, in its highest form, of guiding the human soul to an encounter with ultimate reality. After a discussion of what might constitute good and bad speech-writing, of the prerequisites for composing good speeches, and of the shortcomings of contemporary rhetorical teaching, the conversation returns to Lysias' speech and the defects that Socrates perceived in it. One of these, he says, was that it had no clear logical structure; there was no particular reason for the arguments to be presented in that order rather than any other. In fact, he tells Phaedrus (264c–e),

εὑρήσεις αὐτὸν τοῦ ἐπιγράμματος οὐδὲν διαφέροντα, ὃ Μίδᾳ τῷ Φρυγί φασίν τινες ἐπιγεγράφθαι.
ΦΑΙ. Ποῖον τοῦτο, καὶ τί πεπονθός;
ΣΩ. Ἔστι μὲν τοῦτο τόδε —

> Χαλκῆ παρθένος εἰμί, Μίδα δ' ἐπὶ σήματι κεῖμαι.
> ὄφρ' ἂν ὕδωρ τε νάῃ καὶ δένδρεα μακρὰ τεθήλῃ,
> αὐτοῦ τῇδε μένουσα πολυκλαύτου ἐπὶ τύμβου,
> ἀγγελέω παριοῦσι, Μίδας ὅτι τῇδε τέθαπται.

ὅτι δ' οὐδὲν διαφέρει αὐτοῦ πρῶτον ἢ ὕστατόν τι λέγεσθαι, ἐννοεῖς που, ὡς ἐγῷμαι.

You will find that it is no different from the epigram that some people say is inscribed as an epitaph for Midas the Phrygian.
PHAE. What kind of epigram is that, and what's unusual about it? [or 'what's wrong with it?']
SO. It's this one:

> I am a girl of bronze, and I am placed on Midas' grave [or 'marker', *sêma*].
> As long as water flows and trees grow tall
> Staying here where I am on the much-lamented tomb
> I will tell passers-by that Midas is buried here,

and the fact that it makes no difference which bit of it is spoken first or last is something you'll have noticed, I should think.

In the form quoted by Socrates, it is indeed true that the lines of the epigram can be rearranged in any order without damaging the syntax or changing the overall sense (it is a 'cyclical' poem). This is not the only form in which this epigram has come down to us, however. It was much quoted in antiquity, and attributed by some to the archaic tyrant of Lindus, Cleobulus (one of the 'Seven Sages'), and by others to Homer himself. Here is another version:[55]

> Χαλκῆ παρθένος εἰμί, Μίδου δ' ἐπὶ σήματος ἦμαι.
> ἔς τ' ἂν ὕδωρ τε νάῃ καὶ δένδρεα μακρὰ τεθήλῃ
> καὶ ποταμοὶ πλήθωσι, περικλύζῃ δὲ θάλασσα,
> ἠέλιος δ' ἀνιὼν φαίνῃ λαμπρά τε σελήνη,
> αὐτοῦ τῇδε μένουσα πολυκλαύτῳ ἐπὶ τύμβῳ
> σημανέω παριοῦσι Μίδης ὅτι τῇδε τέθαπται.

> I am a girl of bronze, and I sit on Mides' grave.
> As long as water flows and trees grow tall
> And rivers swell, and the sea washes the shore,
> And the sun rises and shines, and the bright moon too,
> Staying here where I am on the much-lamented tomb
> I will signal to passers-by that Mides is buried here.

With these two middle lines in place, Socrates' point about the poem does not work. The lines can no longer be rearranged at will, and the epigram has a clear development, from the monument's self-introduction, through its claim that it will last as long as a series of progressively larger natural processes (the flowing of streams, the growth of trees, the flowing of rivers, the movements of the sea, the rotation of heavenly bodies), to the final revelation of its reason to desire such immortality, namely its mission to identify Midas' tomb. It is clear that the poem was known in a number of versions, and of course it is perfectly possible that Plato did not know, or had forgotten, the middle two lines here that make it non-cyclical. It is tempting, though, to suppose that he has Socrates deliberately suppress them to make his point.

The poem's opening words, 'I am a girl of bronze', draw attention strikingly to the artificiality of inscriptional conventions, seeming to invite the literal-minded objection that girls are not made of bronze,

---

[55] *Contest of Homer and Hesiod*, lines 265–70 in Allen 1963, vol. 5. For information on the other ancient authors who cite the lines and on the numerous textual variants (they were probably often quoted from memory), see Allen's apparatus to the *Herodotean Life of Homer*, lines 135–40, in the same volume. On the epigram's popularity in antiquity see also Janko 1988, who finds a significant echo of it in Aeneas' first speech to Dido in Vergil's *Aeneid*.

and bronze objects cannot say 'I am'.[56] In doing so, they point forward to a later stage of the discussion in Plato's dialogue, the famous critique of writing and written texts. Written texts, Socrates tells Phaedrus, are like statues, in that they have the appearance of life but are unable to answer questions (275d, clearly reminiscent of the epitaphic motif of the 'voice of the stone' or, as here, the 'voice of the statue'). A written text circulates willy-nilly and cannot discriminate between the right and the wrong sort of readers; when mistreated, it 'always needs its father', that is, its author, 'to defend it' (275de). Thus Lysias' speech is like the Midas epigram not so much because of its lack of structure as because, just as the epigram is vulnerable to Socrates' misquotation, so the speech is unable to defend itself in the absence of its author. Further, written texts promise memory but cannot deliver it (275a), by contrast with the deathless 'living word' of philosophical dialectic (277a). Similarly, Midas' bronze girl vaunts the durability of her message, but the epigram, separated from the monument, is unable to deliver it: the poem tells us nothing at all about Midas, not even where he is buried.[57]

The way we know that the omitted middle lines, in some form, existed early enough for it to be possible that Plato knew them is through the testimony of another early critic of the poem, no less a person than Simonides, our source for the poem's attribution to Cleobulus of Lindos. Simonides rebukes Cleobulus in lines quoted by Diogenes Laertius (third century CE?) in his biography of Cleobulus (1.90 = Simonides 581 *PMG*):

τίς κεν αἰνήσειε νόῳ πίσυνος Λίνδου ναέταν Κλεόβουλον
ἀενάοις ποταμοῖσ' ἄνθεσί τ' εἰαρινοῖς
ἀελίου τε φλογὶ χρυσέας τε σελάνας
καὶ θαλασσαίαισι δίναισ' ἀντία θέντα μένος στάλας;
ἅπαντα γάρ ἐστι θεῶν ἥσσω· λίθον δὲ
καὶ βρότεοι παλάμαι θραύοντι· μωροῦ
φωτὸς ἅδε βούλα.

---

[56] See Tueller 2008: 159, describing this as 'compact irony'; also 155–65 on the larger question of how epigrams deal with the relationship between representation and reality.

[57] I am only partly convinced by Petrovic's reading of this epigram as an early example of the *Ergänzungsspiel*, or 'game of completion', of later literary epigram, whereby readers are required to deduce or supply pieces of information not offered by the text. The poem does require us to imagine the monument but it does not pose any significant unanswered questions, or offer any great encouragement to the modern scholars whose attempts to reconstruct the monument in detail Petrovic reports (Petrovic 2007a: 62). Failing discovery of the actual monument (which I strongly suspect never existed), 'Is the "maiden of brass" a Siren, a Sphinx, or a Ker?' is not a real question.

> What man relying on his wits would commend the inhabitant of Lindus,
>     Cleobulus,
> Who, against ever-flowing rivers and the flowers of spring
> And the flame of the sun and of the golden moon
> And the currents of the sea, set up the might of a stele in opposition?
> All things are weaker than the gods; but a stone
> Even mortal hands can shatter; a foolish
> Man's is this plan.

Questioning Cleobulus' reputation for wisdom, Simonides introduces his name in the first line and makes a play on it in the last: 'Cleobulus' (*kleos* + *boulê*) suggests 'famed for plans', but *this* one is a foolish man's plan (*boulá*). Simonides' point is partly that the monument's claim to permanence is foolish in view of the transience of all things mortal ('all things are weaker than the gods'), but is partly also aimed specifically at poets who work (or pretend to work) in the perishable medium of stone ('might of a stele', *menos stálás*, is a striking paradox, *menos* being the vital energy and fighting spirit that gods breath into warriors on the Homeric battlefield: not something to be found in a stone). It is foolish for them to try to usurp the fame-giving function of poetry composed for oral performance, from epic onwards. For him, as for Plato, it is only 'living' oral communication that can guarantee everlasting *kleos*. So when writers of inscriptional epigram link the durability of their compositions to the durability of the medium in which they are written, it is folly, because it is an admission of their own weakness. But is it? Simonides' poem only works if his audience are aware of the poem to which it refers; even if the monument really exists, presumably we are not meant to imagine Simonides performing next to it. It is thus an implicit acknowledgement that inscribed (or in this case, I suggest, 'inscribed') epigram is perfectly capable of escaping from the stone.[58]

### Winged words: epigram takes flight from stone to book

This brings us back to the significance of Herodotus' naming of Simonides in connection with the epitaph for Megistias. Hitherto, the

---

[58] For more detailed discussion of the Simonides poem, see Ford 2002: 105–9 (also 101–2 on the Midas epigram). See also D. Steiner 1999: 388 with n. 33, and Rutherford 1996: 189 on Simonides 20 W²: for Simonides, Homeric epic, unlike the Midas epigram, *can* aspire to last for ever.

poet of inscribed epigram had regularly been anonymous, and modern scholars have taken this as a sign of its status as a lesser literature, lacking the prestige of orally performed verse.[59] Now Herodotus does not in fact say that Simonides composed the poem, just that he had it inscribed; but it seems very unlikely that this great poet would have commissioned four verses for a friend's grave from someone else, and it is generally agreed that it is natural to infer Simonides' authorship from the text.[60]

The proposition that Megistias' epitaph is by Simonides has a number of important implications.[61] It suggests that inscribed epigrams are worth collecting: what other works of Simonides might be out there? It establishes a prestigious precedent for epigram-writers of later generations: if Simonides does it, there is no need for epigram to be a subordinated genre. And it foreshadows the later scholarly, and poetic, game of attributing epigrams to famous authors.

The early history of epigram collections is obscure.[62] The Byzantine *Suda* lexicon (s.v. *Φιλόχορος*, *Φ* 441 Adler) tells us that the works of the local historian of Attica, Philochorus (c.340–c.260 BCE), included one identified as *Attic Epigrams*; we know nothing further about it, but the obvious guess is that these were inscriptional epigrams collected by Philochorus in the course of his historical studies.[63] Then there is

[59] See e.g. Fantuzzi 2004b: 288. On the earliest exceptions to the principle of anonymity (the first probably in the early fourth century), see Bing and Bruss 2007b: 4 with n. 18, and 6 n. 24 on Ion of Samos; also Fantuzzi 2004b: 290–1.

[60] Even by the generally sceptical Page (*FGE* p. 196). As Page points out, however, it does not follow from the supposition that Herodotus believed the poem to be by Simonides that he *knew* the poem was by Simonides. His information is only as reliable as his informant, which Page plausibly takes to be oral tradition (some at least of Simonides' works may have circulated in writing from an early date, but it seems doubtful whether a written source would have furnished the additional information about Megistias and Simonides being friends). We cannot exclude the possibility that Herodotus simply invented the attribution: it is very neat, for the purposes of his Thermopylae triad, that the author of the third poem should be, on the one hand, a great poet famous throughout Greece, and, on the other, an individual making a private dedication for a friend. The correctness or otherwise of the attribution does not, however, alter the significance of Herodotus' move in linking the poem with the name of Simonides. Sider 2007: 117 uses Simonides' penchant for self-praise as an argument in favour of the idea that Simonides may himself have disseminated his epitaphs and other works in writing, for purposes of (literal) self-advertisement.

[61] Which is not, of course, to suggest a relationship of cause and effect: the Herodotus passage is a signpost, or a straw in the wind.

[62] See Bing and Bruss 2007b: 6–7 n. 26 for the interesting suggestion (made to them in a personal communication by J. Lougovaya) that we should think in terms of a transition from fifth-century copybooks made for the use of professional epigrammatists (e.g., perhaps, Simonides: see below, p. 47) and containing useful formulae (they could perhaps also have been used to show prospective customers a range of options) to fourth-century collections made to be read for pleasure.

[63] On the other hand, David Kovacs has suggested that Philochorus' *Epigrammata Attika* may be the ultimate source for Plutarch's attribution to Euripides of 'Euripides' 1 *FGE*, an epitaph for the Athenian dead of the Sicilian expedition (Kovacs 1995: 566). If correct, that would

the shadowy entity known as the *Sylloge Simonidea*. The existence of this collection, which is not attested in antiquity (and whose Greco-Latin title is an invention of modern scholars), is postulated in order to explain the fact that later collectors such as Meleager confidently attributed to Simonides a large number of epigrams (102 across all the texts that survive: there will have been more), including some that could have been written by him, and others that emphatically could not (for instance, because they refer to events after his death).[64] Inscribed epigrams being in principle anonymous, the question is what gave such collectors the connection between poem and author (in the absence of testimony such as Herodotus'), and the answer is sought in the '*Sylloge*'. The subject is highly controversial, and certain knowledge is not to be hoped for, but David Sider has argued convincingly that the origins of this collection may have been quite early (in the fifth century, perhaps even with written texts created by Simonides himself). It must then have gone through a series of mutations (and probably distinct coexisting versions). In the course of this process it accumulated new material, including, for instance, snippets from Simonides' elegies,[65] inscriptional epigrams believed or guessed to be the work of Simonides, and epigrams that had nothing to do with the poet but that came to bear his name, either through deliberate fakery (*pseudepigrapha*, works passed off by one author as the work of another) or simply by virtue of having been added to this collection.[66] As we will see more fully in Chapter 5, a chaotic and colourful reception, with poems being adapted, reattributed, misattributed, or written as if in the voice of a notable figure in the past, characterized the history of this strange ventriloquist genre from its very beginnings.

perhaps rather suggest a collection of epigrams composed, or allegedly composed, by eminent Athenians. On early epigram collections, see further Petrovic 2007b: 92–101.

[64] See *FGE* pp. 119–23; Petrovic 2007b (especially 25–89); and Sider 2007, with useful tables on 129–30.

[65] i.e. longer poems on various themes in elegiac couplets. The generic boundary between 'elegy' and 'epigram' is loosely drawn, and one way in which 'epigrams' might come into existence was by excerpting from elegy: see e.g. Sider 2006: 330 n. 10; Bing and Bruss 2007b: 11–12; Bowie 2007; and Petrovic 2007a: 55 on the usage of the Greek words ἐπίγραμμα and ἐλεγεῖον.

[66] Sider 2007. There is a burgeoning literature on Simonides, partly in the wake of exciting papyrus finds in the 1990s adding to our knowledge of his elegies (on which see Boedeker and Sider 1996 and other essays in this special volume of the journal *Arethusa*), but also including much work on the 'Simonidean' epigrams, e.g. Bravi 2006, Petrovic 2007b; for an overview, see Pelliccia 2009 and other chapters in Budelmann 2009. At the time of writing, a monograph on Simonides by Richard Rawles was forthcoming; an edition with commentary of the whole Simonidean corpus was also being prepared by David Sider and Ettore Cingano.

# II EPIGRAM IN THE HELLENISTIC WORLD

*Μοῦσα φίλα, τίνι τάνδε φέρεις πάγκαρπον ἀοιδάν;*
*ἢ τίς ὁ καὶ τεύξας ὑμνοθετᾶν στέφανον;*

Beloved Muse, who is it for, this Song plucked from every source?
Or who was it who fashioned it, a Garland made from poets?[1]

## Introductory: sailing to Alexandria

As Chapter 1 ended, with questions of collecting and reception, so Chapter 2 begins.[2] The imperial physician and prolific medical writer Galen (second to third century CE) was particularly interested in books and how people used, or misused, them. In the course of a discussion of how a particular set of annotations found their way into the Library of Alexandria's copy of a classic medical text, the third book of Hippocrates' *Epidemics*, he tells an interesting story to illustrate just how avid Ptolemy Euergetes, king of Egypt in the third century BCE, was as a book collector. He ordered that, whenever ships put in at the harbour of Alexandria, any books their passengers were carrying should be confiscated and copied; the copies were returned to the owners, and the originals were placed in the Library. Ptolemy went further than that, though: he borrowed the official copies of the plays of Aeschylus, Sophocles, and Euripides from the Athenian authorities on the security of a large deposit (fifteen talents), promising to make copies and return the originals. Instead, he kept the originals and returned the copies – and told the Athenians they

---

[1] Meleager 1 *HE* = *AP* 4.1, 1–2: Introduction to the *Garland*.

[2] A chapter on this scale cannot do more than capture flashes from the jewelled surface of the great treasure-box of Hellenistic epigram (or, to borrow the ancient collectors' favourite metaphor, to catch a few wafts of perfume from its summer garland). I am much indebted to Gutzwiller 1998, to Marco Fantuzzi's substantial chapter on Epigram in Fantuzzi and Hunter 2004, and to essays in Bing and Bruss 2007a. For a brief, clear introduction, see also Gutzwiller 2007a: 106–20. Every reader and student of Hellenistic epigrams also owes a debt of gratitude to the late A. S. F. Gow and Sir Denys Page for their enormous service to later scholars in collecting, editing, and elucidating these poems in *HE* and *FGE* (as well as later epigrams in *GPh*).

could keep the deposit as well.[3] The story neatly symbolizes shifts in the Greek world after Alexander's conquests, and sets the scene for the age that follows.[4] The cultural centre of gravity moves from the city-states of 'old' Greece (Athens) to the capitals of the new Hellenistic kingdoms (Alexandria). The cultural function of the texts of tragedy is also transformed: from civic records of historic performances and scripts for revived performances,[5] they become, on the one hand, collector's items (assuming that Ptolemy's desire for the *originals* is not grounded purely in a concern for accuracy) and, on the other hand, data in an enormous scholarly archive of information. Ptolemy's behaviour towards the Athenians displays a combination of respect (he acknowledges the importance of their Great Writers), contempt (he has no compunction about tricking them), and, as befits his title (*euergetês* means 'benefactor'), kingly generosity (nothing constrains him to let the Athenians keep his deposit *and* give them the copies he had made – which, Galen tells us, were lavishly produced). In this world of collectors and collections,[6] a genre as eminently collectable as epigram was bound to flourish.

This was not the only respect in which epigram was appealing to the cultural and literary tastes of the Hellenistic world.[7] Callimachus of Cyrene, the dominant literary figure of the third century BCE, spent much of his career at the court (and in the Library) of Ptolemy Euergetes. He used the prologue of his (now sadly fragmentary)

[3] Galen, *Commentaries on Book III of Hippocrates' Epidemics*, 17a.606–8 Kühn; see also Erskine 1989: 39. Galen does not specify *which* Ptolemy Euergetes, but Ptolemy III Euergetes I seems a more likely candidate than Ptolemy VIII Euergetes II a century later.

[4] Suspiciously neatly, in fact: Battezzato 2003 argues that the story is essentially a cultural-historical myth. For a brief introduction to the history and culture of the Hellenistic age, see Gutzwiller 2007a: 1–25; for a larger survey, see Shipley 2000 and essays in Erskine 2003. Readers with some knowledge of Greek wishing to sample the literature of the period should turn to Hopkinson 1988, a selection of some of the most important and enjoyable texts with useful introduction and commentary.

[5] On third-century revivals of 'old' tragedy see e.g. Habicht 1997: 105.

[6] Once again Nita Krevans' formulation, which we have already encountered in the Introduction, is apt: 'the kings collected objects (art, books) and creatures (zoological specimens, scholars). The scholars collected information' (Krevans 2007: 131).

[7] The term 'Hellenistic', originally applied to post-classical forms of the Greek language and ultimately derived from the Greek word Ἑλληνιστής used in the Acts of the Apostles (6:1, 9:29) to refer to Jews who used the Greek language, has come to refer broadly to the period from the conquests of Alexander to Rome's domination and eventual conquest of the Greek world (see *OED* s.v.; for a brief account of the history of the term's use in scholarship, see Shipley 2000: 1). The present discussion follows Gow and Page's definition (*HE* xiii): 'the period between the death of Alexander the Great in 323 B.C. and the compilation by Meleager of Gadara of the anthology which he called Στέφανος', i.e. about 100 BCE. The emphasis will be on the first half of this period: on possible reasons for the under-representation of second-century epigrams in Meleager's *Garland*, see Argentieri 2007: 147–9.

aetiological poem, the *Aitia*, to set out an influential literary manifesto. In it, he replies to detractors, whom he does not name but refers to as 'Telkhines', malevolent mythological beings associated with the island of Rhodes. They have criticized him, he says, for failing to produce a big poem on a big, heroic subject, but instead spinning out verses a little at a time, like a child at play. In reply, Callimachus defends his 'few-lined' (ὀλιγόστιχος) approach to poetry, and outlines an aesthetic that judges poems by skill not by scale, valuing delicacy, lightness, and the quest for new directions. The charge of being childlike also misses its mark. The poet acknowledges that physical old age weighs heavily on him, but he would shake it off if he could; playfulness does not preclude sophistication, and literary play offers a space where the old can continue to be fictionally – and spiritually – young. Epigram clearly passes the test of being 'few-lined'; as I hope this chapter will demonstrate, it also provided Callimachus and other Hellenistic poets with a perfect frame in which to display their inventiveness, wit, and versatility.[8]

Any discussion of Hellenistic epigram is bound to be highly selective and to reflect the tastes and interests of the author, who is, in effect, creating a new *Garland*. In what follows, I aim less to present any kind of comprehensive overview (for which the reader is referred to the works cited in note 2) than to provide an introduction to some of the features that make these poems attractive and interesting, and some ways in which they may be approached.

### Preliminaries: books and poets

Unless otherwise stated, the epigrams discussed in this chapter have been selected from two sources. One is Gow and Page's *Hellenistic Epigrams* (*HE*), which collects epigrams of Hellenistic date transmitted in the *Anthology*, plus others by the same authors that have been preserved by other means: for example, because they were quoted by other ancient authors. The other is the *editio minor* (that is, smaller-scale, and thus handier, edition) of the complete surviving works

---

[8] For discussion of this famous prologue (*Aetia* F 1) see Hunter 2004a: 66–77. Cf. also briefer programmatic statements in epigrams 2 *HE* = 28 P = *AP* 12.43 and 56 *HE* = 27 P = *AP* 9.507, and Theoc. *Id.* 1.47–54, where the boy so engrossed in crafting a toy that he is oblivious to the world around him (including a fox that is trying to eat his lunch) seems likely to be a metaphor for the poet of bucolic verse. For an introduction to Hellenistic aesthetics, see Gutzwiller 2007a: 26–49.

of Posidippus of Pella, including the 'new Posidippus' contained in the Milan papyrus (AB: 1–112 AB is the Milan 'new Posidippus', 113–50 AB are works known to us from other sources). These two sources represent two different ways in which epigrams have come down to us, and in which they circulated in antiquity: in anthologies organized according to the whim of the collector (thematically, for the most part, in the case of *AP*; alphabetically by author in the case of *HE*, with anonymous poems after 'Z' and Meleager set aside as a special case at the very end); or in books of poems created and published by the poet, raising the possibility that the arrangement itself is part of the act of poetic composition, directing the reader's response to the poems not just as individual units, but as a collection. As we saw in the Introduction, the principle of organization in the Milan papyrus is again thematic, but the choice of what themes to include (and, so far as we can judge given the incomplete state of the surviving book, to omit) is strikingly idiosyncratic. The discovery of the Milan papyrus has encouraged scholars in their efforts to reconstruct the original poetry books of other epigrammatists.[9] Such studies can produce fascinating results but are necessarily speculative, while the accumulation of mutually supporting hypotheses can give an appearance of solidity to reconstructions that are in fact rather fragile.[10] For these reasons, the present discussion will not address the arrangement of epigrams in books, actual or hypothetical, in any detail; readers will, however, be referred to such discussions elsewhere, especially in the case of epigrams that are claimed (sometimes very persuasively) to be statements of an author's literary 'programme'.[11]

[9] See especially Gutzwiller 1998; also 2007a, emphasizing the importance of author-edited poetry books (108), but also acknowledging the likelihood of selective reading, which adds to the paradoxical 'fluidity' of the genre (119–20).

[10] There is also a risk of reconstructing the books that we would wish the ancient authors to have composed, displaying the maximum of whatever form of literary artfulness modern critical taste seeks from them (and, insofar as the Milan volume is artful, the precise form of its artfulness is not something that we could ever have predicted from our other evidence). Of course, to say this is in part simply to recognize that every engagement with epigram is, among other things, an act of reception, and thus about us as well as about the ancient poems.

[11] The most important and influential account of the organization of Hellenistic epigrams into books is Gutzwiller 1998: scholarly, closely argued, and often persuasive, but in my view over-confident. In the case of the Milan papyrus, I am largely convinced by Nita Krevans' view, *contra* Gutzwiller 2004, 2005a and others, that the arrangement of the book is more utilitarian than aesthetic or rhetorical, revealing precisely the mindset of a *collector* more than that of an artificer (Krevans uses the metaphor of the 'reference librarian' vs. the 'symphony conductor'). Briefly, she suggests that the organization of poems within each thematic section can be explained by two principles: (1) poems on similar topics are grouped together, and (2) poems that exemplify the given theme most clearly come first, followed by more marginal cases (Krevans 2005, especially 93–6; Krevans 2007). Of course, as GN points out to me, a critic inclined to see the

After the inception of literary epigram, epigrams in books (whether poetry books or collections) continued to coexist with inscribed epigrams throughout antiquity; dedications continued to be made, and tombs and other monuments erected, and, just as book epigram adopted motifs from earlier inscribed epigram, so inscriptions looked to literary epigrams for models.[12] It is often impossible to tell whether a poem transmitted in books was originally meant for inscription on an object or not,[13] and, since ancient readers would have been equally in the dark, it does not really matter (except in cases such as Myron's *Cow*, where a reader who is not aware that the statue has become the subject of a competitive game will not fully get the joke). Many epigrams, on the other hand, make no reference to any real or imagined inscriptional setting. Such epigrams are sometimes described as 'epideictic', a term that goes back to the ancient anthologists and ultimately to Greek rhetorical theory (where it refers to the genre of speeches composed for purposes of display, rather than for use in practical legal or political situations). Since the epigrams in question do not have anything very significant in common, the usefulness of the term is open to question.[14] An interesting example of a clearly literary epigram being turned into an inscription is provided by Callimachus 8 *HE* = 42 P = *AP* 12.118 (an apology from a lover who has beset, or in this case, kissed, his beloved's doorpost), which was painted, sometime in the first century CE, on one of the inner walls of a building (the so-called 'Auditorium of Maecenas') on the Esquiline in Rome.[15]

Since exploration of some of the flavours of Hellenistic epigrams will take us on a zigzagging journey through time and space, it may be

---

organization as artful could argue (for example) that Posidippus teases the reader by presenting apparently straightforward thematic categories, which he then proceeds to stretch to the limits by including odder and odder examples: see e.g. Hunter 2004b: 99 on such 'generic wit'. Which explanation we find more plausible or economical will depend on our beliefs about the culture in which the collection was created.

[12] This two-way process is well outlined in Bettenworth 2007.

[13] See Bettenworth 2007: 80–5 on 'surplus of information' as a possible indication of literariness (i.e. an object, such as the bronze cock in Callimachus 25 *HE* = 56 P = *AP* 6.149 [see below, p. 55], would not need to tell us what it was if it were before our eyes). Real dedications do sometimes provide unnecessary information, however: for instance, on the horses in the Athenian victory offering, 'Simonides' 3 *FGE*, which we encountered in the previous chapter.

[14] See Gutzwiller 1998: 316; Lauxtermann 1998; Rossi 2002.

[15] See Kaibel 1876, and, on the inscription's setting in this building, Patterson 1992 (probably 'a triclinium and/or nymphaeum', p. 206); see also Murray 1985: 43. The poem is discussed further below, pp. 74–7.

helpful to begin by locating, as far as possible, the writers whom we will encounter. Biographical evidence is generally scarce and uncertain; I follow the example of Page (OCT, x–xi; see also Argentieri 2007, 147) in organizing the poets whose work will be discussed into rough groupings according to their likely *floruit* (period of artistic activity):

*c.*310–290: Aeschrion, possibly from Samos or from Mytilene on Lesbos; Anyte, from Tegea in Arcadia; Nossis, from Epizephyrian Locri, a Greek colony near the toe of the boot of Italy; Phalaecus, about whom nothing more than an approximate date is known. Anyte and Nossis are among the few women writers of Hellenistic epigram whose work is known to us;

*c.*275: Asclepiades, from the island of Samos; Callimachus, from the Greek city of Cyrene in modern Libya, but resident for much of his life in Alexandria; Hedylus, possibly an Athenian or possibly from Samos; Posidippus, from the Macedonian capital, Pella;

*c.*250: Leonidas of Tarentum, from the Greek city of Taras (Latin Tarentum, modern Taranto) in southern Italy, so called to distinguish him from another, later, poet of epigram, Leonides or Leonidas of Alexandria;

*c.*250–200: Dioscorides, whose place of origin is obscure. He is said at one point in the *Anthology* to be from Nicopolis, but it is unclear how reliable this evidence is, and in any case Nicopolis ('Victoryville') was a common place name. He is likely to have spent time in Alexandria;

220–180: Alcaeus, from Messene in the Peloponnese, not to be confused with the early lyric poet, Alcaeus of Mitylene;

**second century**: Philetas of Samos, probably in fact Philitas, Greek $\Phi\iota\lambda\acute{\iota}\tau\alpha\varsigma$, but the spelling with an 'e' has become conventional; 'of Samos' to distinguish him from a more famous poet, Philetas of Cos, but the reality of this distinction is not beyond doubt (*HE* 476);

**second/first century**: Meleager, from the Greco-Syrian city of Gadara;[16] his biographical epitaphs for himself tell us that he was educated in Tyre in Phoenicia and later settled on the island of Cos;

**of uncertain, probably third- or second-century, date**: Glaucus, whose name is a common one, and nothing is known of this author of three poems identified by Gow and Page as Hellenistic; Pancrates, also author of three poems in *HE*, and possibly but not certainly the same person as an Arcadian of that name said to have written a poem about fishing.

Finally, one poet not included by Gow and Page in *Hellenistic Epigrams* (or by Meleager in his *Garland*) makes an appearance here: Meleager's near contemporary and fellow countryman, Philodemus of Gadara. This philosopher, scholar, poet, and associate of aristocratic Romans, whose writings on a variety of subjects are gradually emerging from the charred papyrus rolls of the Villa dei Papiri at Herculaneum, was also the author of a number of vivid and clever epigrams transmitted in the *Anthology* that have much in common with those collected in Meleager's *Garland*. Philodemus, who seems to have spent a significant portion of his life in Italy (and around the Bay of Naples in particular), is an important figure in the encounter between Greek and Roman culture in the first century BCE, and may serve to represent the transition between the present chapter and Chapter 4, on Greek epigram in the Roman world.[17]

### Dedicatory and ecphrastic epigrams

As we saw in Chapter 1, the original function of a dedicatory epigram is to articulate in language a ritual act, the pious offering of a gift to a deity; it may also invite the reader to re-enact this giving. The set of relationships involved (between giver, object given, recipient, and reader) is inventively explored in Hellenistic epigram. A humorous

[16] Modern Umm Qays in Jordan, near the Syrian and Israeli borders; a town familiar to readers of the New Testament from the episode in the life of Christ narrated in Matthew 8:28–32, though in fact a variant reading should probably be adopted, which would turn the 'Gadarene swine' into 'Gerasene swine' (see Sider 1997: 3 n. 2).

[17] For a fuller encounter with Philodemus' epigrams, see David Sider's useful commentary, Sider 1997; see also Nisbet 2000 for some cautionary remarks on Sider's attempts to reconstruct Philodemus' life and views.

(but also perfectly 'functional') epigram of Callimachus serves to set the scene (25 *HE* = 56 P = *AP* 6.149):

> Φησὶν ὅ με στήσας Εὐαίνετος – οὐ γὰρ ἔγωγε
>   γιγνώσκω – νίκης ἀντί με τῆς ἰδίης
> ἀγκεῖσθαι χάλκειον ἀλέκτορα Τυνδαρίδησι.
>   πιστεύω Φαίδρου παιδὶ Φιλοξενίδεω.

(The man who set me up, Euainetos, says – since obviously I
   don't know – that it's for my very own victory
that I am dedicated, a bronze cock, to the sons of Tyndareus.
   I take his word for it; he's the son of Phaidros, son of Philoxenos.

With great lightness of touch, the epigram plays on its ability to make the mute bronze figure speak. The words give it a 'voice', but of course the actual 'knowledge' comes not from it but from Euainetos, who made the dedication (and had the epigram attached to it). The figure's 'witlessness' is underlined by its identification with the live cock that won the cockfight for Euainetos: how can it not even know about its *own* victory? The final line turns in a new direction by assigning some cognitive skills to the figure after all, and not just a voice: it can decide who is to be trusted and who is not. This in turn points back, though, to the function of figure and epigram together as a monument: the reason Euainetos is to be trusted is because of his lineage – which it is the epigram's function to record.[18]

Another Callimachean epigram has the inanimate gift speak, this time not addressing the reader but in dialogue with the recipient (22 *HE* = 34 P = *AP* 6.351):

> Τίν με, λεοντάγχ᾽ ὦνα συοκτόνε, φήγινον ὄζον
>   θῆκε – Τίς; – Ἀρχῖνος. – Ποῖος; – Ὁ Κρής. – Δέχομαι.

To you, Lord Lion-Strangler, Boar-Slayer, me, an oak club,
   dedicated – Who? – Arkhinos. – Which? – The Cretan. – I accept.

Here the essential information (and some further information – the object's identity as a club – that would be unnecessary if this were a

---

[18] See Bettenworth 2007: 84–5 and Tueller 2008: 191–2. See Gutzwiller 1998: 190–3 for a reading of this poem as part of what she thinks was a significantly arranged sequence in Callimachus' epigram book; she suggests that a further level of irony is added by the reader's awareness that the real 'speaker' is neither the figure nor Euainetos, but Callimachus. For a slightly different reading of this epigram as 'question[ing] the conventions of the genre', see Köhnken 2007: 308; see also Fantuzzi 2004b: 316–7 and Meyer 2007: 200–1.

real dedication) is provided in a very short space while simultaneously generating a miniature comic drama. The humble object addresses Heracles in a tone that is reverential and incongruously grand, with its compound epithets and resonant form of address ôna ('Lord'). The god, on the other hand, has heard this before, and is unimpressed: the club's rhetoric is merely delaying the essential piece of information, the name of the dedicatee. This information turns out not to be sufficient: Arkhinos is well-known, but not the only Arkhinos around, so the god still does not know whether the offering is acceptable. The answer is the desired one, and the god takes the club.[19]

An athletic dedication by Phalaecus presents a more complex dialogue (2 *HE* = *AP* 13.5):

> α – Νικῶ δίαυλον. β – Ἀλλ' ἐγὼ παλαίων.
>   γ – Ἐγὼ δὲ πεντάεθλον. δ – Ἀλλ' ἐγὼ πύξ.
> ε – Καὶ τίς τύ; α – Τιμόδημος. β – Ἀλλ' ἐγὼ Κρής.
>   γ – Ἐγὼ δὲ Κρηθεύς. δ – Ἀλλ' ἐγὼ Διοκλῆς.
> ε – Καὶ τίς πατήρ τοι; α – Κλεῖνος. βγδ – Ὥσπερ ἄμμιν.
>   ε – Ἔμπη δὲ νικῆς; α – Ἰσθμοῖ. ε – Τὺ δ' ἔμπη;
> β ; – Νέμειον ἂν λειμῶνα καὶ παρ' Ἥρα.


> A – I've won the footrace. B – I've won in wrestling.
>   C – I've won the pentathlon. D – I've won at boxing.
> E – And who are you? A – Timodemos. B – But I'm Kres.
>   C – And I'm Kretheus. D – But I'm Diokles.
> E – And who's your father? A – Kleinos. B, C, D – He's ours too.
>   E – And where did you win? A – At the Isthmus. E – And where did you?
> B – In the meadow of Nemea, and at Hera's [festival].

The epigram, which is in an unusual metre (catalectic iambic trimeters), records victories by four brothers (A: Timodemos, B: Kres, C: Kretheus, and D: Diokles), information about which is elicited from them by the questions of (presumably) a passer-by, the anonymous E.

---

[19] Other translators, following LSJ ποῖος III (where 'Call. *Epigr.* 36' must be a misprint and intend to refer to this epigram, 34 P), have translated ποῖος; in line 2 as the equivalent of ποδαπός; 'where's he from?' Gutzwiller 1998: 194 suggests that the answer 'from Crete' may be satisfactory because Cretans are known for manliness. I think the poem has more point if the word has its more common sense of 'which?': the god takes an interest in strong men, has heard of more than one Arkhinos, and would not take an offering from just any of them. The ethnic is sufficient to identify *this* Arkhinos, and an offering from (presumably, the famous) 'Arkhinos of Crete' is acceptable. This is not to suggest that Callimachus necessarily has a *real* Arkhinos in mind: the whole scenario is probably entirely fictional. For the translation 'which?' see also Ferguson 1970: 69.

It is hard enough to follow with the benefit of clear modern print, and with the useful addition of letters to identify each speaker (which I have borrowed from *HE*). The ancient reader could not expect these, and would also have to manage without conventions such as spaces between words, punctuation, and capital letters for names, thus being faced with something more like:

$$ΝΙΚΩΔΙΑΥΛΟΝΑΛΛΕΓΩΠΑΛΑΙΩΝ$$
$$ΕΓΩΔΕΠΕΝΤΑΕΘΛΟΝΑΛΛΕΓΩΠΥΞ$$
$$ΚΑΙΤΙΣΤΥΤΙΜΟΔΗΜΟΣΑΛΛΕΓΩΚΡΗΣ...$$

that is,

IVEWONTHEFOOTRACEIVEWONINWRESTLING
IVEWONTHEPENTATHLONIVEWONATBOXING
ANDWHOAREYOUTIMODEMOSBUTIMKRES..., etc.[20]

Of course there are some clues, like the repetition of phrases such as 'but I'm', indicating a change of speaker; but it must still have been formidably hard to work out what's meant to be going on.[21] The task is not made easier by the facts that the name of one of the boys is also an ethnic adjective (Kres means 'Cretan', as in the Arkhinos epigram above) and that their father's name, Kleinos, is also an adjective meaning 'famous' or 'glorious' (which may indeed be a pun; the appropriateness of his name is confirmed by the fact that he has four sons all capable of winning victories within a short enough space of time to have a common victory monument). The difficulty of reading the poem probably contributed to damage suffered by the text in the process of transmission: in line 6 I have printed Herman's very doubtful conjecture Ἰσθμόϊ in place of the meaningless transmitted letters ισθμονη, and it seems likely that at least one couplet is missing at the end (we need to be told where the other two boys were victorious).

So where Callimachus 22 effortlessly invites us into a miniature comic drama, Phalaecus 2 presents us with an uphill struggle. There are two ways of looking at this. One is that Phalaecus is not so good an epigrammatist as Callimachus. This is true. Modern scholars are cautious of making such value judgements but, while epigram is a literary genre, it is also a game (we might almost say a sport), and it is a game that Callimachus plays brilliantly (as well as by particularly

---

[20] Cf. Krevans 2007: 137 on the layout of the Milan papyrus.
[21] Cf. Tueller 2008: 195 on the complex, and therefore confusing, character of this poem.

strict rules).[22] Even once we have seen how it works, this poem lacks
the economy of expression and the dramatic immediacy of appeal of
Callimachus'. From another point of view, though, the difficulty of
reading is precisely the point of the poem: it is the challenge that the
poet makes to the reader and, if we examine that challenge further,
it turns out to be rather clever. The problem of the poem consists
in working out how many people are talking. Once we have worked
out that 'Kres' here doesn't mean 'Cretan' but is a proper name
(since otherwise there would be no explanation for the equivalence
of pattern between lines 3 and 4), we have four named individuals,
who, so far, could be introducing themselves to each other. In line 4,
though, there is nothing to restrict 'He's ours too' to any subgroup of
those named so far, so it becomes clear that they must *all* be sons of
Kleinos, and therefore are all obviously known to each other. Thus
it is revealed that there is another person 'in' the epigram, namely
the person asking the questions – in other words, the reader, who
becomes identified with the anonymous passer-by. The poem invites
us (and indeed compels us, if we choose to read it in the first place)
to become involved in it by solving its puzzle, and thus to locate
ourselves within it. It resembles the riddle of the Sphinx, whose solver
is also its solution. The role of the reader is to find the reader, and the
poem presents a self-contained literary game, whether to be played at
dinner parties or in the library we cannot say (see below, pp. 68–71,
on sympotic epigram).

The subjects of some dedicatory epigrams are frankly bizarre, such
as Anonymus 43 *HE* = *AP* 6.45, in which a hedgehog caught stealing
grapes by impaling them on its prickles is dedicated live to Dionysus.
One important category related to those by victorious athletes
consists of dedications by workers, of various kinds, of the tools of
their trade. Thus, in Philetas of Samos 1 *HE* = *AP* 6.210, an elderly
*hetaira* ('courtesan') dedicates clothes and other equipment 'which
a gentleman may not speak of' to Aphrodite on her retirement; in
Leonidas of Tarentum 7 *HE* = *AP* 6.204, a carpenter similarly offers
his tools to Athena; in Pancrates 1 *HE* = *AP* 6.117, a smith offers
tools to Hephaestus, and so on. Such poems provide an opportunity
for portraits or stories in miniature. Consider, for example, two

---

[22] On Callimachus' fastidiousness in following metrical 'laws', see Fantuzzi 2004a: 35–37 and
Magnelli 2007: 180–1.

consecutive poems from the anthology, also by Leonidas (41 *HE* = *AP* 6.288, 42 *HE* = 6.289):

Αἱ Λυκομήδευς παῖδες Ἀθηνὼ καὶ Μελίτεια
    καὶ Φιντὼ Γλῆνίς θ’, αἱ φιλεργόταται,
ἔργων ἐκ δεκάτας ποτιθύμια τόν τε πρόσεργον
    ἄτρακτον καὶ τὰν ἄτρια κριναμέναν
κερκίδα, τὰν ἱστῶν μολπάτιδα, καὶ τὰ τροχαῖα
    πανία κἀργαστὰς τούσδε ποτιρρόγεας
καὶ σπάθας εὐβριθεῖς, πολυάργυρε· τὼς δὲ πενιχραί
    ἐξ ὀλίγων ὀλίγαν μοῖραν ἀπαρχόμεθα.
τῶν χέρας αἰὲν, Ἀθάνα, ἐπιπλήσαιο μὲν ἴσως
    θείης δ’ εὐσιπύους ἐξ ὀλιγησιπύων.[23]

The daughters of Lykomedes, Atheno and Meliteia,
    and Phinto and Glenis, women devoted to their work,
as a tithe of their work dedicate gifts to your liking: their workmate
    the spindle, and she who parts the warp,
the shuttle, singing dancer through the web, and the running
    bobbins, and these hard-working weights,
and the hefty beaters, goddess rich in silver! Thus, poor as we are,
    of the little we have we offer a little share.
For this may you, equally, Athena, keep our hands ever full,
    and make our breadbasket plentiful, instead of scanty.

Αὐτονόμα, Μελίτεια, Βοΐσκιον, αἱ Φιλολάδεω
    καὶ Νικοῦς Κρῆσσαι τρεῖς, ξένε, θυγατέρες,
ἁ μὲν τὸν μιτοεργὸν ἀειδίνητον ἄτρακτον,
    ἁ δὲ τὸν ὀρφνίταν εἰροκόμον τάλαρον,
ἁ δ’ ἅμα τὰν λεπτῶν εὐάτριον ἐργάτιν ἱστῶν
    κερκίδα, τὰν λεχέων Πανελόπας φύλακα,
δῶρον Ἀθαναίᾳ Πανίτιδι τῷδ’ ἐνὶ ναῷ
    θῆκαν Ἀθαναίας παυσάμεναι καμάτων.

Autonoma, Meliteia, Boïskion, Philolaides’
    and Niko’s three Cretan daughters, stranger –
the first, her yarn-making, ever-whirling spindle;
    the second, her night-watching wool-guarding workbasket;
the third too, the strong-weaving worker of light webs,
    her spindle, the protector of Penelope’s bed –

---

[23] The text of this poem is seriously problematic in two places: line 6 (MSS κερταστὰς τούσδε ποτιρ(ρ)όγεας) and line 7 (MSS πολυάργυρα). For the sake of producing a continuous translation, I print the conjectures that Gow and Page seem to regard as closest to defensible, but neither is altogether satisfactory. ἴσως in line 9 has also been questioned, and I am not confident about the translation of this final couplet.

as a gift to Athena of the Bobbin, in this temple,
dedicated, when they ceased from Athena's toils.

Both poems use rare poetic words combined with variations on the technical terminology of spinning and weaving to create an atmosphere that is poised between the homely and the remote.[24] The semi-personification of the tools (the shuttle as dancer in 41, the basket [if my translation of the slightly obscure Greek phrase, guided by Gow and Page's note in *HE*, is correct] as guardian of the wool while its owners sleep) underlines the women's seclusion, again with a slightly ambivalent effect: an image of security and familiarity, with the friendly tools as constant companions, or of loneliness and monotony, with the tools as their *only* companions? In each case, we are invited to supply or conjecture additional bits of information, to play the *Ergänzungsspiel* ('game of completion'). Neither poem, for instance, gives us any direct indication of the age or status of the women,[25] apart from the fact that Autonoma, Meliteia, and Boïskion are able to stop working whereas Atheno, Meliteia, Phinto, and Glenis are not. Also, what is being dedicated? It makes sense for Autonoma and her sisters to dedicate their work tools, but not for Atheno and hers, who will still need them to effect their hoped-for escape from poverty.[26] Might the dedication actually consist of images, or a painting, of the tools? In the latter case, the epigram will become a kind of ecphrasis (word picture) of the painting. Such a dedication would cost money and/or time that the sisters can ill afford, but perhaps such a symbolic dedication to the goddess might make the real tools more efficacious, thus helping them in the future to win the bread they now lack.

Obviously these are questions that do not in reality have answers; they are part of the game that the epigram sets in play. Again, we might ask, how is it that Autonoma and the others *are* able to give up work? Is it because they are going to be married, to husbands

---

[24] In 41, *potithumia* ('to [your] liking'), *molpâtida* ('performer of a μολπή [a song and dance performance])', *eubritheis* ('hefty'), and *eusipuous* ('having a full breadbasket') are *hapax legomena*, that is, words not attested elsewhere in Greek. Of this last adjective's opposite, *oligêsipuôn* ('having a scanty breadbasket'), only one other instance is known, in another of Leonidas' dedicatory epigrams, 36 *HE* = *AP* 6.300. In 42, *eirokomon* is a borrowed Homeric *hapax* (here in the narrower sense of the term, meaning a word that occurs only once in the Homeric poems: Hom. *Il.* 3.387), while *orphnitan* (which I have translated as 'night-watching' but whose sense is uncertain) is a *hapax* in the wider sense, as is Athena's epithet *Panitidi* ('of the Bobbin').

[25] Unless *paides* ('daughters'/'children') in line 1 of 41 should be taken as bearing sense II in LSJ ('in relation to Age') as well as sense I ('in relation to Descent').

[26] See Gow and Page's introductory note to Agis 1 *HE*, pointing to similar examples, including poems that imitate this one.

rich enough that their wives will not need to weave? That might be suggested by the Homeric allusion in 42.6 (to Penelope's ruse of employing an unfinished piece of weaving, which she worked on by day and secretly unravelled by night, as an excuse to put off marrying one of her suitors: *Od.* 19.137–55); if weaving is characterized as a delayer of marriage, perhaps the women are setting aside their weaving equipment because marriage is imminent. It is remarkable, though, if they are all getting married at once. Another possible reason would be old age, as in the case of the elderly musicians who dedicate their instruments on retirement in Leonidas 43 *HE* = *AP* 5.206; but ancient Greeks tended to think of old age (short of death, that is) as troublesome, not as the 'ceasing from toils' referred to in the final line. In fact, as Kathryn Gutzwiller points out, such expressions have more of the resonance of an epitaph;[27] and as she says, retirement from a profession is indeed the end of one life and the start of a new one – and so too is marriage.

Finally it is worth pointing out how the different voices with which the two epigrams address the reader once again set a different tone. Atheno and the others address the goddess directly, which is appropriate in a dedication that is also a prayer for help; the reader's position is thus slightly voyeuristic, looking in on an intense moment in the lives of strangers. The second poem, by contrast, addresses the reader directly as 'stranger': this is a scene that we are *meant* to see.[28] The women can properly take pride in this (imagined) public monument to their improved circumstances; at the same time, the impersonal, third-person voice helps them avoid giving any impression that they are over-proud or complacent in their prosperity.

Focussing on such imaginary scenes should not beguile us into thinking that epigram and history part company in the Hellenistic period. Nossis commemorates a victory of her Locrian countrymen over the Bruttians in a striking epigram (2 *HE* = *AP* 6.132):

Ἔντεα Βρέττιοι ἄνδρες ἀπ᾿ αἰνομόρων βάλον ὤμων
θεινόμενοι Λοκρῶν χερσὶν ὕπ᾿ ὠκυμάχων,
ὧν ἀρετὰν ὑμνεῦντα θεῶν ὕπ᾿ ἀνάκτορα κεῖνται
οὐδὲ ποθεῦντι κακῶν πάχεας οὓς ἔλιπον.

---

[27] Gutzwiller 1998: 93.

[28] Tueller 2008: 101 suggests that this may be the earliest surviving dedicatory epigram to adopt the funerary convention of the 'address to the passer-by' (one that Leonidas himself does not use in his funerary epigrams).

> These arms men of Bruttium cast off from shoulders doomed to die
>    as they were rained with blows at the hands of the Locrians, swift in
>       battle;
> singing in praise of their valour they are dedicated in the gods' temples,
>    and feel no yearning for the cowards' forearms they left.

There is no reason to doubt (but equally no means of establishing) the reality of this battle, of which nothing else is known, between the Locrians and their non-Greek south Italian neighbours. In its pride and ferocious scorn for the defeated enemy, the poem recalls the Athenian dedication 'Simonides' 3 *FGE*, quoted by Herodotus, that we encountered in Chapter 1. There are several respects, however, in which the technique, if not the effect, is more subtle and less direct. In its opening words, for instance, by placing the 'men of Bruttium' in the nominative case, it adopts the perspective of the Bruttians, and indeed suggests for a moment the possibility that this may be *their* dedication: the sentence could just as well continue 'These arms men of Bruttium dedicated, having conquered…'.[29] The word 'men' (*andres*), has the additional connotation of 'brave men', men who live up to a masculine warrior ideal. It soon becomes apparent that this mark of honour is being given to the Bruttians only the more effectively, and devastatingly, to take it away again. By throwing away their shields they throw away their manhood, a process that we see completed when their very shields label them *kakoi*, 'cowards', in the final line.[30]

Similarly the poem takes up the Bruttians' subject position in the first line only to move in line 3, most unexpectedly, to the subject position of their captured shields: as Gow and Page note, this is the only known instance of the verb *humneô* ('hymn', 'sing in praise

---

[29] Unlikely, of course, in practice, since the Bruttians were not Greek-speakers. In its later line order, 'Simonides' 3 also begins with the defeated, ἔθνεα Βοιωτῶν καὶ Χαλκιδέων ('peoples of Boeotia and Chalcis'); but, while the neuter plural *ethnea* ('peoples') could be either nominative (indicating subject) or accusative (indicating object), the use of this word as opposed to the honorific *andres* would make it instantly clear to an Athenian reader that these must be the losers and that the word should therefore be understood as accusative.

[30] The idea that a *rhipsaspis*, a soldier who casts off his shield, loses his masculinity by doing so is famously encapsulated in the apocryphal story of the Spartan mother saying to her son, on handing him his shield as he leaves for battle, ἢ ταύταν ἢ ἐπὶ ταύτας, literally 'this or on this', i.e. either bring the shield back safely or return carried on it dead (followed by other similar anecdotes at 241f in the *Sayings of Spartan Women* attributed to Plutarch; on other tellings of this story in antiquity and later, see Hammond 1980). It also has rich literary resonances, for example with Archil. 5, a daring expression of indifference by the soldier-poet who has left his shield behind in a retreat; on the relationship between Nossis' poem and Archilochus' see Tueller 2008: 100–1.

of') being used with something inanimate as its subject. The shields now have more claim to subjectivity, and a voice, than their former human owners, and they use their new-found powers to sing the praises of the victors.[31] As the opposition of *andres* ('men') in line 1 to *kakôn* ('cowards') in line 4 marks the beginning and end of the process whereby the life force moved from the Bruttians to their shields, so the contrast between *ap'...balon ômôn* ('they threw from their *shoulders*') and *pakheas...elipon* ('they left the *forearms*') provides a remarkable close-up on the moment it happened: at the beginning of the movement, volition was with the Bruttians, who cast their shields down off their shoulders in order to run away faster; but at the moment they made this cowardly decision, volition passed to their disgusted shields, which (or rather who) completed the movement, from lower arm to ground, and left their former owners of their own accord.[32]

Meanwhile, the victorious Locrians, who might be thought in danger of disappearing from view in the midst of this strange drama, are picked out by the epithet *ôkhumakhos* ('swift in fighting'), which has an authentic Homeric ring but in fact turns out to be a *hapax* (a word used nowhere else in surviving Greek). There is a striking correspondence of sound, and equivalence of metrical quantity, between *ap' aino-morôn* ('from doomed-to-die') in line 1 and *hup' ôku-makhôn* ('by swift-fighting'[33]) in line 2, and it is tempting to

---

[31] I am not entirely convinced by Gutzwiller's suggestion that Nossis makes the shields voice the victors' praise in order to express masculine values while preserving her own distinctly feminine persona (Gutzwiller 1998: 80.). As a parallel for ὑμνεῦντα, Gow and Page cite Anyte 4 *HE*, where a stone tomb 'sings' (ἀείδει) the verse that records the dead man's brave death in battle. The personification of the shields is perhaps further underlined by the unusual use of the plural verb κεῖνται with a neuter plural subject. Exceptions to the rule that n. pl. subject take singular verb are usually (a) where the n. pl. noun refers to people or other living creatures or (b) where it refers not to a cohesive group of things but to things distributed over space or time: KG 2.1 pp. 65–6; the latter explanation might also apply if, in view of 'the gods' temples', we are meant to think of the shields as dedicated in several different places, a possibility raised by Gow and Page.

[32] As GN points out to me, this physical movement is accompanied by a poetic movement into semantic focus: what the Bruttians threw from their shoulders could have been various kinds of equipment (e.g. swords slung on sword belts); what leaves their forearms is clearly their shields. While the forearm goes through the handle of the shield, the weight is borne by the shoulders, and it is 'on their shoulders' that warriors are generally said to carry shields (Hom. *Il.* 11.527, etc.), so, in a culture in which arms and armour were a matter of everyday experience, the reference to their forearms perhaps contributes to capturing the Bruttians' humiliating situation. A rare case in which someone is said to hold a shield on the forearm is Posidippus 36 AB 6 (ἐν πήχει κοῖλον ἔχουσα σάκος), where the holder is Queen Arsinoe II Philadelphus. To have the shield slung on her shoulders would perhaps masculinize the queen too much.

[33] Though in fact if Gow and Page are right 'by' belongs grammatically with the preceding word *khersin* 'hands'.

suggest that the two together sound an underlying elegiac note by suggesting *ôkumorôn*, the corresponding grammatical form of a much more familiar word, the Homeric adjective *ôkumoros* ('swift to die'):[34] winners or losers, death comes too soon to us all.

A famous epigram by Posidippus on an equally famous allegorical statue by the sculptor Lysippus provides a convenient transition to the genre of ecphrastic epigram[35] (Posidippus 19 *HE* = 142 AB = *AP* 16.275):

Τίς πόθεν ὁ πλαστής; – Σικυώνιος. – Οὔνομα δὴ τίς;
— Λύσιππος. – Σὺ δὲ τίς; – Καιρὸς ὁ πανδαμάτωρ.
— Τίπτε δ' ἐπ' ἄκρα βέβηκας; – Ἀεὶ τροχάω. – Τί δὲ ταρσούς
ποσσὶν ἔχεις διφυεῖς; – Ἵπταμ' ὑπηνέμιος.
— Χειρὶ δὲ δεξιτέρη τί φέρεις ξυρόν; – Ἀνδράσι δεῖγμα
ὡς ἀκμῆς πάσης ὀξύτερος τελέθω.
— Ἡ δὲ κόμη τί κατ' ὄψιν; – Ὑπαντιάσαντι λαβέσθαι
νὴ Δία. – Τἀξόπιθεν δ' εἰς τί φαλακρὰ πέλει;
— Τὸν γὰρ ἅπαξ πτηνοῖσι παραθρέξαντά με ποσσίν
οὔτις ἔθ' ἱμείρων δράξεται ἐξόπιθεν.
— Τοὔνεχ' ὁ τεχνίτης σε διέπλασεν; – Εἵνεκεν ὑμέων,
ξεῖνε, καὶ ἐν προθύροις θῆκε διδασκαλίην.

– Who's your sculptor, and where's he from? – From Sikyon. – And his name?
    – Lysippus. – And who are you? – All-conquering Opportunity [*Kairos*].
– Why are you standing up on tiptoe? – I'm always on the run. –Why do you have
    a pair of wings on your feet? – I'm flying, borne by the wind.
– Why are you holding a razor in your right hand? – As a sign to men
    that I am more acute than any blade.
– Why do you have hair over your face – For anyone who meets me to grab me by,
    by Zeus. – And why is the back of your head bald?
– Because once I have run past on my winged feet
    no-one, however much he wants to, can then seize me from behind.
– What did the artist make you for? – For people like you,
    stranger, and he put me up as a lesson, here in the portico.

---

[34] Used by Thetis of Achilles in a series of memorable scenes in the *Iliad*: 1.417, 1.505, 18.95, 18.457.

[35] On the meaning of the term 'ecphrasis' in antiquity and in modern scholarship (briefly: in antiquity, any vivid description; in modern scholarship: an extended description of a work of art), see Gutzwiller 2002: 85 n. 1; on the category 'ecphrastic epigram', see further Männlein-Robert 2007: 251–2.

The epigram has some, but not all, of the outward form of a dedication. It names the 'dedicator'/artist who erected the statue, and *thêke* ('put [me] up') in the last line echoes the standard dedicatory *anethêke* ('put up = dedicated'). There is no divine dedicatee, though; in a sense, the onlooker for whom the statue is a lesson takes the place of the dedicatee. What the epigram essentially does, however, is evoke and interpret the allegorical statue through the device of the dialogue between monument and passer-by. Its epigrammatic 'point' consists in the wide-eyed naïveté of the questioner, who needs every detail explained to him; this in turn points to the paradox of the statue, aiming to 'capture' fleeting, abstract Opportunity in static, figurative bronze. The figure's last utterance gives vent to the statue's exasperation that, because of the interrogator's inability to 'read' its visual signs, it is unable to do its didactic job without the assistance of the epigram.[36] At the same time, by its use of the plural pronoun *humeôn* ('you [plural]', translated 'people like you' above) in juxtaposition with the singular form of address *xeine* ('stranger'), it draws attention to the role of the reader.[37] In a literal sense, obviously, it can be interpreted as 'you and other passers-by' ('people like you'), but it also signals that the audience for its lesson extends beyond the individual imagined as being in the presence of the statue: that is, it includes us, the readers of the epigram. The epigram has thus effectively replaced the statue: insofar as we are 'like' the internal reader, the imaginary passer-by, it enables us to understand and learn from the statue just as well as if we had seen it, and without the epigram's help we would not be able to make sense of the statue even if it were before our eyes.[38]

The Kairos epigram is typical of Hellenistic 'ecphrastic' epigram in that, by contrast with rhetorical ecphrasis, its concern is primarily with the significance, interpretation, and 'point' of the artwork rather

---

[36] On the wider question of the relationship between the kind of supplementation required of the viewers of Hellenistic art and the readers of Hellenistic epigram, see Zanker 2004: 72–102 (99–100 specifically on Kairos). It has been suggested persuasively that the Kairos statue's declaration that it is located *en prothurois* ('in the portico') contains a pun, because it suggests the use of *prothura* ('the parts before the door') to refer to the early stages of a programme of study: 'a lesson in the portico' is thus also 'a lesson for beginners' (Prauscello 2006).

[37] Cf. Gutzwiller 2002: 96: 'the plural ὑμέων...pulls the reader into the group represented by this viewing ξεῖνος'.

[38] For other interpretations of this poem, see e.g. Gutzwiller 2002: 95–6 and Männlein-Robert 2007, 260–2. Tueller 2008: 196–7 notes that all but the last of the statue's replies could actually be 'spoken' by Kairos/Opportunity himself. In fact this is true of the last reply as well, if we supply 'my statue' instead of 'me' as the object of θῆκε ('placed'), though on this occasion the question is unambiguously *addressed to* the statue.

than with vivid and detailed evocation of its visual appearance.[39] This contrast can, however, be overstated; some of the poems in the Milan papyrus collection, in particular, do seem concerned to create intense visual effects, as in this example from the section devoted to *Lithika*, 'Poems About Stones' (Posidippus 7 AB):

ἐξ Ἀράβων τὰ ξάνθ' ὀ[ρέων κατέρ]υτα κυλίων,
  εἰς ἅλα χειμάρρους ὢκ᾽ [ἐφόρει ποτα]μὸς
τὸν μέλιτι χροιὴν λίθ[ον εἴκελον, ὃ]ν Κρονίο[υ] χεὶρ
  ἔγλυψε· χρυσῷ σφιγκτ[ὸς ὅδε γλυκερ]ῇ
Νικονόη κάθεμα τρη[τὸν φλέγει, ἧ]ς ἐπὶ μαστῷ
  συλλάμπει λευκῷ χρωτὶ μελιχρὰ φάη.

As it swept tawny-coloured debris down from Arabian mountains
  the river, swollen with winter rain, brought swiftly to the sea
the stone with a surface like honey, which the hand of Kronios
  carved: bound in gold, for sweet
Nikonoe it sets fire to her inlaid necklace, as on her breast
  its honeyed light shares radiance with her pale skin.

The poem has a double development. One is from the tumultuous evocation of stones borne headlong from exotic mountains, via the painstaking art of the jeweller who tames or civilizes the gem by carving it and mounting it in gold, to the tableau of the jewel resting on Nikonoe's breast. The other is through a succession of colour images, from the rubble in the Arabian river (described as *xanthos*, an adjective applied to human hair as well as, for example, to lions and horses, and often translated 'blond' or 'tawny' but hard to pin down precisely), via the honey simile, the placement in the gold mount, and the fire metaphor, once again to the climactic juxtaposition with Nikonoe's skin. Here, visual evocation of the stone's colour (though not of its precise form) is clearly crucial to the poem, but it is still subordinated to a 'point', an exploration of the oppositions between nature and culture, life and art.[40] The 'wild' stone is captured, carved, and bound, but bursts out again with 'natural' energy when it reaches

[39] Cf. Männlein-Robert 2007: 252. This point is well illustrated by contrasting Posidippus' epigram on Lysippus' Kairos statue with a later rhetorical ecphrasis of the same work, by Callistratus (writing possibly in the fifth century CE), *Descriptions of Statues* 6. Three-quarters of Callistratus' account is devoted to the statue's miraculously lifelike appearance; the interpretation of the allegory is relegated to a sentence at the end and put in the mouth of another person, an expert who 'happened to be present'.

[40] See Hoffman 2004 on the vividness and 'real-world' qualities of poems in the Milan papyrus; there is a danger of overstatement. On 7 AB see Bing 2005: 125–7, and Kuttner 2005: 145 (and Kuttner's chapter more generally on the *Lithika* as a 'cabinet of curiosities').

its intended place on Nikonoe's breast (it is not a coincidence that its colour is that of honey, a substance liminal between nature and culture). The interplay of the etymologically related and semantically overlapping words *khroia* ('surface') in line 3 and *khrôs* ('skin') in line 6 underlines the juxtaposition of honeyed stone with pale skin and the placement of one exquisite surface upon another, but also suggests an affinity, or blurring of identity, between the jewel and its wearer. On the one hand, the gem is alive; on the other hand, Nikonoe is herself a jewel.[41]

A theme common to both ecphrastic epigram and rhetorical ecphrasis is the miracle, or paradox, of Life captured in the lifeless media of Art, as in the Myron's Cow epigrams and, for instance, in another poem on a statue from the Milan papyrus, this time from the *Hippika* ('Poems About Horses') section (Posidippus 72 AB):

> τοῦ πώλου θηεῖσθε τὸ λιπαρές, ὡς πνόον ἕλκει
> πάντι τύπῳ καὶ πᾶς ἐκ λαγόνων τέταται
> ὡς νεμεοδρομέων· Μολύκῳ δ᾽ ἤνεγκε σέλινα
> νικήσας ἄκρῳ νεύματι καὶ κεφάλῃ.

> Look at the colt's determination, how it draws breath
>     through its whole form, and its whole body is stretched out from the
>     flanks
> as when running the race at Nemea; for Molykos it took the celery-crown
>     when it won by a nod of the tip of its nose.

The figure of a horse flying to victory is praised for capturing precisely those qualities that, on the face of it, plastic art cannot convey: its abstract quality of eagerness to win, its accentuated drawing of breath, even the place and nature of its victory. As with the Kairos poem, however, what this ultimately reveals is that we need to be told (see the opening imperative 'look') how to view the statue, it *requires* commentary; and since the commentary conjures the statue by forcing the reader to imagine it, the plastic artwork itself becomes dispensable.[42]

---

[41] See also Kuttner 2005: 163 on the logic of reproduction and copying at work in these poems, whereby the ultimate answer to the question 'what is the truly lasting gem?' is the poem itself; as Kuttner puts it, 'gem poetry is perhaps gem magic'.

[42] Papalexandrou 2004: 253–5 emphasizes the interdependency of poem and artwork; perhaps with a literary scholar's prejudice, I am inclined to see the poem as taking the place of the artefact. For an image of a bronze figure perhaps similar to the one described in the epigram, the 'Artemision horse', see Acosta-Hughes, Kosmetatou, and Baumbach 2004, Figure 2.

## Sympotic, amatory, and erotic epigrams

Wine, love, sex, and the symposium or men's drinking party (with male and female entertainers) do not always go together in epigram but they often do, and for that reason these fluid categories of epigrammatic poetry will be discussed together. The association of inscribed verse with sympotic, or possibly sympotic, activities goes back to a very early date, as attested by two famous early graffiti: the 'Dipylon oinochoe' and 'Nestor's cup'. The first, one of the very earliest Greek inscriptions known to us, was written in the eighth century BCE on the shoulder of a wine jug found in a grave near the Dipylon gate in Athens (*CEG* 432 = IG I² 919, SEG 39: 41[a]):[43]

> hὸς νῦν ὀρχεστôν πάντον ἀταλότατα παίζει,
> τô τόδε κλῖμιν

that is,

> ὃς νῦν ὀρχεστῶν πάντων ἀταλώτατα παίζῃ,
> τῷ τόδε [six letters of uncertain interpretation]
>
> Whoever now of all the dancers performs [lit. 'plays'] most sweetly,
> [?]For him is this...

The inscription, Homeric in style, appears to identify the vessel as a prize in a dancing contest, and the fact that the verb used underlines the playfulness of the performance makes it tempting to imagine a sympotic context.[44]

'Nestor's cup' (not the only archaeologically discovered vessel to have been given this name, but perhaps the one with the best title to it; see Hom. *Il.* 11.632–7 for the fictional cup on which they are presumably modelled, which 'another man would struggle to raise from the table when it was full, but the old man Nestor lifted effortlessly') is a drinking vessel also found in a grave, this time on the island of Pithekoussai (modern Ischia) off the cost of Italy, on which the following lines (the first either prose or metrically unusual

---

[43] I print Hansen's text from *CEG*. Numerous attempts have been made to read and interpret the letters in the second line, but it remains enigmatic; the reading of the first line, however, is clear.

[44] For discussion of the vessel and its possible sympotic context, see e.g. B. Powell 1991: 158–63; Fantuzzi 2004b: 285–6 with 286 n. 7; Day 2007: 35–6; Henrichs 2003: 45–6 (envisaging a religious context); and Osborne and Pappas 2007: 133–4 (with photograph).

verse, the second and third hexameters) are inscribed (*CEG* 454 = IGASMG III 2):[45]

> Νέστορός ε[ἰμ]ι εὔποτον ποτέριον.
> hὸς δ' ἂν τôδε πίεσι ποτερί[ο] αὐτίκα κêνον
> hίμερος hαιρέσει καλλιστε[φά]νο Ἀφροδίτες.

that is,

> Νέστορός εἰμι εὔποτον ποτήριον.
> ὃς δ' ἂν τῶδε πίῃσι ποτηρίῳ, αὐτίκα κεῖνον
> ἵμερος αἱρήσει καλλιστεφάνου Ἀφροδίτης.

I am Nestor's cup, good for drinking.
Whoever drinks from this cup, he will at once
be seized by desire for fair-crowned Aphrodite.

This inscription echoes other kinds of inscription: the very common and simple ownership inscription 'I am so-and-so's', and curse inscriptions: an oft-quoted parallel is IG XIV 865, on a pot about half a century later in date found at Cumae, not far from Ischia: 'I am Tataie's lekythos ['flask']. Whoever steals me will go blind'. It is tempting to see in this small vessel's self-description as *eupoton*, 'good for drinking' (or 'easy to drink from'), a playful reference to the Homeric passage, in which Nestor's huge cup is *hard* for anyone other than Nestor to drink from. The likelihood of such an allusion has been questioned, and the inscription has been variously interpreted;[46] at the very least, it is clear that we have here some inscribed verses linking the themes of wine and love.

These intriguing beginnings do not, however, inaugurate a tradition of inscribed verses on amatory or sympotic subjects; in fact, apart from them, Hellenistic sympotic and erotic epigram have almost no direct antecedents, which has led to much debate about how these genres originated. One possible hypothesis is that this is a case of the principle we have already encountered, that epigram arises when

---

[45] Note that, in *CEG*, the dates '535–20' and '525–20' are misprints for '735–20' and '725–20' respectively: see *CEG* II, p. 304.

[46] For discussion see e.g. B. Powell 1991: 163–7 (clever sympotic humour); West 1994, Faraone 1996, and Henrichs 2003: 46–7 (all seeing the inscription as a magic charm; West suggests a connection with lost epics telling of Nestor's earlier career); Fantuzzi 2004b: 286–7 ('certainly a product of the world of the symposium'); and Osborne and Pappas 2007: 134–5 (with photograph; 'plays with both the conventions of curses and knowledge of the epic tradition').

elegy meets scissors. Love and wine were certainly prominent in the repertoire of early elegy. Ancient books required quasi-editorial effort from their readers, and it would be natural for readers to look out for self-contained excerpts quotable, say, at a symposium; it would be an easy transition from finding excerpts to modifying such excerpts in order to make them *more* self-contained, and thence to creating 'excerpts' (that is, epigrams), from scratch. The story is unlikely to have been anything like this simple, but some connection between these epigrams and elegy seems extremely likely.[47] Another influence, directly or indirectly, is likely to have been an inscriptional practice that definitely *was* associated with the classical symposium, namely the game of writing on pots or potsherds variations on the formula 'X *kalos*', ('so-and-so [is] beautiful/ attractive').[48]

However it was that epigram found its way to the symposium, and whether the parties at which it made itself at home were real or fictional ones, it undoubtedly flourished in its new environment, adopting motifs both from earlier erotic verse and from other epigrammatic forms, and establishing many of the characteristic themes of later love poetry in both Greek and Latin (and in other languages thereafter). An epigram of Hedylus (5 *HE*, not in the *Anthology* but quoted by the second- to third-century-CE writer Athenaeus, 11 472f) serves to set the scene:

> Πίνωμεν· καὶ γάρ τι νέον, καὶ γάρ τι παρ' οἶνον
> εὕροιμ' ἂν λεπτὸν καί τι μελιχρὸν ἔπος.
> ἀλλὰ κάδοις Χίου με κατάβρεχε καὶ λέγε, 'παῖζε
> Ἡδύλε'· μισῶ ζῆν ἐς κενὸν οὐ μεθύων.

Let's drink! You know, something new, something wine-inspired
  is bound to come to me, some subtle, honey-coloured talk.
Drench me with vats of Chian and say: 'Play,
  Hedylus!' I loathe living emptily, not being drunk.

---

[47] On the 'editorial' demands that ancient books made of their readers, see Krevans 2007: 135–6; on elegy and epigram, see especially Bowie 2007, with references to earlier discussions; see also Aloni 2009, especially 179–82, envisaging epigram as entering the sympotic repertoire alongside elegy at an early date (182). As this chapter and the preceding one will have made clear, I do not fully share Aloni's view of epigram as having a 'character of completeness' by contrast with the 'dialogic structure' of elegy, and thus inviting a relatively passive response, though he is of course right to stress that the two forms invite a different kind of response.
[48] On *kalos* inscriptions, see e.g. Lissarague 1999. For uncertain but intriguing evidence of a particularly elaborate *kalos* game in an Athenian public building in the early fifth century, possibly involving parody of the process of ostracism, see A. Steiner 2002.

The poem sets a high standard of sympotic extravagance: *kadoi* ('vats') are storage vessels, not drinking vessels (sizes varied, but one ancient reference indicates a capacity of approximately nine gallons/ forty litres: see *HE* p. 293); and the fact that the wine is coming 'straight from the *kados*' has the further implication that it is unmixed. Drinking unmixed wine seems to have been a practice more common at fictional symposia (cf. Callimachus 8, discussed below) than at real ones, where mixing wine with water in varying proportions was an important piece of social ceremony. The alcoholic soaking the poet calls for also seems in tension with his hope that wine will bring witty inspiration; as will be seen, the effect of wine on the wits of the scholar-poet is another recurrent epigrammatic theme. Finally, there is a characteristic ambiguity, or gap left to be filled in by the reader, in the poem's closing words: what sort of filling of the void are we to envisage? Will drinking remedy the emptiness of Hedylus' life, or merely make him oblivious to it?

A calmer but equally ambivalent sympotic scene is evoked with characteristic vividness and economy by an epigram of Callimachus (13 *HE* = 43 P =*AP* 12.134):

Ἕλκος ἔχων ὁ ξεῖνος ἐλάνθανεν· ὡς ἀνιηρόν
    πνεῦμα διὰ στηθέων – εἶδες; – ἀνηγάγετο,
τὸ τρίτον ἡνίκ' ἔπινε, τὰ δὲ ῥόδα φυλλοβολεῦντα
    τὠνδρὸς ἀπὸ στεφάνων πάντ' ἐγένοντο χαμαί.
ὤπτηται μέγα δή τι. μὰ δαίμονας, οὐκ ἀπὸ ῥυσμοῦ
    εἰκάζω, φωρὸς δ' ἴχνια φὼρ ἔμαθον.

The stranger has a wound we hadn't noticed: how painfully
    he drew that breath – did you notice? – up into his breast,
as he drank the third cup, and the roses were shedding their petals
    off the man's garlands, and they all ended up on the ground!
He's got the fever badly. In the gods' name, that's no haphazard
    guess: I know a thief's tracks, I'm a thief myself.

The speaker's address to his fellow guest, with the urgent aside 'did you notice?', achieves the mise-en-scène immediately; the poem's dramatic development hinges on the speaker's instinctive identification with the stranger as a fellow lover, and on the pathetic fallacy of the corresponding 'droopiness' of the garland and its wearer. The proverbial ending rounds the poem off neatly, but does so with ambiguity, again demanding more work from the reader. The primary sense is clear enough, as in the English expressions 'set a thief to catch a thief' or 'it takes one to know one', but what are the implications of likening lovers to thieves? Is it a reminder that, for all their suffering and self-pity, lovers are always to some extent predatory, 'raiders on the flock', seeking to snatch favours from the objects of their affection?[49] Or does the man's thief-like 'furtiveness' consist in his attempt to conceal his love instead of telling his fellow guests all about his latest infatuation, thus breaking the rules of commensality? If so, the poem's ending activates an ambiguity inherent in the word *xeinos* in line 1, Greek for both 'stranger' and 'guest/friend'. At the same time, it points a questioning finger at the poet's own persona as well: has he drawn attention to the other man's lovesickness simply as a distraction strategy from his own?

Another frequent theme is the irresistible power of love and the extremities to which it drives the lover. In Asclepiades 11 *HE* = *AP* 5.64, a man in love defies the elements:

Νεῖφε, χαλαζοβόλει, ποίει σκότος, αἶθε, κεραύνου,
  πάντα τὰ πορφύροντ' ἐν χθονὶ σεῖε νέφη·
ἢν γάρ με κτείνῃς τότε παύσομαι, ἢν δέ μ' ἀφῇς ζῆν
  κἂν διαθῇς τούτων χείρονα, κωμάσομαι·
ἕλκει γάρ μ' ὁ κρατῶν καὶ σοῦ θεός, ᾧ ποτε πεισθείς,
  Ζεῦ, διὰ χαλκείων χρυσὸς ἔδυς θαλάμων.

Snow, hurl down hail, make darkness, send thunder and lightning,
  shake every cloud that hangs purple over the earth;
if you kill me, then I will stop, but if you let me live
  you can make worse weather than this, and I'll still revel [go on a *kômos*]:
what pulls me is the god who rules even you, at whose persuasion,
  Zeus, you once slipped as gold into a bronze bedroom.

The speaker's forthright tone when addressing the Father of Gods and Men demands explanation, which line 5 provides: he need not fear Zeus, or rather is incapable of heeding him, because the force that

[49] Cf. Socrates' words at Pl. *Phdr.* 241d: ὡς λύκοι ἄρνας ἀγαπῶσιν, ὡς παῖδα φιλοῦσιν ἐρασταί ('just as wolves are fond of lambs, so lovers like a boy'), a slight misquotation (or affected misquotation, since it may well be Plato's own composition) of a proverbial-sounding hexameter; and see Luck 1959 on later developments of this motif, including a possible one in Callimachus' *Iambics* and several in later epigram.

impels him, Love, is more powerful than them both. The final line provides an added twist: Love's power over Zeus took the precise form of transforming the weather god into a different kind of 'weather', the golden rain-shower that he became in order to make love to Danaë. At the same time, the epigram's closing lines enact the power of Love: the moment he enters the poem, the storm clouds and violence of the first four lines are replaced by the tranquil, if slightly sinister, tableau of Danaë's miraculous impregnation.

This is one of many epigrams that evoke the *kômos*, the outdoor revel following the symposium that might, among other possibilities, lead the lover, intoxicated with love and wine, to the beloved's door. If the latter remains shut, as in Callimachus 63 *HE* = 36 P = *AP* 5.23 (a poem whose attribution to Callimachus has been questioned),[50] the result is a *paraklausithyron* or 'song at the closed door' (sometimes Latinized: *paraclausithyron*), a form much imitated by Roman love poets:

Οὕτως ὑπνώσσαις, Κωνώπιον, ὡς ἐμὲ ποιεῖς
  κοιμᾶσθαι ψυχροῖς τοῖσδε παρὰ προθύροις·
οὕτως ὑπνώσσαις, ἀδικωτάτη, ὡς τὸν ἐραστήν
  κοιμίζεις, ἐλέου δ᾽ οὐδ᾽ ὄναρ ἠντίασας.
γείτονες οἰκτείρουσι, σὺ δ᾽ οὐδ᾽ ὄναρ· ἡ πολιὴ δέ
  αὐτίκ᾽ ἀναμνήσει ταῦτά σε πάντα κόμη.

I hope you sleep as comfortably, Konopion, as you make me
  lie, here in this cold doorway.
I hope you sleep as comfortably, brute, as the resting place you give
  your lover – but you don't even dream of pity.
Your neighbours are sorry for me, but you don't dream of it. Turned grey,
  though, your hair will soon remind you of all this.

The poem promises a reversal of roles: the girl will be sorry when she is old, a commonplace of later (if this poem is by Callimachus) love poetry. This poignant future reversal is in tension, however, with another, more humorous, one in the present: the girl, a *hetaira* ('prostitute'/'escort'), has a professional name that can be translated 'Mosquitina', little biting insect (GN suggests 'Gnatalie'), a creature whose usual role is to keep an otherwise sound sleeper awake by buzzing around and threatening to bite (and a name which is perhaps meant to suggest Konopion's skill in 'irritating' her customers into

---

[50] For one thing because Callimachus' self-presentation elsewhere in his epigrams is as a lover of boys, not girls: Gutzwiller 1998: 213–4.

sexual arousal). Here, though, Konopion is sleeping soundly (in spite of her lover's wishes), while he is the one creating the nocturnal noise (and keeping the neighbours awake).[51]

In the poem mentioned earlier as having been incorporated in the decor of an elite Roman dining room, Callimachus varies the *paraklausithyron* theme, with clear interplay with Asclepiades 11, discussed above (Callimachus 8 *HE* = 42 P = *AP* 12.118):

> Εἰ μὲν ἑκών, Ἀρχῖν', ἐπεκώμασα, μυρία μέμφου,
>     εἰ δ' ἄκων ἥκω, τὴν προπέτειαν ἔα.
> Ἄκρητος καὶ Ἔρως μ' ἠνάγκασαν, ὧν ὁ μὲν αὐτῶν
>     εἷλκεν, ὁ δ' οὐκ εἴα τὴν προπέτειαν ἐᾶν·
> ἐλθὼν δ' οὐκ ἐβόησα τίς ἢ τίνος, ἀλλ' ἐφίλησα
>     τὴν φλιήν. εἰ τοῦτ' ἐστ' ἀδίκημ', ἀδικέω.

> If I chose to come on a revel [*kômos*], Arkhinos, blame me a million times,
>     but if I had no choice but to come, then let the impulse alone.
> It was Unmixed Wine and Love who compelled me, and of the two of them
>     one pulled me on, while the other would not let me let the impulse alone;
> and when I arrived, I didn't give my name or my surname,[52] but kissed
>     your doorframe; if that's a crime, I'm a criminal.

The poem is a 'cancelled' paraclausithyron: far from lamenting outside the closed door, the lover/speaker has merely kissed it, and now defends himself for his behaviour. The precise situation is slowly revealed by the play of tenses: aorists (a part of the Greek verb used to mark an action as complete) in lines 1, 3, and 5 indicate that the *kômos* behaviour, that is, the intoxicated arrival at the beloved's door, is over; the verb *hêkô* in line 2 implies 'I have come (and am now here)'; the present tense of the imperatives in lines 1 and 2 and of the

---

[51] On the question of the attribution to Callimachus see Tarán 1979: 91–2; on the name Konopion, ibid. 91 n. 110, quoting an article by K. J. McKay that I have not been able to consult. McKay's interpretation of the name's significance, surprisingly seldom mentioned in discussions of this poem, is clearly correct. The interpretation and text of line 3 are disputed (see *HE* p. 215 and Taran 1979: 90 with n. 104). I suspect that, in this poem of sleep and sleeplessness, there is further play with the expression *oud' onar* ('not even [in] a dream', repeated in line 4), which in Greek is usually a dead metaphor meaning 'not in the slightest'. The unexpected sense provided if we construe the verb ἀντιά(ζ)ω with the genitive ἐλέου (which would have the girl failing to *receive*, instead of failing to feel, pity) brings the metaphor back to life by forcing us to reinterpret ὄναρ as the verb's direct object: she has not 'met even a dream of pity', i.e. she is sleeping so soundly in spite of everything that her lover's plight does not even impinge on her dreams. See Tueller 2008: 130–1 on this poem's exploitation of funerary motifs.

[52] Literally 'my father's name', serving to identify a visitor in answer to the question 'who's there?'

indicatives in the final line show the speaker addressing the beloved directly. The speaker has come to the house in usual *kômos*-fashion but, instead of staying obdurately behind closed doors, the beloved has come out, without even being summoned, and asked what he is doing there. Callimachus uses this 'doorless' paraclausithyron, with the conventional barrier between the desirer and the object of desire removed, as an opportunity for reflection on problems of self-control, passion, and free will.

The word *propeteia* ('impulsiveness', 'rashness', 'unmeditated action') in line 2 is ambiguous. It could mean '*your* impulse to blame me', the impulsiveness of which has already been suggested by the use of the hyperbolic word *muria* ('a million times'; strictly 'ten thousand times', but the standard word in Greek for a number too big to count) in line 1; or it could mean '*my* impulsiveness in coming here', which is the sense it takes on unambiguously when the word is repeated in line 4.[53] The text of line 4 is uncertain in the manuscript tradition but the reading, with its almost exact repetition of the second half of line 2, is confirmed by the Roman wall inscription of the poem mentioned earlier. The inscription's publisher, Georg Kaibel, pointed out that the word *propeteia* also carries suggestions of the vocabulary of Stoic logic, and proposed that we might think of the boy Arkhinos as being pupil to an austere Stoic tutor, and of the speaker of the poem as celebrating his own freedom from such constraints.[54] Gow and Page in *HE* (p. 163) gently mock the suggestion that Arkhinos 'was being twitted with a Stoic education' as far-fetched. We do not, however, need to presuppose any biographical reference (or indeed any very specific reference to Stoic doctrine) in order to recognize how the poem parodies, or plays with, philosophical discussions of motivation and free will (the technical vocabulary of philosophy was later to become a frequent target of epigrammatic wit).

A scholastic, logic-chopping tone is established by the mannered presentation of alternatives in the openings of lines 1 and 2 ('if on

[53] Bücheler, as reported in Kaibel 1876: 5, noting this ambiguity, points out (4) that there may be yet another sense latent in the word; προπέτεια is formed from the root of the verb προπίπτω, 'fall forward', and we may be invited to think of the drunken lover as having literally fallen on the ground at the beloved's doorpost. Bücheler's discussion of the poem, exploring its intertextuality with earlier and later literature (esp. Prop. 1.3.13–14), is still well worth reading. For a qualified defence, which I do not find convincing, of one of the manuscript readings of this line, see Tarán 1979: 67–8.

[54] Kaibel 1896: 266–8. For an introduction to the philosophical schools of the Hellenistic period, see Mitsis 2003; for a more detailed survey of Hellenistic philosophy, see Algra, et al. 1999, and on the Stoics in particular, see Inwood 2003.

the one hand by-choice…if on the other hand not-by-choice', *ei men hekôn…ei de âkôn*). It is underlined by the etymological wordplay suggested by the juxtaposition *âkôn hêkô* ('not-by-choice I have come'), by the near repetition of the line-ending from line 2 to line 4 (*tên propeteian eâ…tên propeteian eân*), suggestive of the iteration of technical terms in philosophical treatises, and finally by the convolutedness (pronounced 'unattractive' by Gow and Page) of the double use of the verb *eaô* ('allow, let, let alone') in line 4: *ouk eiâ tên propeteian eân*, ('would not let me let the impulse alone'), further emphasized by the jingling assonance of *eiâ…-eian…eân*. And it is not only at the stylistic level that the poem has suggestions of the philosophical schoolroom: indeed, it is argumentative from the start.

The question at stake is: 'who has shown himself to be governed by reason: Arkhinos or the speaker?' Line 1 implies that this is a question that Arkhinos himself has prejudged: reproach is already on his lips. But, it points out, he has done so without first considering the speaker's psychological state. Did the latter act by choice? If not, it is irrational to blame him – all the more so to blame him excessively (*muria*), thereby showing lack of restraint. The change of verb in line 2, from *epekômasa* ('I came on a revel') to *hêkô* ('I have come'), draws attention to a further respect in which Arkhinos has failed the rationality test. He omitted to consider not only the speaker's motivational state but also the correct description of his action. Was it a *kômos* at all? We will soon see that it was not, since he did not even announce himself or knock on the door. It thus becomes increasingly unclear whether it is the speaker or Arkhinos who has a case to answer on the charge of impulsiveness (*propeteia*).

In line 3, the agents who compelled the speaker are introduced: Wine and Love. As we have seen in Asclepiades 11, it is a truism that no-one, not even Zeus, can resist Love; lovers' excuses of this kind are commonplace, often mentioning wine as well.[55] Here, though, the argument that the poem develops gives new point to this commonplace idea. Love alone was not in fact sufficient (the imperfect tense of the verb *heilken* ['was dragging', 'tried to drag'] in line 4 marks the action as uncompleted and thus dramatizes the speaker's resistance as well as Love's deployment of force). Wine, and not just wine but wine in its extreme, unmixed form, was required as well; and even then, the effect

---

[55] All-conquering Love is mythologically articulated in the 'deception of Zeus' scene in the *Iliad* (14.153–351; see esp. line 294, 'as he saw her, so Love enfolded his shrewd wits'); cf. e.g. Eur. *Hipp.* 443–58. See Gow and Page's note (*HE* 163) for similar excuses on behalf of a lover.

on him is expressed in surprisingly negative terms, as debilitating rather than overwhelming. It 'would not let him let [the impulse] alone'. Far from being spontaneously impulsive, the speaker is revealed as having shown extraordinary resistance against overwhelming odds. Finally, as the last couplet indicates, the power Love and wine were able to exert was over his body alone, not his mind or power of speech, and did not extend even to producing impulsive physical treatment of any *sentient* creature. He came to the door, but did not say anything. He kissed – not the beloved, but the doorpost. That is all. He is able to rest his case.[56]

Another debate about the impulse to go on a *kômos*, this time in the form of an internal dialogue, appears in Meleager 19 *HE* = *AP* 12.117, a poem that brings together motifs from both Asclepiades 11 and Callimachus:

> Βέβλησθω κύβος· ἅπτε· πορεύσομαι. – Ἠνίδε τόλμαν·
> οἰνοβαρές, τίν' ἔχεις φροντίδα; – Κωμάσομαι,
> κωμάσομαι. – Ποῖ, θυμέ, τρέπῃ; – Τί δ' Ἔρωτι λογισμός;
> ἅπτε τάχος. – Ποῦ δ' ἡ πρόσθε λόγων μελετή;
> – Ἐρρίφθω σοφίας ὁ πολὺς πόνος· ἓν μόνον οἶδα
> τοῦθ', ὅτι καὶ Ζηνὸς λῆμα καθεῖλεν Ἔρως.

> Let the die be cast! Light torches: I'm on my way. – What recklessness!
>     you drunkard, what's your idea? – I'm going to party [go on a *kômos*]!
> I'm going to party! – Where are you heading for, my heart? – What does
>     Love care for reasoning?
>     Light torches, quickly! – Where's your past commitment to reason?
> – To hell with all the hard work of wisdom! There's just one thing
>     I know: that Love brought low the courage even of Zeus.

In this poem the rare adjective *oinobares* ('weighed down by wine', 'drunkard') in line 2 is a clear reminiscence of the abuse addressed by Achilles to Agamemnon during their famous argument in Book 1 of the *Iliad* (1.225):

> οἰνοβαρές, κυνὸς ὄμματ' ἔχων, κραδίην δ' ἐλάφοιο

> You drunkard, with the eyes of a dog and the heart of a deer!

and thus suggests the other two accusations, of shamelessness and lack of courage, as well as that of drunkenness; it also connects the poet's

---

[56] See also Gutzwiller 2007b: 324 on this poem as an example of Callimachus' evocation of deflected desire.

inner struggle, perhaps comically, with another argument in which
an external force (in that case *Atê*, 'Infatuation') deprived one party
of reason, thus precipitating the events of the epic and, ultimately
the death of Achilles and the fall of Troy. The Homeric allusion is
appropriate both to the solemnity and to the bookish preferences of
the 'voice of reason'; it prepares for, and is trumped by, the other
voice's appeal to the example of Zeus at the end of the poem ('I may
be no better than an Agamemnon, but then again I am no worse than
a Zeus').[57]

Erotic epigrams are not always as subtly concerned as Callimachus
8 with the rights and wrongs of the lover's behaviour. Some poems
describe the attractions of the beloved, as in Philodemus 12 *GPh* = 12
Sider = *AP* 5.132:

> Ὦ ποδός, ὢ κνήμης, ὢ τῶν ἀπόλωλα δικαίως
>     μηρῶν, ὢ γλουτῶν, ὢ κτενός, ὢ λαγόνων,
> ὢ ὤμοιν, ὢ μαστῶν, ὢ τοῦ ῥαδινοῖο τραχήλου,
>     ὢ χειρῶν, ὢ τῶν μαίνομαι ὀμματίων,
> ὢ κατατεχνοτάτου κινήματος, ὢ περιάλλων
>     γλωττισμῶν, ὢ τῶν θυέ με φωναρίων·
> εἰ δ' Ὀπικὴ καὶ Φλῶρα καὶ οὐκ ᾄδουσα τὰ Σαπφοῦς,
>     καὶ Περσεὺς Ἰνδῆς ἠράσατ' Ἀνδρομέδης.

> Her foot! Her calf! Her truly knock-me-out
>     thighs! Her buttocks! Her mound! Her waist!
> Her shoulders! Her breasts! Her slender neck!
>     Her hands! Her driving-me-crazy eyes!
> Her so-professional action! Her incomparable
>     tonguework! Her kill-me-for-them whisperings!
> So what if she's Italian and called 'Flora' and can't sing Sappho's songs.
>     Perseus fell in love with an Indian, Andromeda.[58]

The poet catalogues Flora's charms from the ground up, foot to eyes,
symmetrically centred on her waist as item six out of eleven; having
reached the head, he goes on to her intellectual qualities, that is, her

---

[57] There is probably also a reminiscence, conscious or unconscious, of the use of the word
in an epigram likely to have been included in Meleager's *Garland*, 'Simonides' 3 *HE* = 66 *FGE*
= *AP* 7.24, where the poet Anacreon is described (without any pejorative implication) as ὁ
φιλάκρητός τε καὶ οἰνοβαρὴς φιλόκωμος ('the neat-wine-loving and wine-heavy lover of the
*kômos*', line 5). This and Meleager's poem seem to be the only instances of the adjective (other
than in quotations or discussions of the *Iliad* passage) in surviving Greek literature down to
Oppian in the second century CE (Oppian *Halieutica* 2.412, 4.671).

[58] The exclamation marks in my translation aim to convey the effect of the repeated use of
the exclamatory word ὤ in the Greek.

love-making technique. There is a humorous tension between the rather matter-of-fact list and the poet's extravagant interjections expressing the effect the girl has on him; this is developed by the change of tack in the final couplet, from the infatuation suggested by 'kill-me-for-them' (literally 'offer me as a sacrifice for them') in line 6 to the cool acknowledgement of 'defects' in line 7 and the rationalizing appeal to a mythological precedent in the final line. This poem fits loosely in the category of Philodemus' erotic epigrams that Sider labels 'dark-but-comely',[59] which could be seen as a development of the tension between Love and Reason that we have seen explored by Callimachus: the scholar-poet is too realistic to imagine his beloved to be perfection – but is attracted to her nonetheless. Another example is Philodemus 8 *GPh* = 17 Sider = *AP* 5.115:

μικκὴ καὶ μελανεῦσα Φιλαίνιον, ἀλλὰ σελίνων
    οὐλοτέρη καὶ μνοῦ χρῶτα τερεινοτέρη
καὶ κεστοῦ φωνεῦσα μαγώτερα καὶ παρέχουσα
    πάντα καὶ αἰτῆσαι πολλάκι φειδομένη.
τοιαύτην στέργοιμι Φιλαίνιον ἄχρις ἂν εὕρω
    ἄλλην, ὦ χρυσέη Κύπρι, τελειοτέρην.

She's tiny and dark-skinned, is Philainion; but her hair is curlier
    than celery leaves, and her skin is softer than down,
and her voice is more seductive than the Girdle, and she does
    everything, and often doesn't bother to ask for pay.
I'm happy with such a Philainion until I find
    another, golden Cypris, closer to perfection.

Again there is humour in the way the poem veers between infatuated enthusiasm and cynicism. The Girdle of line 3 is the *Kestos*, Aphrodite's Girdle, familiar to any educated Greek from *Iliad* 14.214–17 (part of the 'deception of Zeus' episode mentioned earlier):[60]

Ἦ, καὶ ἀπὸ στήθεσφιν ἐλύσατο κεστὸν ἱμάντα
ποικίλον, ἔνθα δέ οἱ θελκτήρια πάντα τέτυκτο·
ἔνθ' ἔνι μὲν φιλότης, ἐν δ' ἵμερος, ἐν δ' ὀαριστὺς
πάρφασις, ἥ τ' ἔκλεψε νόον πύκα περ φρονεόντων.

---

[59] See Sider 1997: 33 and 123.
[60] On the *Kestos*, see further Sider 1997: 124–5.

> She [Aphrodite] spoke, and from her breast she loosed the girdle strap[61]
> of many colours, in which all her charms were stored:
> in it was affection, in it was yearning, in it was flirtatious
> persuasion, which deceives the minds even of the most strong-witted.

If Philainion's voice is more seductive than the *Kestos*, it is very seductive indeed – but the next moment the speaker's mind turns, with an effect of bathos, to much less lofty aspects of the girl's appeal.

Other epigrams are positively raunchy, such as Dioscorides 5 = *AP* 5.55, described by the lemmatist (that is, the author of the headings to the poems) in *AP*, whether disapprovingly or appreciatively we shall never know, as *pornikôtaton* ('highly pornographic'). Its speaker describes having sex with a woman in the position known as *kelês* ('horseback'), in which, against the grain of the Greek male tendency to imagine women as animals needing to be tamed, the man is the horse and the woman is the rider:

> Δωρίδα τὴν ῥοδόπυγον ὑπὲρ λεχέων διατείνας
>   ἄνθεσιν ἐν χλοεροῖς ἀθάνατος γέγονα.
> ἡ γὰρ ὑπερφυέεσσι μέσον διαβᾶσά με ποσσίν
>   ἤνυσεν ἀκλινέως τὸν Κύπριδος δόλιχον,
> ὄμμασιν νωθρὰ βλέπουσα· τὰ δ' ἠύτε πνεύματι φύλλα
>   ἀμφισαλευομένης ἔτρεμε πορφύρεα,
> μέχρις ἀπεσπείσθη λευκὸν μένος ἀμφοτέροισιν
>   καὶ Δωρὶς παρέτοις ἐξεχύθη μέλεσι.

> When I stretched pink-bottomed Doris out wide over my bed
>   among spring flowers, I became immortal.
> Straddling her extraordinary legs across me
>   unswervingly she ran Love's endurance race to the end,
> with a languid look in her eyes, which, like leaves in the wind
>   sparked in their brilliance as she tossed forward and back,
> until the pale vigour poured itself out for both of us
>   and Doris sprawled off me, her limbs relaxed.[62]

---

[61] While the phrase *kestos himas* probably really means 'embroidered strap', the adjective *kestos* was later reinterpreted as a noun referring to the girdle itself; see LSJ s.v. 2.

[62] There are some uncertainties of interpretation: in addition to Gow and Page (whose suggestions I have mostly followed), see Schrier 1979, Baldwin 1980, Schrier 1982, and Zanker 2007: 247. The usage of the verb διατείνω ('stretch out/across') in line 1 is unusual; there may be a pun between a metaphorical sense, 'put her to full stretch', i.e. employed her talents to the full (developed by ἤνυσεν ἀκλινέως ['unswervingly ran...to the end'] in line 4), and a literal, physical sense, 'stretched her out across me' (developed by διαβᾶσα ['straddling'] in line 3). In line 4, the δόλιχος, which I have translated 'endurance race', is a long-distance foot race. τὰ... πορφύρεα in lines 5–6 has been much discussed: Gow and Page suggest a reference to Doris' breasts, Baldwin argues for her buttocks or thighs; I am persuaded by Schrier's defence (based

The poem's paradox is that the 'immortality' that the poem's speaker says he acquired from his experience with Doris seems largely to take the form of detachment from it: he observes and describes, while the energy and concentration of the sex act (indicated by the abstracted gaze), and the final exhaustion, all belong to the woman.[63] It is interesting that the one moment of mutuality, underlined by *amphoteroisin* ('for both [of us]') at the end of the penultimate line, is the moment of climax. In orgasm, the poet's subjectivity and the objectifying gaze that he directs at the woman are simultaneously, but momentarily, annihilated.

This moment, the discharge by both love-makers of their 'pale vigour', is also the moment when the poem declares its own literary relationship with another poem, once lost but now famous, by the archaic poet Archilochus (seventh century BCE).[64] Archilochus, of whose work tantalizingly little has survived, was famous in antiquity for his (supposed) courtship of a girl called Neoboule and for the viciously abusive poems he wrote about her and her family after being rejected. In the fragmentary poem F 196a West (sometimes known as the 'Cologne Archilochus' from its discovery on a papyrus there), the poet narrates an episode in which he meets a young girl (possibly Neoboule's younger sister) in an isolated spot. At the start of the fragment the girl is speaking: the poet has clearly propositioned her and she is trying to persuade him to turn his attentions elsewhere. He tries again to persuade her, promising that he will stop short of penetration and contrasting the girl's honest simplicity with Neoboule's harshness and withered charms; finally, whether by persuasion or coercion, he induces the girl to join him in a sexual embrace among the summer flowers, and, in the final lines, reports how he 'released his pale vigour

---

on taking πορφύρεα to mean 'shining', 'sparkling' rather than 'deep red/purplish in colour') of early scholars' assumption that the reference is to her eyes. On the nautical metaphor contained in the *hapax* ἀμφισαλευομένης ('being tossed about'), see Murgatroyd 1995: 15. In an article that provides a detailed and fascinating survey of the sea as sexual metaphor in Greek and Roman poetry, he suggests a reference here to Doris' mythological namesake, Doris the Oceanid, wife of Nereus (Hes. *Theog.* 240–2), whose name can stand for the sea, e.g. *Doris amara* at Virgil *Eclogues* 10.4.

[63] On the poet's stance as spectator and the 'exchange of perspectives' in this poem, see further Zanker 2007: 247; see also Acosta-Hughes and Barbantini 2007: 450 n. 97 for the persuasive idea (with reference to the allusion to Archilochus to which we will turn shortly) that Dioscorides 'transfers the elements of the *locus amoenus* [idyllic natural location]...to the landscape of Doris' body'.

[64] See Acosta-Hughes and Barbantini 2007: 450 with n. 97.

(*leukon menos*), touching her blond hair' (51–2).[65] The allusion sets up a striking contrast on the one hand between the vehemently emotional and sexually aggressive archaic poet and the half-detached, indulgent epigrammatist, and on the other hand between the inexperienced, passive young girl ambushed by Archilochus and Dioscorides' energetic sexual professional.[66] At the same time, it provides a gloss on Dioscorides' claim at the end of line 2 that he 'became immortal': his encounter with Doris is a literary encounter, and it is by evoking it in an epigram that the poet is able to share literary immortality with the ancient Archilochus.

Another encounter with a sexual professional is dramatized in Philodemus 4 *GPh* = 20 Sider = *AP* 5.46:

> Χαῖρε σύ. – Καὶ σύ γε χαῖρε. – Τί δεῖ σε καλεῖν; – Σὲ δέ; – Μήπω
>    τοῦτο φιλοσπούδει. – Μηδὲ σύ. – Μή τιν' ἔχεις;
> Αἰεὶ τὸν φιλέοντα. – Θέλεις ἅμα σήμερον ἡμῖν
>    δειπνεῖν; – Εἰ σὺ θέλεις. – Εὖ γε· πόσου παρέσῃ;
> – Μηδέν μοι προδίδου. – Τοῦτο ξένον. – Ἀλλ' ὅσον ἄν σοι
>    κοιμηθέντι δοκῇ, τοῦτο δός. – Οὐκ ἀδικεῖς.
> – Ποῦ γίνῃ; πέμψω. – Καταμάνθανε. – Πηνίκα δ' ἥξεις;
>    –Ἢν σὺ θέλεις ὥρην. – Εὐθὺ θέλω. – Πρόαγε.

Hi there. – Hello to you too. – What's your name? – What's yours? You needn't
    worry about that just yet. – Then you needn't either. – Are you with someone?
– With my boyfriend...whoever he is at the time. – Would you like to have dinner with me
    today? – If you like. – Excellent! How much will you charge?
– Don't pay me in advance...– That's unusual! –...but once we've
    been to bed, pay me what you think best. – That's a fair deal!
– Where will I find you? I'll have you picked up. – Work it out. – When will you come?
    Whatever time you like. – I'd like it right now. – Let's go.

This vivid street-scene is a virtuoso performance in the art of accommodating the choppiness and informality of everyday dialogue

---

[65] Some caution is necessary because crucial letters are lost on the papyrus, and Dioscorides' poem constitutes part of the case for Merkelbach's supplement *leuk]on aphêka menos (therm]on* 'hot' would be another possibility); but the case seems to me to be very strong.

[66] On the Archilochus poem see e.g. Carey 2009: 156–8. While capturing the (in my view sinister and disturbing) gentleness of the scene, Carey seems to me to overstate the extent to which the girl is presented as 'allowing' herself to be seduced, or indeed as having any effective agency in the episode at all.

within the formal structure of the elegiac couplet (the language, in Gow and Page's words, is 'largely if not wholly vernacular, with one or two poetical liberties in the word-order', *GPh* p. 376).[67] The atmosphere is that of New Comedy, the tone relaxed and urbane; I do not detect the 'professional's hauteur' attributed by Sider 1997: 132, to what he calls the 'saucy prostitute', nor much sign of the manipulation on her part to which he refers; the transaction seems to me much more matter-of-fact and reciprocal. The delicacy with which the male speaker elicits the information that the woman's services are indeed for sale evokes the edginess of the demi-monde; compare and contrast Philodemus 21 Sider = Antiphilus 14 *GPh* = *AP*, dramatising an encounter in which a man attempts to accost a female passer-by, gets no reply, but vows to continue pursuing her. Humour is generated by the contrast between the polite circumlocutions ('have dinner', 'been to bed') and the directness of the practical arrangements, as well as by the urgency suddenly discovered in the final line.

Nossis declares the primacy of love in a poem that may have been programmatic, perhaps opening her epigram collection (1 *HE* = *AP* 5.170):

Ἅδιον οὐδὲν ἔρωτος, ἃ δ᾽ ὄλβια δεύτερα πάντα
    ἐστίν· ἀπὸ στόματος δ᾽ ἔπτυσα καὶ τὸ μέλι.
τοῦτο λέγει Νόσσις· τίνα δ᾽ ἁ Κύπρις οὐκ ἐφίλασεν
    οὐκ οἶδεν κήνα τἄνθεα ποῖα ῥόδα.

Nothing is sweeter than love, other blessings all
    come second: even honey I spit from my mouth.
This is what Nossis says: but anyone whom the Cyprian has not kissed
    is a woman who does not know what roses Love's flowers are.[68]

---

[67] In line 7, the imperative καταμάνθανε ('work it out', more literally 'learn' or 'understand') leaves several possibilities open. Sider suggests that the man interrupts the woman in his eagerness, i.e. καταμάνθανε in effect means 'I'll tell you', but the speaker is stopped before she can do so. Gow and Page (*GPh* p. 377) tentatively opt for 'you can find out', an indication that the woman's address is common knowledge. I am inclined to agree with the suggestion of Kaibel 1885: 7–8 that the word points to some form of extra-textual communication. Following Jacobs, he suggests a 'calling-card'; another possibility would be an imagined gesture, either pointing to her lodgings or indicating that she is currently at the spot where she regularly solicits business, and will not move until hired.

[68] See Gutzwiller 1998: 75–9 for an interesting if slightly dogmatic interpretation of this poem; I am not convinced that spitting honey is to be read as 'reject[ing] the tradition of Hesiodic epic' (76). I tentatively accept Gutzwiller's defence of the MS text in line 4 (78 n. 82), though, *pace* Gutzwiller, the sense must then be 'does not know what sort of roses the flowers [of Love] are', not 'does not know what sort of flowers roses are' (which would be e.g. οὐκ οἶδεν ποῖα ἄνθεα (τὰ) ῥόδα). I agree with Gutzwiller that it is not necessary to assume an explicit

The poem belongs in a long tradition of 'priamels' (poems listing items implicitly or explicitly compared with one another) on the subject of what is best or most desirable. Famous early examples include the opening of Pindar, *Olympian I* ('Water is best...') and, a particularly important model for the present poem, the first lines of Sappho 16: 'Some say a force of cavalry, others of infantry, others of ships, to be the fairest thing on the dark earth; but I say it is whatever someone loves...'.[69] Like Sappho, Nossis underlines the assertion of her own view ('I say'/'Nossis says') but, where Sappho then goes on to state that the surpassing beauty of the love object 'can easily be made understandable to anyone' by means of a mythological example, Nossis takes a different line. She sees no point in trying to explain or persuade: there is no substitute for personal experience. Another likely model for Nossis' poem, also modelled on Sappho's and following its structure more closely, is Asclepiades 1 *HE* = *AP* 5.169:

> Ἡδὺ θέρους διψῶντι χιὼν ποτόν, ἡδὺ δὲ ναύταις
>     ἐκ χειμῶνος ἰδεῖν εἰαρινὸν Στέφανον·
> ἥδιον δ' ὁπόταν κρύψῃ μία τοὺς φιλέοντας
>     χλαῖνα, καὶ αἰνῆται Κύπρις ὑπ' ἀμφοτέρων.

> Pleasant is snow to drink when thirsty in summer, and pleasant to sailors
>     is the sight, after winter, of a sign of spring, the Crown;
> more pleasant, though, is when lovers are hid by a single
>     cloak, and Cypris wins approval from them both.[70]

Thus through imitation and reminiscence epigrams accumulate additional layers of meaning.[71] These poems of Asclepiades and Nossis

---

sexual reference in order to understand the poem, but am not certain that such an interpretation should be ruled out.

[69] Cf. also the poem reported by Aristotle, *Eudemian Ethics* 1214a 1–8 as being inscribed on the propylaea of the Letöon at Delos: κάλλιστον τὸ δικαιότατον, λῷστον δ' ὑγιαίνειν·/ πάντων ἥδιστον δ' οὗ τις ἐρᾷ τὸ τυχεῖν, 'The most beautiful thing is what is most just, and the best thing is to be healthy;/ but the sweetest thing is to get what one desires.'

[70] The Crown (Greek *Stephanos*, the same word used later by Meleager for his 'Garland') is apparently the constellation known as the Northern Crown, *Corona Borealis*, which, as the sixth-century-CE astrological writer John Lydus reports, sets at dawn on the Nones (7th) of March, and may thus be a sign of spring (see *HE* 118, Lydus *De Ostentis* 61.12 = p. 122 line 16 Wachsmuth; '192.8' in *HE* appears to be an error; 'evening rising' presumably indicates Gow and Page's silent approval of Merkel's conjecture, reported but rejected by Wachsmuth, of φαίνεται... ἑσπέρᾳ in place of δύεται...ὄρθρου). For an interesting, if not entirely persuasive, reading of this poem as a commentary on Epicurean theories of pleasure, see Clayman 2007: 508–9.

[71] As Acosta-Hughes and Barbantani 2007: 450 put it, 'especially effective in Nossis' recollection of Asclepiades is her perception of Asclepiades as reader of Sappho'.

may in turn allude to two poems by Anyte that exemplify her interest in rustic and pastoral scenes, and which may again be programmatic:

Ἷζε᾽ ἄπας ὑπὸ καλὰ δάφνας εὐθαλέα φύλλα
    ὡραίου τ᾽ ἄρυσαι νάματος ἁδὺ πόμα
ὄφρα τοι ἀσθμαίνοντα πόνοις θέρεος φίλα γυῖα
    ἀμπαύσῃς πνοιᾷ τυπτόμενα Ζεφύρου.

Sit down, everyone, under the beautiful dense leaves of the laurel
    and draw sweet drinking-water from the lovely stream,
to give your limbs panting from summer toil
    relief, struck by the gusts of the West Wind.
                                      Anyte 16 *HE* = *AP* 9.313

Ξεῖν᾽, ὑπὸ τὰν πέτραν τετρυμένα γυῖ᾽ ἀνάπαυσον –
    ἁδύ τοι ἐν χλωροῖς πνεῦμα θροεῖ πετάλοις –
πίδακά τ᾽ ἐκ παγᾶς ψυχρὸν πίε, δὴ γὰρ ὁδίταις
    ἄμπαυμ᾽ ἐν θερμῷ καύματι τοῦτο φίλον.

Stranger, rest your wearied limbs under the rock –
    it is pleasant, the sound of the breeze in the fresh leaves –
and drink cold water from the stream; for travellers
    enjoy this relief in the midst of summer heat.
                                      Anyte 18 *HE* = *AP* 16.228

The two poems' inscriptional setting, whether real or imaginary, is a spring by the wayside; the address to the passer-by is clearly borrowed from the earlier tradition of funerary epigram. Anyte offers water and green shade to the passer-by – and thus, by implication, her poetry to the reader – as a pleasantly cooling relief from toil; Asclepiades and Nossis use her as a foil in expressing their preference for the more hectic pleasures of love.[72]

We conclude this section with two poems in which the lover's gaze is linked with celestial objects. The first is 'Plato' 1 *FGE* (attributed to the philosopher Plato in antiquity, but generally agreed to be of Hellenistic date):

Ἀστέρας εἰσαθρεῖς, ἀστὴρ ἐμός· εἴθε γενοίμην
    οὐρανός, ὡς πολλοῖς ὄμμασιν εἰς σὲ βλέπω.

You are gazing at the stars, my star: I wish I could become
    the sky, to look at you with many eyes.

---

[72] On Anyte, see Gutzwiller 1998: 54–74 (on these poems, esp. 68–73); for discussion of 'pastoral' or 'bucolic' as a subgenre of epigram, a good starting-point is Stanzel 2007.

The poem is full of light. The reader is invited to envisage the face of the addressee, presumably a boy, turned up to the stars; the light of the stars shining on his face and illuminating it, confirming his status as the 'star' of the lover's universe; the returning gaze of the innumerable stars, now reconfigured as the eyes of heaven; and, finally, the insatiable longing gaze of the speaker-lover, excluded from the tranquil reciprocity of 'star' and stars in his extravagant, unrealizable wish to multiply his own vision.[73] The image of the stars as innumerable amorous eyes is adapted in Catullus 7, the famous kiss-counting poem, where the stars have become innumerable voyeurs, lines 7–8: *aut quam sidera multa, cum tacet nox, / furtivos hominum vident amores* ('or as many as the stars which, in the silence of night, / observe the secret love affairs of humans').

A different heavenly encounter is involved in the peaceful love scene of Philodemus 9 *GPh* = 14 Sider = *AP* 5.123:

> Νυκτερίνη δικέρως φιλοπάννυχε φαῖνε, Σελήνη,
>      φαῖνε δι' εὐτρήτων βαλλομένη θυρίδων·
> αὔγαζε χρυσέην Καλλίστιον. ἐς τὰ φιλεύντων
>      ἔργα κατοπτεύειν οὐ φθόνος ἀθανάτῃ.
> ὀλβίζεις καὶ τήνδε καὶ ἡμέας, οἶδα, Σελήνη·
>      καὶ γὰρ σὴν ψυχὴν ἔφλεγεν Ἐνδυμίων.

> Two-horned night-watcher, friend of night parties, shine! Selene,
>      shine, casting your light through the latticed shutters.
> Cast your rays on golden Kallistion. For an immortal
>      to spy on lovers' work is no affront.
> You think both her and me happy, I know, Selene:
>      your soul too caught fire for Endymion.

Here both the speaker and the moon-goddess Selene are spectators of Kallistion in her sleep, a reminder to the latter of her love for the sleeping Endymion. The mythological precedent invites comparison with the poems that we have already encountered in which lovers invoke the example of Zeus as an excuse, but Selene is assumed not merely to understand the speaker's feelings but to congratulate him. It is a remarkable move to make a deity call mortals happy; similarly 'affront' or 'resentment' (*phthonos*) is an attitude more naturally feared

---

[73] 'Plato' 2 *FGE* is another 'star' poem, this time an epitaph: ἀστὴρ πρὶν μὲν ἔλαμπες ἐνὶ ζωοῖσιν ἑῷος, / νῦν δὲ θανὼν λάμπεις ἕσπερος ἐν φθιμένοις ('Once you shone as the morning star among the living, / and now you are dead you shine as an evening star among the perished'); the epitaph adds to the poignancy of the love poem and it is likely that the two were conceived as a pair: see Scodel 2003: 264.

by mortals from gods than vice versa. Selene's role is transformed from that of light-giver to that of onlooker, an effect that is brought into focus by the ambiguity of the verb *katopteuein* in line 4: as well as meaning 'act as a spy on' (Gow and Page, *GPh* p. 380), it is also used of astronomers 'observing' the heavenly bodies (Sider 1997: 115). Through this series of inversions, the epigram invites us to see the brightest light in the imagined room as emanating, not from the moon addressed in its first and final couplets, but from 'golden Kallistion' at its centre, whose epithet *khrusee* ('golden') is, as Gow and Page observe, one commonly associated with the goddess of love herself.[74]

The Roman elegist Propertius alludes to this epigram of Philodemus in the famous third poem of his first book. In this poem, Propertius (or rather 'Propertius', his poetic persona) comes home inebriated after a night out to find his girlfriend Cynthia asleep, and stands in contemplation until Cynthia, woken by the light of the moon entering her bedroom, wakes up and scolds him for deserting her. In a detailed discussion of the relationship between the two poems, Joan Booth suggests that the effect of Propertius' treatment is to activate sinister undercurrents beneath the apparently perfect surface of Philodemus' poem.[75] How can the poet 'know' (line 5) that Selene's attitude is sympathetic rather than jealous, that the moonlight is a benign rather than a baneful or disruptive presence? And how can we, as readers, be sure that the speaker of the poem and Kallistion are as united as line 5 suggests, or indeed that he is really a gentle and solicitous lover rather than a drunken delinquent (cf. line 1, 'friend of night parties') like Propertius' persona in his poem, or worse still, the would-be assailant imagined by that narrator as troubling Cynthia's dreams? Another interesting comparison can be made with John Donne's poem *The Sunne Rising*, where the celestial visitor, this time the sun, is at first an intruder, an unwelcome reminder that the night of love is over:

> Busie old foole, unruly Sunne,
> Why dost thou thus,
> Through windowes, and through curtaines call on us?

but, as the poet reflects on love's ability to transcend space, time, and convention, becomes by the end of the poem an accepted part of the

---

[74] This association is underlined by the following phrase φιλεύντων / ἔργα ('works of lovers'), which, as Sider notes, evokes expressions such as ἔργα / πολυχρύσου Ἀφροδίτης ('works of greatly golden Aphrodite') at Hes. *Op.* 521: Sider 1997: 115.

[75] Booth 2001, especially 543–4.

lovers' universe-in-miniature, being subsumed into their world rather as the moon's light is subsumed by Philodemus' Kallistion:

> Shine here to us, and thou art every where;
> This bed thy center is, these walls, thy spheare.

### Funerary epigrams

Having explored some of Hellenistic epigram's innovations, we should observe briefly that it was no less successful in developing epigram's most traditional form, the epitaph. As we saw in the case of inscriptional epigrams, epitaphs can be no less effective for being simple, for example Callimachus 46 *HE* = 17 P = *AP* 7.453:

> Δωδεκέτη τὸν παῖδα πατὴρ ἀπέθηκε Φίλιππος
> ἐνθάδε, τὴν πολλὴν ἐλπίδα, Νικοτέλην.

> His son aged twelve years old father Philippos set aside
> here, his abundant hope, Nikoteles.

The closeness of father and son, and thus the sadness of their separation, is suggested both by the placing of their names at line-end and by the juxtaposition *paida patêr* ('son father') in the first line, which is also a *hysteron proteron* (reversal of order: here, object before subject, son before father) underlining the violation of the norm that it is the duty of children to bury their parents. The choice of the verb *apethêke*, here translated 'set aside', is unexpected,[76] and triggers a range of possible meanings. Most basically, Philippos is setting aside his son – being parted from him for ever. He is also laying aside his hope, and there may be additional grim irony in the word's association with storage of precious objects: Nikoteles was a prospect for the future that will now never be realized. The use of a verb not commonly associated with burial may also suggest the father's inability to accept what has happened. In the final line, *ten pollên elpida* ('his abundant hope') is given heavy, lingering emphasis by alliterative sounds, by the long syllables and double consonant of *pollên*, and by its grammatical

---

[76] The active voice, used here (and nowhere else in Callimachus' surviving work), usually means simply 'put away' (e.g. in a chest: Hom. *Il.* 16.254), while the much more common middle voice has a range of senses including 'lay aside', 'put in storage', or (rarely) 'bury'. See *GPh* p. 199, and Hopkinson 1988: 247 for suggested interpretations.

separation, indicated by the editorial commas, from the other words in the line. The adjective *pollên* ('abundant', more literally 'much', 'great in quantity') is also carefully chosen, pointing to the open-endedness of parental hope: limitless but also, as Nikoteles' fate shows, of unforeseeable outcome.

The stillness evoked by this poem may be contrasted with the drama of another Callimachean funerary epigram, this time without specific reference to a place of burial (32 *HE* = 20 P = *AP* 7.517):[77]

Ἠῷοι Μελάνιππον ἐθάπτομεν, ἠελίου δέ
    δυομένου Βασιλὼ κάτθανε παρθενική
αὐτοχερί· ζώειν γὰρ ἀδελφεὸν ἐν πυρὶ θεῖσα
    οὐκ ἔτλη. δίδυμον δ' οἶκος ἐσεῖδε κακὸν
πατρὸς Ἀριστίπποιο, κατήφησεν δὲ Κυρήνη
    πᾶσα τὸν εὔτεκνον χῆρον ἰδοῦσα δόμον.

At break of day we were burying Melanippos, and as the sun
    was setting the girl Basilo died
By her own hand: to live when she had put her brother on the fire
    she could not bear. It was a twin sorrow for the house to see
Of father Aristippos, and Cyrene was cast down in silence,
    the whole city, having seen the child-blessed household empty.

The beginning and ending of the opening line set the time-frame of the drama, from sunrise to sunset, and with their keening vowel sounds (*êôoi...êeliou...*) make us hear the mourning cries (Greek cries of grief encountered in tragedy include *ô, ômoi, iô, iou*, and *êe*). The first person plural verb 'we were burying' draws the reader into the ritual action. The two four-syllable words *parthenikê, autokheri* ('unmarried', 'by her own hand'), enjambed across lines 2 and 3, present with devastating directness the pathos of a life (by ancient Greek standards) unfulfilled, but also of Basilo's preservation of autonomy in death, untouched by any hand but her own; they may remind us of Phrasikleia's epitaph encountered in Chapter 1. It is no coincidence that the adjective *autokheir*, of which *autokheri* ('by her own hand') is the adverb, occurs repeatedly in the most famous drama of an unmarried girl who dies because of love for her brother, Sophocles' *Antigone*.[78] Basilo might

---

[77] As with dedicatory epigram, it is generally very hard to tell whether literary funerary epigrams were in fact also inscribed, though in this case there is evidence to suggest that the dramatis personae were real people (*HE* p. 190).

[78] The adjective has a broad sense meaning someone who 'acts for themselves' or 'does something with their own hands', a narrower sense of 'perpetrator' or 'killer', and a specific sense of 'suicide'. It occurs five times in this play, more often than in any other surviving tragedy

be said to outdo the tragic heroine in her sisterly devotion: Antigone
dies as a result of her attempt to bury her brother; Basilo successfully
completes the ritual, but still cannot bear to live without him.

As the poem develops, the scene presented to the reader pans out,
from the graveside to the household to the whole city of Cyrene. It
then fades with *katêphêsen* ('was cast down in silence') in line 5: this
verb implies a mute lowering of the eyes, and thus both drops the
viewer's gaze and hushes the cries of mourning. The last line drives
home the poem's point with another powerful juxtaposition, *euteknon
khêron* ('blessed-with-children empty', or 'bereft').

In a famous pair of epitaphs, Callimachus sketches his own family
history (29 *HE* = 21 P = *AP* 7.525; 30 *HE* = 35 P = *AP* 7.415):

> Ὅστις ἐμὸν παρὰ σῆμα φέρεις πόδα, Καλλιμάχου με
>  ἴσθι Κυρηναίου παῖδά τε καὶ γενέτην.
> εἰδείης δ' ἄμφω κενρ ὁ μέν κοτε πατρίδος ὅπλων
>  ἦρξεν, ὁ δ' ἤεισεν κρέσσονα βασκανίης.

> You who make your way past my marker [*sêma*], know that of Callimachus
>  of Cyrene I am the son and father.
> You may know them both: one once led his country's arms
>  in battle, the other sang songs stronger than jealousy.[79]

> Βαττιάδεω παρὰ σῆμα φέρεις πόδας εὖ μὲν ἀοιδήν
>  εἰδότος, εὖ δ' οἴνῳ καίρια συγγελάσαι.

---

(followed by *Oedipus the King* and Euripides' *Electra*, each with three instances). It is applied to
all three characters who die: of Haemon (1175) and Eurydice (1315) to report their suicides,
and by Antigone of herself, in the final scene in which she appears, but this time referring to
her burial of her parents and brother 'with her own hands'. These instances are foreshadowed
by two occurrences in the mouth of Creon: referring to the deaths of Eteocles and Polynices at
172, and referring to the 'perpetrator' of Polynices' attempted burial at 306. For a close reading
of this poem as a 'tragedy in miniature' echoing *Antigone*, see Ambühl 2002, especially 9–11
(10 n. 43 on *autokheir*); also Harder 2007: 409 for a brief summary in English of Ambühl's
conclusions. Ambühl further suggests that the poem's theme of devotedness between siblings is
ideologically connected with the Ptolemaic monarchs' practice of sibling marriage, reflected in
the epithet Philadelphos ('brother-/sister-loving'). On epigrams honouring Ptolemaic kings and
queens (there are many in the Milan papyrus), see Ambühl 2007.

[79] This epigram as transmitted in *AP* has two additional lines that correspond to lines 37–8
of the *Aetia* prologue and that do not connect easily in sense here with what has gone before:
οὐ νέμεσις· Μοῦσαι γὰρ ὅσους ἴδον ὄθματι παῖδας / μὴ λόξῳ, πολίους οὐκ ἀπέθεντο φίλους
('never mind [or 'no wonder'], because those whom the Muses have looked at in childhood
/ with no sidelong glance, they do not reject as friends when they are grey'). I follow Pfeiffer,
Gow and Page, and others in assuming that these lines have been added here in error. For an
interpretation based on the assumption that they do belong here (as well as in the *Aetia*), see
Fantuzzi 2004b: 297–9.

> You are making your way past the marker [*sêma*] of Battiades, an expert
> in song, but also in well-timed laughter accompanying wine.

The first is for Callimachus' father, the second for Callimachus himself; the closely matching formulae in line 1 strongly suggest that they are designed as a pair. It is, as usual, impossible to say whether the poems were designed for inscription, but this formula, with the address to the passer-by, clearly invokes the conventions of inscribed epitaphs and the poems proceed to play with those conventions. The epitaph for the father names the son and grandfather (both called Callimachus) but not the father himself; the epitaph for Callimachus provides the name of his father (Battos) but not the poet's own.[80] In the father's epitaph, momentary puzzlement is created by the claim to be the same person's 'son and father', before *amphô* ('both') reveals that two people of the same name are in question; the fact that the poem says nothing whatsoever about its supposed 'subject' (reflected in the lemmatist's misidentification of it in *AP* as an epitaph for the poet himself) is surely a joke.[81] Instead, with the balanced clauses in lines 2 and 3 and the sound correspondences between *êrxen* ('led') and *êeisen* ('sang'), it proposes an equivalence between the older Callimachus' career as a general in the service of his country and the younger Callimachus' career as a poet whose work conquers jealous critics: a *militia carminis* that points the way to the *militia amoris* ('military service of Love'), a central motif of Latin love poetry.[82] The poet's own epitaph uses the limited space left in the distich by the quasi-inscriptional formula to announce his expertise with exquisite brevity, as a scholar, poet, and witty symposiast possessing the judgement to balance these roles in due time and measure. The word *eidotos*, which I have translated 'expert', is in fact a participle, 'having knowledge of', normally present in tense (and thus paradoxical in an epitaph); it is tempting to see it as instructing the reader to reflect on what kind of *sêma* ('marker') this is. Now it has entered a book, the poet's mark

---

[80] Battos is also the name of the legendary founder of Callimachus' home city, Cyrene, and it has been suggested that the patronymic 'Battiades' in this poem should be understood as a poetic nickname, 'scion of Battos', rather than as evidence that Callimachus' father was indeed called Battos. No conclusive answer is possible, but the epigram pair has more point if it is his father's name. See further Fantuzzi 2004b: 297–9.

[81] It is also interesting, as GN points out, that the younger Callimachus, author of the epitaph, is referred to in the past tense, 'sang'. This usage, which may have contributed to the lemmatist's error, perhaps evokes an inscriptional setting projected into the future, and a resulting sense of timelessness or of being outside time.

[82] On the development of the *militia amoris* theme, see Murgatroyd 1979 and Gutzwiller 1993.

or trace with which we are presented as readers is independent of his own life, and of his own mortality.[83]

As has been seen, funerary epigrams can be intensely emotional, but they do not have to be deadly serious. Sometimes they offer a puzzle, as in Alcaeus 16 *HE = AP* 7.429:

> Δίζημαι κατὰ θυμὸν ὅτου χάριν ἁ παροδῖτις
>   δισσάκι φεῖ μοῦνον γράμμα λέλογχε λίθος
> λαοτύποις σμίλαις κεκολαμμένον. ἦ ῥα γυναικί
>   τᾷ χθονὶ κευθομένᾳ Χιλιὰς ἦν ὄνομα;
> τοῦτο γὰρ ἀγγέλλει κορυφούμενος εἰς ἓν ἀριθμός.
>   ἢ τὸ μὲν εἰς ὀρθὰν ἀτραπὸν οὐκ ἔμολεν,
> ἁ δ' οἰκτρὸν ναίουσα τόδ' ἠρίον ἔπλετο Φειδίς;
>   νῦν Σφιγγὸς γρίφους Οἰδίπος ἐφρασάμαν.
> αἰνετὸς οὐκ δισσοῖο καμὼν αἴνιγμα τύποιο
>   φέγγος μὲν ξυνετοῖς ἀξυνέτοις δ' ἔρεβος.

I'm asking myself in my mind for what reason this roadside
  stone has received Phi twice as the only inscription
carved on it by the stone-carver's chisels. Is it that the woman
  hidden under the earth went by the name of Khilias ['Thousand']?
That's the report the number gives, added up as a single sum.
  Or did that idea not go down the right road
and was the woman who lives in this sad tomb called Pheidis ['Phi
  Twice']?
  That's it! I'm Oedipus, I've solved the Sphinx's riddle.
All credit to him, the man who made a riddle from two signs,
  light for the clever but darkness for the stupid.

The poem plays self-consciously with the fact that it is *not* the (imagined) inscriptional epitaph, the text of which is simply ΦΦ, the Greek letter phi twice over. The 'point' is that the dead woman's name Φειδίς (Pheidis), can be reinterpreted in Greek as φεῖ δίς ('phi twice'), but also means 'sparing', 'thrifty', and thus the very short inscription represents both the sound of her name and the character trait that it implies. The speaker initially goes down the 'wrong road' of interpreting the signs according to the Greek system of using letters as numbers, in which Φ equals 500 and ΦΦ would thus be a possible way of writing 1000. There is additional humour, perhaps underlined by the congratulatory final couplets, in the fact that the result is a long

---

[83] See also Gutzwiller 1998: 213; her suggestion that this was the concluding poem of a collection is attractive.

epigram (much longer than most real epitaphs) that conspicuously lacks the economy of the inscription it describes.[84]

In an epigram in the unusual choliambic metre, the *hetaira* Philaenis is made to deny authorship of a famous book on sexual technique that circulated under her name (Aeschrion 1 *HE* = *AP* 7.345):

> Ἐγὼ Φίλαινις, ἡ 'πίβωτος ἀνθρώποις,
> ἐνταῦθα γήρᾳ τῷ μακρῷ κεκοίμημαι.
> μή μ', ὦ μάταιε ναῦτα, τὴν ἄκραν κάμπτων
> χλεύην τε ποιεῦ καὶ γέλωτα καὶ λάσθην,
> οὐ γάρ, μὰ τὸν Ζῆν', οὐ μὰ τοὺς κάτω κούρους,
> οὐκ ἦν ἐς ἄνδρας μάχλος οὐδὲ δημώδης.
> Πολυκράτης δὲ τὴν γονὴν Ἀθηναῖος,
> λόγων τι παιπάλημα καὶ κακὴ γλῶσσα,
> ἔγραψεν οἷ' ἔγραψ' ἐγὼ γὰρ οὐκ οἶδα.

> I, Philaenis, the one everyone talks about,
> have been laid to rest here, far into old age.
> You cheeky sailor, as you round the headland
> don't jeer at me or make me a rude joke:
> I swear by Zeus, I swear by the Boys below,
> I wasn't randy with men or an easy lay.
> It was Polycrates, an Athenian by race,
> a jerker-out of words, a filthy tongue,
> who wrote – whatever he wrote: I personally don't know.[85]

The Athenian Polycrates to whom Philaenis is made to ascribe the book must be the rhetorician of that name, famous for speeches (now lost) on paradoxical subjects, including a spoof prosecution speech against Socrates, and thus a reasonable choice as author of an outrageous book, though it is not clear why he is chosen in particular. The poem is innovative in asking the passer-by *not* to do something, by contrast with the conventional request to 'stand and pity' or the like. This points to a further paradox. Normally, the function of an epitaph is to tell us who it commemorates and thus keep their name, at least, alive. Philaenis has a different problem: her name is (so the

---

[84] For a more extensive discussion of this poem, interpreting it as a statement of Alcaeus' literary programme, see Bruss 2002/3.

[85] The reference of the oath 'by the Boys below' is unclear: see *HE* p. 5. 'The *Kouroi*' would normally be the Dioscuri, Castor and Polydeuces, but they do not belong 'below' in the Underworld; we might expect μὰ τὴν κάτω κούρην ('by the Girl below', i.e. 'by Persephone'), and this has been suggested as an emendation, but the corruption in the manuscripts would be hard to explain. It is possible that there is a joke in the idea that Philaenis, because of her profession, cannot swear as other women do by the chaste Persephone, but there is no obvious parallel.

poem says) on everyone's lips already, but in connection with a false story, which the epigram attempts to refute. The irony is that, in denying Philaenis' association with the book, the imagined inscription and the actual poem serve instead to perpetuate it.[86] There is also obvious humour in Philaenis being made to accost a sailor – indeed, every passing sailor – precisely in order to assure him that she is not 'that sort of girl', and perhaps also in her being made to do so in a metre particularly associated with an author of distinctly raunchy verse, the poet Hipponax of the sixth century BCE.

Needless to say Hellenistic funerary epigram does not waste the opportunity to play with dramas involving multiple voices in dialogue. An example that is particularly enjoyable, if grim in its way, is Callimachus' epigram on Kharidas (31 *HE* = 13 P = *AP* 7.524):

> Ἦ ῥ᾽ ὑπὸ σοὶ Χαρίδας ἀναπαύεται; – Εἰ τὸν Ἀρίμμα
>     τοῦ Κυρηναίου παῖδα λέγεις, ὑπ᾽ ἐμοί.
> –Ὦ Χαρίδα, τί τὰ νέρθε; – Πολὺ σκότος. – Αἱ δ᾽ ἄνοδοι τί;
>     – Ψεῦδος. – Ὁ δὲ Πλούτων; – Μῦθος. – Ἀπωλόμεθα.
> Οὗτος ἐμὸς λόγος ὔμμιν ἀληθινός, εἰ δὲ τὸν ἡδύν
>     βούλει, Πελλαίου βοῦς μέγας εἰν Ἀίδῃ.

> Is it true that Kharidas is resting under you? – If it's Arimmas
>     of Cyrene's son you mean, yes, under me.
> – Kharidas, what's the Underworld like? – Very dark. – And the Upward
> Roads?
>     – A lie. – And Pluto? – A fairy-story [*muthos*]. – We're done for!
> – That's the true account I have for you, but if it's the nice one
>     you're after, a whole ox costs one Pellan coin in Hades.

The poem offers sophisticated play on the obviously absurd, but conventionally well-established, idea that the epitaph is spoken by the dead person, and takes it a step further by creating a dialogue.[87] The

---

[86] See Rosen 2007: 475 n. 30, and, on the negative request to the passer-by, see Tueller 2008: 65–6; see also 192. The poem is imitated by Dioscorides 26 *HE* = *AP* 7.450, on the same theme. Fragments of the book attributed to Philaenis have been found on a papyrus, P. Oxy. XXXIX 2891: see Beta 2007: 313 n. 11, with references. On Polycrates, see Livingstone 2001: 28–40. 'Exculpatory' poems such as this one are on the fringes of a much larger genre of imaginary epitaphs for famous people from the past (writers of tragedy and comedy, philosophers, etc.): on such poems see e.g. Rosen 2007, on poems about the poets Archilochus and Hipponax; Fantuzzi 2007, on poems with theatrical themes; and Clayman 2007, on philosophers in epigram.

[87] On Callimachus' 'conversations with the dead', see further Fantuzzi 2004b: 322–8. Another example in which the passer-by asks the dead person for information about conditions in the Underworld is Callimachus 51 *HE* = 4 P = *AP* 7.317, on the legendary misanthrope Timon: Τίμων, οὐ γὰρ ἔτ᾽ ἐσσί, τί τοι, σκότος ἢ φάος, ἐχθρόν; / – τὸ σκότος· ὑμέων γὰρ πλείονες εἰν Ἀίδῃ ('Timon, since you're not alive any more, which do you really hate, the Dark or the Light? – The

'passer-by' initially addresses the stone, rather like someone knocking on a door and asking whether they have got the right address; the stone politely replies, again rather like a slave answering the door, and the passer-by accordingly turns to its 'master', Kharidas.[88] Kharidas obligingly replies to each question, but his answers fail to oblige the questioner because they knock away one by one the props supporting his belief in an afterlife – and thus, of course, also demolish the possibility that Kharidas could in fact have a voice to speak with.[89] The final line reveals Kharidas' irritation, understandable especially in view of the passer-by's tactless remark in line 4, where *apôlometha* 'we're done for!' could also be translated 'we're dead'. *We* (that is, the passer-by and we the readers) by definition are not. Kharidas is, and it is impolite, as well as unnecessary, to draw attention to this inequality of status between us and him.

The point of the 'whole ox' reference in the final line has been much discussed; it seems likely to have a double meaning. On the one hand, it offers the questioner not content with the truth a 'nice' version instead ('food is dirt cheap in Hades'; or, as GN suggests we might put it, 'Hell as an all-you-can-eat steak buffet'). On the other hand, and more obscurely, it plays simultaneously on the expression 'a great ox has stood on my tongue' (which goes back to the watchman's prologue in Aeschylus' *Agamemnon* [36–7] and means 'I can't possibly tell you') and on the Greek burial practice of placing a coin in the dead person's mouth with which to pay Charon, the ferryman, in the Underworld. In this sense, the resultant meaning is that the coin in his mouth (perhaps a coin with a figure of an ox on it, or a low-value coin made of oxhide) has turned into a 'great ox' preventing him from speaking, so he *cannot* offer a comforting account; or, to put it another way, he cannot speak because he is dead.[90] The punning reply, containing a comforting answer for the simple-minded and a more

---

Dark, because there are more of you people in Hades'); see also 33 *HE* = 2 P = *AP* 7.520. Such poems provide a likely model for the second-century-CE writer Lucian's *Dialogues of the Dead*.

[88] On the unusual role of the stone as intermediary, see Tueller 2008: 114.

[89] In this interrogation and in another related poem, 33 *HE* (which effectively gives an 'address' for anyone wishing to trace the dead person in Hades, explaining that he will be found 'among the pious': see Fantuzzi 2004: 323–4), it is tempting to see a parody of ritual texts buried with initiates which instruct the dead person on what he or she must say in answer to certain questions in order to reach a better place in the next world, e.g. : 'Ahead you will find from the Lake of Memory cold water pouring forth; there are guards before it. They will ask you, with astute wisdom, what you are seeking in the darkness of murky Hades. Say, "I am a child of Earth and starry Sky..."'. On such texts see Graf and Johnston 2007 (quotation from p. 17).

[90] This is essentially the interpretation of Livrea 1990: 319–24; see also Gutzwiller 1998: 210–11. On Charon's fee, see Sourvinou-Inwood 1995: 303–21.

honest one, which contains no comfort, for those able to understand, will remind alert readers of the lines of the *Agamemnon* that follow the 'great ox' proverb: 'the House itself, if it were to acquire a tongue, could give the clearest answer; since I, of my own free will, speak for listeners who understand, but am silent for those who do not' (37–9). The dead Kharidas is as likely to acquire a tongue as the House of Atreus; the answer given by 'Kharidas' in the poem, like the watchman's answer in the play, addresses two different audiences on two different levels.

Once we notice the questioner's mistake in saying *apôlometha* in line 4, it becomes clear that the whole dialogue has in a sense arisen from a misunderstanding, caused by insufficient attention to the various ways of saying 'dead' in Greek. My translation of line 1 takes advantage of the fact that in Greek, as in English, to say that someone is 'resting' (*anapauetai*) is a euphemistic way of saying that they are dead. Thus the poem's opening question is ambiguous. If it is taken as meaning 'Is it true that it's under *you* that Kharidas is "resting" [i.e. "lying dead"]?', then the stone's reply, 'yes', is accurate. If, on the other hand, it is taken to mean 'Is it true that what Kharidas is doing under you is "resting"?', then the correct answer would be 'no, he's dead', and the poem should properly end here.

A common type of poem that plays on the locatedness of inscriptional epigram and the contrasting circulation of epigram in book form is the 'message epitaph', for example, Asclepiades 31 *HE* = *AP* 7.500:[91]

> Ὦ παρ' ἐμὸν στείχων κενὸν ἠρίον, εἶπον, ὁδῖτα,
>   εἰς Χίον εὖτ' ἂν ἴκῃ πατρὶ Μελησαγόρῃ
> ὡς ἐμὲ μὲν καὶ νῆα καὶ ἐμπορίην κακὸς Εὖρος
>   ὤλεσεν, Εὐίππου δ' αὐτὸ λέλειπτ' ὄνομα.

> You who walk past my empty grave, report it, traveller,
>   when you come to Chios, to my father Melesagoras
> that me, and my ship, and my cargo, the cruel East Wind
>   destroyed, but that my name, Euippos, is left.

Of course, this sort of message has its model in the 'tell them at Sparta' motif of the epitaph for the Spartan dead that we encountered in Chapter 1; but the Battle of Thermopylae was big news, the fallen Spartans were heroes of Greece (or at any rate the epigrammatist

---

[91] On such poems see Tarán 1979: 132–49; on this poem and the related poem Callimachus 38 *HE* = 18 P = *AP* 7.272, see Bruss 2005: 104–10.

intended that they should be so), and Sparta was a powerful presence throughout the Greek world. What reason does Euippos have to believe that the reader of his epitaph is going to Chios, and why should he expect anyone to trouble to find his father? The answer is clearly that he cannot; such poems underline the radical sense in which the dead are lost and scattered. At the same time, they point to the ability of the book, portable and durable through copying, to gather them together again in fictional, literary form: to re-collect them.[92]

We conclude this section, and this chapter, with a poem that is not funerary at all, but that is an intriguing variation on the message-epitaph (Nossis 11 *HE* = *AP* 7.718):

> Ὦ ξεῖν᾽, εἰ τύ γε πλεῖς ποτὶ καλλίχορον Μιτυλήναν
>    τᾶν Σαπφοῦς χαρίτων ἄνθος ἐναυσόμενος
> εἰπεῖν ὡς Μούσαισι φίλαν τήνᾳ τε Λόκρισσα
>    τίκτεν· ἴσαις δ᾽ ὅτι μοι τοὔνομα Νοσσίς. ἴθι.

> Stranger, if you are sailing to Mitylene, place of beautiful dancing,
>    to take inspiration from the flower of Sappho's graces,
> say that a daughter dear to her and to the Muses a woman of Lokris
>    bore. You need to know that my name is Nossis. Go.[93]

Unlike Asclepiades' epitaph, this poem does provide the addressee with a motive for going to Lesbos, and a plausible one: the addressee is by definition a reader of Nossis, and a reader of Nossis might reasonably be expected to have an interest in poetry in general and in Sappho in particular. Nossis does not specify the intended recipient of her message, but she surely wishes to be known not to the people of Mitylene in general but to its most famous daughter in particular. Her poem thus replaces Asclepiades' implausible request to take information about a dead person to a living person with an impossible request to take information about a living person to a dead person.[94]

---

[92] See Bruss 2005: 106–7 on the poem's self-conscious fictionality.

[93] On this poem, see especially Gutzwiller 1998: 65–6; also Acosta-Hughes and Barbantani 2007: 445–6. There are significant textual uncertainties; the text I have printed follows Gutzwiller (with a minor change of punctuation in line 4), who in turn follows Gallavotti. Gutzwiller's theory that this poem imitating Asclepiades closed Nossis' epigram collection, just as Nossis 1 *HE*, also imitating Asclepiades and likewise signed with the poet's name, opened it, goes beyond what we can hope to prove from present evidence but is nonetheless extremely tempting.

[94] I do not mean to imply that Nossis' poem is directly modelled on Asclepiades'. On this see Tueller 2008: 64, arguing against Gutzwiller 1998. Unlike Tueller, I think that the two poems are clearly related, but I agree with him that the relationship need not be one of imitation (in either direction). Tueller rightly emphasizes the echo in ὦ ξεῖν᾽ ... εἰπεῖν of the Thermopylae epitaph

In what is simultaneously self-advertisement, an assertion of literary genealogy, and a fan letter, Nossis imputes to literary epigram the potential not just for space travel but for time travel. The following chapters will explore some of the ways in which she may have been right.

---

'Simonides' 22b *FGE* ὦ ξεῖν, ἀγγέλλειν..., which underlines the programmatic quality of the epigram and its mission to establish a link with the past; the classical heritage to which Nossis lays claim is poetic rather than military.

## III EPIGRAM FROM GREECE TO ROME

### The Cyzicene epigrams: Rome as Greek myth

'Epigrams at Cyzicus': the enigmatic title of the *Anthology*'s third and shortest Book introduces a sequence of nineteen sequentially numbered epigrams (one of them a broken scrap) purportedly inscribed by or on behalf of two royal brothers in the early second century BCE. Eumenes II and Attalus II were the sons of Attalus I of Pergamum, a small but culturally and politically dynamic Hellenistic kingdom in western Turkey. Just five years after Attalus II died, his nephew left Pergamum to Rome in his will, introducing the Romans to power politics in the Greek East.[1] The Cyzicene epigrams are alleged by the introduction to *AP* 3 to have been incised on the *stulopinakia* – whatever they are – in Cyzicus' shrine to Apollonis, the deified mother of Attalus and Eumenes; but the introduction is a confusing text of uncertain provenance, consisting of a single sentence of extraordinarily bad Greek.[2]

If we can take what it says at face value, each epigram was originally a kind of verse subtitle to a carved scene illustrating a story from Greek myth, and each scene-and-epigram combination was incised on one of the supporting columns of the temple. In the written-up version of *AP* 3, a short prose preamble stands in for each carved image (narrating the content in lieu of illustration) and so supplies a context for each poem. The decorated columns run in a continuous sequence, like a Hellenistic Stations of the Cross, and we are told when the sequence turns a corner of the building; the book thus invites us to have a

---

[1] For a concise and gripping account of Attalid history, see Shipley 2000: 312–19.

[2] Στυλοπινάκιον is an odd compound found only here. 'Pillars with figures on them' is LSJ's best try; Paton in the Loeb guesses at 'tablets of the columns'. The most glaring problem in the Greek is the use of εἰς (into or to) to mean 'on' or 'in'; there are no parallels for this, not even late, bad ones. Cameron 1993: 147–8 follows Demoen 1988 in assigning a post-Hellenistic date. Conversely, the editors of a recent collection of inscriptional epigrams from the Greek East accept the Cyzicene epigrams at face value as authentic transcripts: Merkelbach and Stauber 2001. Kuttner 1995: 168 splits the difference – there really were *stulopinakia* (whatever those were) with inscribed captions on them, but the *AP* 3 epigrams are not the real inscriptions.

go at reconstructing the temple's floor-plan. With nineteen columns, Apollonis' temple would seem to have been architecturally eccentric (if we believe a word of this story), but its decoration was thematically consistent and appropriate to the dedicators and dedicatee. The mythic scenes all illustrated the virtuous love of parents for sons, and sons for parents – mostly mothers. Most of these myths are very obscure to a modern readership but the final, and thus climactic, episode is still famous: its loving sons are Romulus and Remus. We present the epigram together with its preamble:

On the nineteenth [column are] Remus and Romulus, protecting their mother, Servilia by name, from the punishment of Amulius. For Ares [i.e. Mars] seduced her and fathered them by her, and a she-wolf suckled them when they were exposed. And so, when they became men, they rescued their mother from her chains, founded Rome, and restored Numitor to his throne:

> You delivered this secret birthing of children to Ares – Remus and
> Romulus of the shared couch – and a brute she-wolf nursed them and
> raised them in a cave, and they snatched you from toils hard to heal.

The prose preamble segues from describing the moment from myth represented in the carved scene ('Remus and Romulus, protecting their mother') to recapitulating the larger themes expressed in the epigram. It clarifies the events that have led up to the incident in the carving (Mars's seduction of Servilia); usefully for the modern reader, other preambles in the book do much the same. But the nineteenth preamble and epigram both also foreshadow the *future* of this particular mother and her sons. No other poem in *AP* 3 has done this; that it happens here, in the final poem, and that the story cues up the larger narrative of Rome's foundation can hardly be coincidental.

'Epigrams at Cyzicus' justifies and explains the rise of Rome in Greek terms; it figures the city's founders as the logical endpoint of Greece's own tradition of heroically dutiful sons. That it must struggle to *manufacture* such a tradition (as we indicated, most of these myths are desperately obscure) is significant. In *AP* 3 we see Greek myth succumbing to the gravitational pull of Roman elite ideology of the family; it is reconfigured as a series of prototypes for the moral and social values of the new Mediterranean superpower. *Pietas*, filial duty – the defining trait of Vergil's 'pious Aeneas' – underwrites the city's ascension to supremacy over the old Hellenistic kingdoms. Still, the writer carefully leaves space for dissident readings. In this version, the boys have the 'wrong' mother; and Remus is placed *before* the brother who slew him and gave his name to the city. For Remus and Romulus, read Greece and Rome?[3]

If these epigrams really are Hellenistic – and this is *extremely* unlikely – they are uncanny in their prescience. Their function of cultural translation would instead be more characteristic of the cosmopolitan Greek literary culture that flourished under the Roman empire in the early centuries CE – a culture that additionally revelled in visually evocative literary descriptions (*ekphrases*) of works of art and their architectural settings.[4] We explore the wider contexts of epigram in this 'Second Sophistic', and later periods, in Chapter 4. Here, however, the way in which *AP* 3 constructs an imaginative scenario to accommodate Rome in a formerly Greek genre, explaining each culture to the other, is very much to the point. Epigram *did* cross between cultures early; it *was* associated with important mediators of Hellenistic Greek culture to the Roman elite; and it talked about, and directly *to*, imperial power in a way that few if any other Greek genres could. Later, with Martial, it would claim recognition as the ultimate outsider's critique of the Roman urban experience.

### Epigram and the Neoterics

As a specifically Hellenistic genre, epigram had huge appeal to the Neoteric ('avant-garde' or 'new wave') poets of the late Republic, most famously Catullus. This was metropolitan poetry on an accessibly personal scale, and without the heavy baggage of being part of the canon of Classical Literature – a category that Hellenistic scholarship and standardized school curricula had already summoned into existence.[5] But the Neoterics were always an anomaly, not least in their own reckoning. Self-consciously edgy, they appropriated (and

---

[3] On Remus as Rome's narrativized Other, see provocatively Wiseman 1995. In the standard version of the story, Romulus' and Remus' mother is of course Rhea Silvia. 'Servilia' might charitably be explained as a misheard version – if so, and if it was actually inscribed where Roman tourists could see it, this would have been an embarrassing gaffe. Or perhaps Rhea Silvia is being conflated – whether accidentally or with mischievous intent – with Servilia Caepionis, mother of Brutus and mistress of Julius Caesar (fictionalized as the 'Servilia' of HBO's *Rome* [2005–7]).

[4] On slightly mischievous mediation between Greek and Roman cultures as a defining trait of prose literature in this period, see e.g. Elsner 2001 and Preston 2001; key ancient texts include Plutarch's *Greek and Roman Questions*. On imaginary ecphrasis in a key Second Sophistic text, see Bryson 1994.

[5] On Hellenistic canon-formation see Pfeiffer 1968: 203–8 (noting in passing that κανών never means 'canon' in antiquity); Cribiore 2001: 192–205.

perhaps travestied) versions of Hellenism for shock and pose value. The showy erudition of Catullus *Carmen* 7 (encountered briefly in the preceding chapter) is a case in point, reckoning Lesbia's kisses by the grains of sand in the desert at 'silphiophorous Cyrene' beside the tomb of 'ancient Battus', ancestor of Callimachus. ('Silphiophorous' – *lasarpiciferus* – is just the kind of one-off neologism or *hapax legomenon* that Callimachus himself would have appreciated.) This is of a piece with Catullus' hype for the learned mini-epics ('epyllia') of fellow Neoterics – poems that in his account are so intricately planned, so exquisite in their refinement, that most of them never quite get written for real. The smart girlfriend who distracts Caecilius from his epyllion on the goddess Cybele (worshipped at Rome as the *Magna Mater*, 'Great Mother') in *Carmen* 35 is characterized as an idealized Alexandrian *hetaira*, provocatively out of place in Roman culture. We may also be meant to see a comic paradox in Caecilius getting distracted from his subject matter by sex – in Hellenistic literary sources at least, drawn on by Catullus in *Carmen* 63, male worshippers of Cybele prove their devotion by castrating themselves. Implicitly in this account, pithy situational epigram (of which the poem is itself an example) is one kind of poetry that the Neoterics *can* actually deliver:

> Papyrus, please tell my drinking-buddy Caecilius, the tender poet, to come to Verona... For ever since he read me the outline draft of his 'Lady of Dindymus', I've been burning up. I forgive you, girl more learned than the Sapphic muse: Caecilius' 'Great Mother' *is* suave – for an outline draft.

The Catullus of the epigrams (particularly the elegiac material of *Carmina* 69–116) announces his own status as a countercultural outsider, turning epigram composition into an un- or even anti-Roman activity. His self-characterization as *delicatus* in *Carmen* 50 connotes an effeminate pleasure-addict, all surface manners and no moral substance – the polar opposite of a good Roman son and heir:

> Yesterday, Licinius, with time on our hands, we played [*lusimus*] for hours on my writing-tablets – just the thing for us metrosexual types [*delicatos*]. Each of the two of us scribbled little ditties, dabbling now in this metre, now in that; and each gave fair return as we drank and fooled around. Licinius, I came away from there fired up by your urbanity and witty comments...

In trying on the role of a Hellenistic Greek scholar-poet at play, Catullus is writing himself into a Republican Roman fantasy scenario of dangerous foreign decadence. (Ptolemaic Egypt is still a notionally independent player in Mediterranean politics; Cleopatra is Catullus' younger contemporary by around fifteen years.) This narrative coincidentally plays to the modern scholarly desire to fit Hellenistic epigram into a sympotic frame, but we would do well not to treat poems like this as documentary 'evidence' for what Posidippus and Callimachus actually got up to – or, necessarily, Catullus himself. It is naïve to read him as a transparent reporter of social practice, or to take all his bad-boy posing at face value; his poetics are a provocation, a move in a game.

Catullus *is* of course often read naïvely, and very partially: his relatively easy Latin has turned him into a standard school author, aided by his reputation for Romantic melancholy and sweetness (all those kisses, and it helps that he died young). Many students still approach him through Fordyce's winnowed 'Oxford Red' ('A few poems which do not lend themselves to comment in English have been omitted'), and our early training as Classicists tends to deliver a Shelley-esque Catullus in a floppy shirt, anguished and discreetly consumptive. This modern figment is brilliantly debunked by Wiseman (1985); but the elegiac epigrams typically do not feature heavily in school collections anyway.[6] In search of lyric sensibility and a biographical love affair, we endlessly revisit Lesbia's sparrow, her countless kisses and fickle heart. Many readers are surprised (and a little put out) to be told that Catullus is an epigrammatist at all.

## Epigrams for Piso

Looking outside the Neoteric bubble, we find epigram thriving within specific elite networks. The Epicurean philosopher-poet Philodemus of Gadara, encountered in Chapter 2, is one of the most important mediators of Hellenistic Greek culture to the poets of the late Republic; the recovery and ongoing decipherment of his prose theoretical works from the villa of his patron Piso at Herculaneum, where they had been buried by the eruption of Vesuvius in 79 CE, is even now changing our

---

[6] 'A few poems': Fordyce 1961: v, justifying the omission of about a quarter of the poems. Critics have had a field day with his wording ever since. On the making of his commentary, see now John Henderson 2006. Wiseman 1985: 1–14, 211–32 punctures the myth. This Catullus is also a mainstay of historical fiction – see, among others, Thornton Wilder's epistolary novel, Wilder 1948.

ideas about ancient literary theory.[7] Philodemus writes witty erotic epigrams in imitation of the Hellenistic big names, but with some up-to-the-minute touches – at least two epigrams respond to poems by Meleager, his near contemporary and a fellow Gadarene.[8]

Philodemus' epigrams are not particularly influential *as* epigrams, within their own genre. Instead he shapes Latin poetry through being there and communicating the ideas of the senior culture.[9] This wider, vaguer influence is part of a more general picture of diffusion and transposition. Catullus' famous *Odi et amo* poem – 'I hate and I love... and I don't know why' (*Carmen* 85) echoes Philodemus 1: *nescio* ('I don't know') more or less translates οὐκ οἶδα.[10] Epigram's themes of sex and death filter into Roman erotic elegy, which shares its typical metre, but also into Horatian lyric and even serious epic. Philodemus himself is an important influence on Vergil and others, and a suggestive recent study links Posidippus' shipwreck poems to the epitaph-like lament for Aeneas' helmsman, Palinurus, in the *Aeneid*. These Roman poets were engaging actively with Hellenistic epigram and refashioning its topics in the image of their own culture.[11] A poem humorously requesting financial support under the pretext of inviting Piso to dinner in unpretentious Epicurean style (Philodemus 27) becomes the model for an entire micro-genre in Latin, from Catullus to Horace to Martial and Juvenal.[12] Sow's udder was an expensive delicacy, and Chian wine was some of the best – at least in Roman estimation. Piso may be the notional guest here, but as Philodemus' patron he is presumably footing the bill, and reference to the Phaeacians of the *Odyssey* is calculated to remind him of king Alcinous, a model of generous hospitality to the Greek wayfarer cast up upon his foreign shore:[13]

> Tomorrow, dearest Piso, your Muse-loving friend is hauling you off to his frugal hut at the ninth hour, celebrating your year-round largesse with a

---

[7] For a lively account see Gigante 1995; more soberly, the introduction to Sider 1997.

[8] Philodemus 5 and 10, on which see Sider 1997: 78–80, 98–100.

[9] Sider 1997: 24–5 on Philodemus' own poetic models; 18–24 on his role as catalyst for Latin literary culture.

[10] On Philodemus 1 and its relation to Catullus 85 ('a far better poem') see ibid.: 62–4.

[11] On Philodemus' influence, see Sider 1997: 18–24. Sider identifies specific examples at e.g. 79 (Propertius); 104, 131, and 143 (Ovid); 139 (Horace). Thomas 2004 teases out Posidippan connections in lyric and elegy in addition to Vergilian epic (Vir. *Aen.* 5.870–1, 6.355–62).

[12] This poem and its influence on Latin poetry are discussed by Sider 1997: 152–60. Ancient recipes for udder: 158; Apicius' Roman cookbook also gives instructions for cooking womb.

[13] On Roman appreciation of Chian wine and stuffed sow's udder, a dish fit for a Caesar, see Dalby 2000: 136, 221, and 248–9.

dinner party. Although you won't get udders or Bacchus' Chian-born wine, you will see true and trusty friends and hear words sweeter by far than the land of the Phaeacians. And if ever you turn your eyes towards us also, Piso, we'll throw you a richer celebration as a change from the hut.

A tiny amount of Latin epigram has also begun to appear, independently of Philodemus and well before trendy Catullus: epitaphs in the native Saturnian metre; isolated translations and versions of Hellenistic originals. This hardly amounts to a 'Latin epigram tradition', despite the valiant efforts of Martial scholars to package it as one. Domitius Marsus and Albinovanus Pedo are the only names that stand out. This is largely because Martial subsequently talks up their supporting role as minor predecessors in genre, eclipsed in his account by the influence of Catullus.[14] However, little if anything that Martial says about his place in genre (or in society for that matter) can be taken at face value. He writes a great deal about these topics, and not just in his elaborate prefaces and long opening sequences – but most of the time he is just trying to be funny, not accurate or fair.

## Martial as translator: skoptic epigram

A case in point – perhaps *the* case in point – is Martial's relationship to his Greek models. Modern scholars have catalogued the correspondences between Martial's epigrams and pre-existing material by Lucillius and Nicarchus, Greek skoptic poets of the mid-first century CE, whose surviving epigrams largely come to us through the eleventh book of the *Anthology* (Martial was writing towards the end of the same century).[15] Martial 6.12 is one example among many:

Fabulla swears that her hair is her own – the hair she bought. You tell me, Paulus, is she a hypocrite?

---

[14] Sullivan 1991: 93–100 – informative as far as it goes but feel the lack of width, in a book of 388 pages. Sullivan does his best but the material simply is not there.

[15] Skoptic is not quite (or not just) satirical: Nisbet 2006. We touched on Book 11 and its preface in the Introduction. For a detailed account of Martial's relation to the surviving poems of Lucillius and Nicarchus, see Burnikel 1980; Sullivan 1991: 85–93 is more accessible, but underplays the importance of the Greek poets to shore up Martial's 'Classic' credentials. For a general study of skoptic epigram, see Nisbet 2003a.

There are minor difficulties in the second line of the Latin text, but
the overall sense is clear enough, as is Martial's source. The epigram
is a blatant reworking of a Lucillian original, *AP* 11.68:

> Nikulla, some people say you dye your hair – the raven-black hair you
> bought at the market.

Earlier in the corpus, Martial has (to put it charitably) alluded to
this and other poems by Lucillius – in, of all things, a complaint
against plagiarists. This is deliberate cheek for comic effect. The joke
anticipates and rewards an ideal reader who knows Martial's sources
(1.72):

> Do you think yourself a poet because of my verses, Fidentinus? Do you
> ache to be believed one? That's the way Aegle can reckon she has teeth
> (she bought bones and Indian ivory), and Lycoris can like the look of
> herself in white lead (she's blacker than a falling mulberry). By the same
> rationale that makes you a poet, you'll have a full head of hair when you're
> bald.

We cannot even guess at the true extent of Martial's debt to these
near-contemporary Greek skoptic epigrammatists; essentially we only
know Lucillius and Nicarchus through the poems that make it into the
*Anthology*, and most of their work is probably lost for ever. The point
is made clearer by a tantalizing exception – a single surviving column
containing five poems from what was probably an epigram book by
Nicarchus, recovered on papyrus from Oxyrhynchus.[16] If this papyrus
is anything to go by, Nicarchus and Lucillius were *much* smuttier
poets than the *Anthology*, the product of an intensely Christian age, is
letting on. (Cephalas compiles for an erudite minority; a later age of
piety would winnow the *Anthology*'s selection still further to make it
suitable for a mass readership: see Chapter 5.) In Nicarchus' version
of the Riddle of the Sphinx, solved in myth by Oedipus, the answer is
not 'man' but the *pathikos* – an adult man who, contrary to the norms
of Greek culture, submits to sexual penetration by other men:

> 'What creature walks the earth on two legs, and four, and three?' At first
> it stumped them all – but it's the poof. Standing, he's a biped; face down
> and taking it on hands and knees, a quadruped; and with that dick of his,
> the boy-buggering beast is three-legged... No-one could decipher it more

---

[16] P. Oxy. LXVI 4501.

smartly than me. If I'd been around back then, my friends, I'd have taken possession of seven-gated Thebes.

Perhaps much of Martial's notorious Roman smut started life in the books of an Egyptian Greek. Although largely a phenomenon of the early centuries CE, skoptic epigram ultimately derives its sexual and scatological humour from the Old Comedy of Athens.[17] As well as inventive dirty jokes, it brings a new non-occasionality to the genre of epigram. The butts of its jokes are social stereotypes rather than identifiable individuals, and are often given comically appropriate names (so-called 'speaking names'). This technique imitates the New Comedies of playwrights such as Menander; like the dirty jokes, it feeds into Martial's idea of how to write epigram and thus into the later Western tradition.

Other aspects of skoptic epigram do not outlive it; for instance, many of the poems are not meant to be laugh-out-loud funny but instead advise their listeners on appropriate behaviour at the symposium and in daily life. (Cephalas approved of these, and included a lot of them; unsurprisingly, modern anthologists tend to leave them out.) The social stereotypes of the more obviously joke-like poems seem to address the same function indirectly, by illustrating undesirable behaviour getting its comeuppance; these fates are often violent. Many of these epigrams are hard going for a liberal modern reader because they are openly and strongly misogynistic – older women who seek to retain a sexual identity come in for particularly vicious second-person tirades.[18]

Potential fellow-symposiasts – which is to say, men – are steered more gently towards virtue by reference to third-person Others who embody the fears of their culture, often literally. For instance, the advisory humour in poems about *leptoi* ('wimps') – a frequent skoptic stereotype of extreme physical slenderness – only kicks in when we situate them within the context of the early years of the Second Sophistic (see Chapter 4) and its obsessive pursuit of a balanced Greek identity: an educated mind in a toned and active body. Study is necessary for the educated mind, but pursued to excess it destroys mental stability as well as bodily strength. If Diophantus (*AP* 11.111)

---

[17] Bowersock 1994: 33–5 sees Lucillius' exuberant comic anti-realism as a direct throwback to Aristophanes. For an invaluable systematic guide to Old Comic sexual and scatological humour, see Jeffrey Henderson 1991.

[18] Richlin 1983, a classic feminist response, is still valuable; see also Nisbet 2003a: 10–13, 76–81.

had gone easy on the books and spent more time at the gymnasium, he would have been fine:

> Diophantus the *leptos* once got the urge to hang himself – so he got a strand from a spider's web and did it.

And athletes have it just as bad – they need to spend *less* time at the gym.[19] Skoptic epigram's repertoire of types thus hints broadly at the recurrent anxieties of its first- and second-century clientele, making it an invaluable source for cultural history (and as rotten a source for *factual* history as Martial is himself). 'Skoptic' is often translated as 'satirical', but this equation is misleading – skoptic epigram is both more and less than satire.[20]

### Martial as 'satirist'

*Satura quidem tota nostra est* – 'Satire, at least, is completely our own.' Quintilian, a Roman literary scholar of the late first century CE (and thus Martial's contemporary), here famously identifies *satura* as Rome's own literary turf – the one genre the Greeks had not invented.[21] Martial is of course not a satirist in this sense; capital-'S' Satire is by definition longer poetry in hexameters, as written by Lucilius (its major Republican exponent) and most famously by Juvenal, another contemporary of Martial. One might say that Martial gets roped into accounts of Latin satire to make Juvenal look good. Gilbert Highet's mid-twentieth-century Juvenal (Highet 1954) fearlessly exposed Roman degeneracy and vice; his 'nasty little' Martial (encountered briefly in our Introduction) was a disgusting pornographer who flattered a vicious tyrant, Domitian. Best not read at all, really, or (as we will shortly see) only in expurgated selections.

This negative modern version of Martial has nineteenth-century roots. The poet had an established role in Victorian narratives of decline, in which literary and racial 'degeneracy' went hand in hand.[22] The literary culture of the Augustan age had always had a smooth ride

---

[19] On *leptoi* and athletes, see Nisbet 2003b. Recent studies of athletics and Greek identity in the Roman Empire include König 2005 and Newby 2005; on body issues generally, see Barton 1995 and Gleason 1995.

[20] On the advisory role of skoptic epigram, see Nisbet 2006.

[21] *Institutio Oratoria* ('Foundation Course in Rhetoric') 10.1.93, much-quoted.

[22] See briefly the preface to Fletcher 1980: 9.

in European reception – as (not coincidentally) had its conservative politics; but Nero and Domitian were conventionally deprecated as 'bad' Emperors, and the literature of their era ('Silver' to the Augustans' 'Golden') was viewed as a sad symptom of moral collapse. Juvenal's redeeming quality, in this account, was that he clung to enough residual decency to rage against the dying of the light.

Highet's moral-crusader version of Juvenal now appears almost comically naïve in the light of the new wave of scholarship that reanimated the study of Latin satire in the 1980s and 1990s. The whole edifice was suddenly revealed as a house of cards. The 'Juvenal' of the *Satires* was not, as previously imagined, a biographically real and psychologically complete Juvenal, telling the unvarnished truth as he saw it. Instead he was a persona, a fictional mask – actually a whole series of personae. Some of these masks were clearly intended to be figures of fun in themselves, cranky and inconsistent: the author was sending himself up, and deliberately undermining satire's purported claims to moral truth-telling. Juvenal's noisy and dangerous metropolis was not even terribly realistic, once you started checking into background detail and social trends; bits of it were obviously out of date, again sapping the credibility of his narrating personae.[23]

Martial is not a satirist, but he writes the same kind of Rome as Juvenal does, using many of the same techniques. All the critical insights of the current approach to satire translate well to his books of epigrams, and scholarship on Martial is beginning to take them on board. Some older material on Martial, like that on Juvenal, now reads as very silly: one is startled at the simple literalism of biography-writers who assure us that Martial was 'living from hand to mouth and occupying a garret three flights up' while being simultaneously 'pointed out to foreign visitors, plagiarized at Rome and abroad, read and sung all over the Roman Empire'.[24] This was always an unlikely combination, but persona-theory now enables us to bypass the messy dead end of biography, instead seeing the poet's ongoing concern with his own literary practice and status as a 'pervasive fiction'. There is no 'real' Martial that we can access behind the mask:

[Martial] develops fully articulated fictional scenarios depicting the nature of his writing and its role in society... Both the image of the degraded poet-journeyman, whose parasitical existence undermines his work's integrity, and that of the dignified

---

[23] The pivotal essay is Braund 1989a; her subsequent work on Martial is also very valuable.
[24] Nixon 1927: 46, 52.

author, who enjoys the friendship of literary patrons in a spirit of polite urbanity, derive from irreducible aspects of Martial's complex self-representation.[25]

If there is resistance, it is in part because the temptation to retain a truthful Martial is so strong. Sullivan's breakthrough modern treatment of Martial as a literary author, while immensely valuable in many ways, doggedly interrogates the poems to reconstruct a 'life and times' of the author that must have seemed a little dated even in 1991: 'Was Martial married?' (On balance probably not, concludes Sullivan, but the epigrams do not seem to present a consistent account; funny, that.)[26] Ancient historians traditionally prioritize Martial's times over his life, reading him for fascinating urban factoids, or even constructing gazetteers of the sites and sights of Rome under Domitian. As we saw in the Introduction, school and student-oriented sourcebooks for daily life in ancient Rome cannot get enough of him. One could even say that we now have two Martials, serving two distinct and irreconcilable markets that, if anything, are growing further and further apart. Literary scholars, respectfully moving on from Sullivan's literal-minded approach, celebrate the ambitious and innovative author who playfully misdirects his readers; urban topographers and encyclopaedia-makers sometimes see instead a passive repository of historical and archaeological fact. 'Why did the chicken cross the road?' asks Martial, and they dutifully note the existence of a street next to a chicken farm.[27]

In fact, these written Romes flicker and shift to serve his literary purpose of the moment. Book Three, for instance, is vividly characterized by Martial in its opening sequence of epigrams as a humble *libellus* sent scurrying to Rome from Cisalpine Gaul along the hot and dusty Aemilian Way, under orders to find a protecting patron among Martial's city friends (3.1–5). The Rome it finds on its arrival is a poetic idyll made up of cool horizontals – shaded porticoes and soothing baths. One potential host is hard to track down:

Is he at ease in the Poets' Seminary, reciting witty verses tinged with Attic charm? Of if he's moved on from there, is he pacing the temple colonnade or dallying in the Portico of the Argonauts? Alternatively, is he sitting or strolling in the sun of the Portico of dainty Europa, free of harsh cares, among box-trees that are beginning to warm in the

---

[25] Roman 2001: 113, 117.

[26] Sullivan 1991: 25.

[27] For a more conciliatory formulation, see Prior 1996. Rodríguez Almeida 2003 goes all out to wring topography from the *libelli*.

afternoon heat? Is he cleansing himself in the warm Baths of Titus or of Agrippa, or the Bath of shameless Tigellinus?        (3.1.20)

It is almost as though Martial is *teasing* his exhausted little book with this vision of a cityscape packed with amenities for the footsore traveller. Martial's third book is objectified at the outset as a *uerna liber* (3.1.6), a 'home-bred [slave] book' under strict instructions from its master. Book Three (the roll) must hurry through book three (the text), encountering at every turn a scripted Rome that at first consists *entirely* of baths and colonnades in which its errand and status will not permit it to linger.[28]

### 'The unexpected Classic' – Martial goes to school

'Martial is my Vergil', declared Lucius Aelius Caesar, Hadrian's adopted son and heir – at least as reported by the *Historia Augusta*, a notoriously unreliable history of Rome's emperors, written in the closing years of the fourth century CE. Whether Aelius really said it or not, Martial's books were certainly being read again by the date of the history's composition, and afterwards he never went entirely out of style. His reception history from antiquity to the twentieth century and his persistence as a model for literary emulation have been mapped out by Sullivan among others.[29]

When Aelius Caesar declared for Martial in the early second century CE – *if* he did – the poet was less in fashion. Greek epigram was popular among Greeks and Romans alike, as we will see in the next chapter; but Martial's influence on it was negligible and may have been nonexistent. Historians with a moral axe to grind have sometimes adduced Aelius' remark as proof of the coarse character of his decadent age – if Martial was so popular, the reckoning goes, then the rot had clearly set in; but Aelius (or the fictionalized 'Aelius' of the *HA*) is clearly showing off by citing an author who is *not* much read. Martial was perhaps a cult favourite: a self-deprecating minor author, a few decades dead and clearly never destined for the 'set book' status that conferred canonicity. Perhaps Aelius picked Martial for his shock

---

[28] See also, in this early part of the book, 3.5, 19, and 25. Fundamental to modern readings of Latin literary constructions of Rome is Edwards 1996; the major recent collection by Larmour and Spencer 2007 opens up the field considerably.

[29] Sullivan 1991: 253–312; in English translation, Sullivan and Boyle 1996.

value, to make a point. (I tell students that Vergil's *Aeneid* is fine, but *Buffy* does more for me; it gets them thinking about questions of cultural value.) Or maybe he was just sucking up to his adoptive father, who was himself a keen epigrammatist in Greek (just like *his* adoptive father, Trajan). Aelius aside, Latin epigram undergoes a centuries-long silence until Ausonius and other poets of Late Antiquity finally come back to the genre; and then, as we shall see in the next chapter, Martial is simply one influence among many.

After Ausonius' post-classical reboot of Latin epigram (see Chapter 4), Martial's influence was continuous; he became Europe's perennial model of epigrammatic wit and 'point'. In time, he also acquired an important educational role. Martial offered a wealth of authentic detail about daily life in ancient Rome (a wealth that now appears half-illusory), and a text already broken up into conveniently sized gobbets for translation and grammar work. Appropriately winnowed, his text became a handy educational tool. A standard school edition of 1906 touts the value of the winnowed corpus as a sourcebook for the historical background of the early Church ('throws a valuable and instructive light on the social life of Rome in the first century of our era') and justifies its many omissions without actually saying what it is that the editors are leaving out.[30] If only Martial could have confined himself to tender epitaphs for dead infants:

> But unfortunately this better mood is rare, and Martial's work as a whole is spoiled by that Roman hardness to which the greater poets rose superior, and of which his grossness is only another side... Ugliness is always bad art, and Martial often failed as a poet from his choice of subject.

In other words, Martial wallows in explicit sex and gratuitous violence; we have cut all the sex (violence never hurt anybody), but we are not going to *tell* you this in so many words, boy, in case you get it into your head to seek out Father's unexpurgated edition. (Similarly, the first 'complete' translation into English assured its readers that Martial's 'constant and severe castigation of the two great vices which prevailed in his time' made him worth reading, but was careful to remain vague

---

[30] Bridge and Lake 1906: iii, xi. The formulaic announcement in the preface that the edition was 'intended for the use of upper forms in schools' (iii) would have told the adult purchasers everything they needed to know, 'over the heads, so to speak, of their children': see Perrin 1992: 112.

on what those two vices were.[31]) Winnowed editions like this kept Britain's youth safe from cunnilingus. Adultery and homosexuality were out; also pretty slaves (male and female), nude bathing, excretory functions, haemorrhoids, drunkenness, belching, the god Priapus, and mention of wedding nights. So much for wealth of detail – and these are just the omissions from Martial's first Book. 'Anyone who reads a hundred epigrams and still wants more, Caedicianus, is a glutton for punishment', Martial jokes in its final poem (1.118). The schoolboys who read Book 1 through Bridge and Lake missed out on twenty poems, a sixth of its total; no hundred epigrams for them. This is if anything a light touch. The editors of Martial's epigrams for the 'Grammar School Classics' series declared that 'not less than a fourth part of them is exceedingly gross' – and played it safe by printing less than half.[32]

Martial had failed to do the decent Romantic thing and die young like Catullus; he had lived too long and written too much. The rare editions that presented him entire tended to leave telltale gaps in the facing translation; in borderline cases they translated into not English but Italian. (An Englishman who could read Italian evidently did not need protection – or perhaps was beyond saving.)[33] Editors cut heavily, routinely and without qualms: the Grammar School Classics edition boasted that it 'omitted hardly any [epigrams] of the readable sort which can fairly be considered important', and until the 1990s the many gaps in its facing translation made the standard Loeb a convenient index for impatient young students wanting to go straight to the dirty bits.[34]

### Bringing Martial to book

The 1990s saw a sea change in attitudes to Martial among scholars. Previously, a widely held theory about the corpus of Martial had

---

[31] Bohn 1860: iii. This important translation, personally compiled by the editor of the Bohn series, was the first 'complete' Martial for the mass market.

[32] Paley and Stone 1868: iv–v. The proportion of obscenity in Martial varies with cultural norms and personal tastes: e.g. for Nixon 1927: 44 'only about one-fifth…are open to objection – but a large proportion of that fifth are very open indeed.'

[33] Bohn 1860 presents eighteenth-century Italian versions for poems 'where an English translation given faithfully would not be tolerable' and assures its readers that even these are 'rather dexterous in refining impurities' (iv).

[34] The old Loeb: Ker 1919/20.

appeared to justify any amount of omission and rearrangement: these were not Martial's books to begin with, or not the ones that really mattered. The original collections, referred to by the poet as his *libelli*, were lost forever. Instead the current 'books' were a series of large and unlovely later compendia in which Martial had recycled the contents of the original *libelli*, abandoning the earlier arrangement in which individual poems made most sense – in effect anthologizing himself, and not particularly well. The most important exponent of this '*libellus* theory' in recent times has been Peter White, but it goes back much further. A 1995 article by the late Don Fowler decisively shut down what in retrospect seems almost another house of cards.[35]

The *libellus* theory rested on an over-literal reading of the terminology with which Martial situated himself within his genre. (This is of course not the first time that we have seen overly literal readings of Martial tie the scholarship in knots.) *Libellus* means literally 'little book', and Martial's books are not unusually small by ancient standards – they contain about the same number of lines as most other ancient poetry books (an optimum length at least partly determined by the practical limitations of the papyrus roll format). It followed (or so the theory went) that the poems in which the poet speaks of his 'little books' must refer to a previous stage of publication in physically smaller books – pamphlets, really. No examples of these *libelli* survive (the theory continued) because they were never intended for general circulation; instead they were poetic gifts, composed by Martial as one-offs and tailored to the interests of specific patrons.

However, in Latin as in English, diminutives are often used ironically ('Little John') or affectionately ('little darling'). The *libellus* theory failed to take into account Martial's elaborate self-fashioning against the earlier epigrams of Catullus, for whom, as we shall see, the word *libellus* is significant. We have already seen how thoroughly Martial misrepresents his debts to Greek models, and his account of Latin epigram is almost as badly distorted – Catullus is actually not nearly as major an influence on Martial as Martial makes him out to be. Instead Martial finds advantage in name-dropping; Catullus becomes the famous predecessor he needs, a founding figure to emulate and surpass, at times to jarring and comic effect.

---

[35] White 1974 is taken on trust by Sullivan 1991: 23 n. 38, but Fowler 1995 deconstructs his argument to devastating effect, as acknowledged in James Holoka's *BMCR* review (http://ccat.sas.upenn.edu/bmcr/1995/95.11.04.html, accessed 5 November 2009) and emphatically endorsed by e.g. Sven Lorenz 2001: 263; see also the important article by Roman 2001.

## Catullan deformations: post-*Classic* Martial

In Martial's very first numbered book, his notional genre-hero ends up taking third place to an amateur poet and, of all things, a devoted lapdog:[36]

> The *Dove*, my Stella's delight, wins out over Catullus' *Sparrow*, and I may say this even if [Catullus' hometown] Verona is listening...    (1.7)

> Issa is naughtier than Catullus' sparrow [or *Sparrow*], Issa is purer than the kiss of a dove [or *Dove*]... (1.109)

The earlier poet's identity is progressively deformed. At 6.69 'Catullus' is a cuckolded husband (6.69) whose daughter is as promiscuous as his wife – potentially a figure for the liberties that Martial is taking with the dead poet's material. At 8.54(53), 'Catulla' has swapped genders and genres, transformed by Martial into a cruel elegiac *domina*. 'Lesbia', the structuring presence/absence of Catullus' *oeuvre*, becomes increasingly abject: fellatrix (2.50), bottle blonde (5.68), monstrously ugly (6.23), hideously old (10.39), a retired prostitute (10.62). The final Lesbia of the corpus (11.99) is grotesquely swollen – Neotericism's antithesis embodied. And still Martial insists that Catullus is the one predecessor whom he really looks up to, by way of a series of clunky cover versions of his greatest hits.[37]

Calling his books *libelli*, a term characteristic of Catullus, helps Martial set the terms of this slightly misleading relationship. *Cui dono lepidum nouum libellum?* ('To whom shall I give this smart new little book?') famously opens the very first poem in Catullus' collection as we have it. The nature of that collection is itself open to doubt,[38] but this programmatic poem was clearly always a well-known opening gambit, packed with Neoteric buzzwords – *lepidus* ('smart') is a case in point. This front-loading of jargon was a trend that had begun with the Neoterics' own declared role models, the trendy Greek poets of Hellenistic Egypt. They boasted of being *leptos*, 'slender', without meaning literally that they were thin and other poets were fat. With

---

[36] On Martial and Catullus see now, with references to earlier scholarship, Fitzgerald 2007: 167–86.

[37] E.g. 7.19; 11.52; and cf. the Catullan referentiality of 11.6 (deliberately shoddy?).

[38] On the Catullan collection see, among others, Wiseman 1985. The collection is too large to fit a single papyrus roll; critics typically divide it into three sections, with some disagreement as to where these begin and end, but there is no parallel for this kind of structure in other ancient authors.

*libellus*, Catullus boasts of having a slender book – rakishly thin in its stylish foreign poetics. Perhaps it was physically thin as well; but its actual dimensions are of no concern to Martial. In a move typical of his Catullan 'misreadings and rereadings', he simply co-opts the earlier poet's Callimachean pose and turns it into a ready-made terminology for the Latin epigram book.[39]

While the *libellus* theory lasted, it justified winnowing and school editions: no violence was being done to the original intention of the author. (We will see the same rationale developed to a far greater extent in our final chapter, which develops the topic of epigram in reception.) Since the abandonment of the theory in the 1990s, a new wave of scholarship has begun to chart the intricate design and order-in-chaos of Martial's books. An important recent monograph even suggests that their jostling semi-randomness makes epigram, in Martial's hands at least, the ultimate literary expression of life in the big city.[40] Juxtaposition has emerged as an important aspect of his technique of composition: adjacent poems invite the reader's wandering eye to make connections that their separate texts neither confirm nor deny. Researchers busy themselves spotting matched pairs, sequences, and even widely spaced cycles of connected poems: 'each book of the *Epigrams* is an interactive semiotic system', a network of mutually referring signs.[41]

They may in time go even further, exploring the structure not just of individual books but of the entire twelve-book corpus of this sophisticated and ambitiously allusive author. It cannot be a coincidence that twelve is also the number of books in Vergil's *Aeneid*: 'the proper frame of reference for exploration of the poems is really the dodecapartite [twelve-part] whole'.[42] It remains to be seen how well such a project will work in practice, but until recently it would have been utterly inconceivable. In little more than a decade we have come from writing off the epigrams as a random mass to seeing Martial's books as artful literary compositions – and entertaining the idea that each book might be merely one element in a much larger scheme, a *magnum opus* coterminous with Martial's self-declared

[39] For 'misreadings and rereadings', see Fitzgerald 2007: 167.

[40] Fitzgerald 2007: 7.

[41] Boyle 1995: 96, in a significant essay mapping out a likely post-Sullivan game plan for Martial studies, subsequently picked up on in the important article by Lorenz 2004.

[42] Lorenz 2004: 276. On juxtaposition and sequences see, brilliantly, Fitzgerald 2007: ch. 4, and see also his ch. 6 on Martial's complex intertextuality.

poetic career.[43] This opens dizzying new prospects; epigram is now the frontier of classical studies, wild perhaps, but a place of opportunity and adventure.

[43] The numbered books of Martial's own corpus explicitly make a clean break, with the earlier publications disowned as juvenilia (*quaecumque lusi iuvenis et puer quondam*, 1.113 – 'whatever I once toyed with as a youth and a child'); see also 1.29, inviting plagiarists to buy them outright. For Martial's new numbering scheme, see 2.93. Modern editions open with his first publication, *De Spectaculis*, but misleadingly place the *Xenia* and *Apophoreta* as Books 13 and 14.

# IV EPIGRAM IN THE SECOND SOPHISTIC AND AFTER

'After [the Alexandrian era] comes nothing new but the jokes of Rome', 'corrupted by the lusts of Rome and the decadence of the East'.[1] These and similar reactions to post-Hellenistic epigram – explicitly teleological[2] and, from a twenty-first-century perspective, often startlingly racist – are typical of the late nineteenth century and much of the twentieth. Scholars felt almost as strongly about Greek epigrammatists under Rome as they did about Rome's own major epigrammatist, Martial (discussed in the previous chapter). His fellow travellers in genre came too late in epigram's history: they could not possibly be any good, and the public were advised to remain at a safe distance to avoid aesthetic and even sexual contamination. The interloper Martial had wrecked ancient epigram's manners and morals, and the Greeks who came after him could only sport grimly in the ruins: 'The brothel and the grave are all that is left for Rufinus and his contemporaries.'[3] This revealingly overwrought response is essentially late Victorian, but its echoes are still felt; our final chapter will follow the trail of panic quotes back to John Addington Symonds and Uranian Love, laying bare the contingency and special pleading that lie behind *any* modern account of ancient epigram.

Our own account of Greek and Latin epigram in the Roman Empire is naturally very different from the pessimism of the Victorians. The early centuries CE are, if anything, epigram's golden age. The genre permeates every level of literate society. Emperors crack jokes in (occasionally wobbly) elegiacs, and compose verse epitaphs for the restored tombs of formerly neglected Hellenistic poets; prefects of Egypt carve Latin tags onto crumbling colossi.[4] New Greek epigrammatists, writing varieties of epigram probably unknown to the Hellenistic age, circulate widely and attract important Roman patrons, and ordinary consumers track and mark favourite poems for personal

---

[1] Lothian 1920: n.p.; Symonds 1920: 527.

[2] By 'teleological' in this context I mean making no attempt to understand ancient Greece on its own terms, whatever those were, but interpreting it as the first chapter of a story predestined to reach its climax in the modern nation-state.

[3] Symonds 1920: 528.

[4] For an engaging survey of epigram under the Antonine emperors, see Bowie 1990.

use. Everyone is now their own anthologist, if they want to be: the papyrus scraps that in our Introduction underpinned the image of a Greco-Roman culture of collecting are all from the early centuries CE.

In part, this chronological clustering in the papyri must reflect the nature of the evidence. At Oxyrhynchus and other sites, survivals of pre-Roman material are very rare simply because the bottoms of the rubbish mounds sit nearer the water table. The older the papyrus, the further down it is in the heap and the likelier it is to turn to mush. Still, we find epigram in *so* many other important contexts in the Roman period that the picture we get from the papyrus record may not be so distorted after all. In a world of increased social and physical mobility, these most mobile of texts were doing very well for themselves.

### The poetry of numbers: new kinds of epigram

Some of epigram's new varieties have seemed strange to modern eyes. Leonides, a former astrologer from Alexandria in Egypt, wrote 'isopsephic' poems under Nero; approximately forty-two of them survive. He courts the emperor's patronage, offering a birthday poem as a bloodless equivalent to the regular sacrifice to his divine ruler (*AP* 6.231 = *FGE* Leonides 1):

> The Nile-dwelling Muse of Leonides dedicates this poem to you on your birthday, Caesar; for Calliope's offerings are always without smoke. If you are willing, next time she will offer a poem outdoing this one.

The term 'isopsephic' means equal in numerical reckoning, as this opening poem explains (*AP* 9.356 = *FGE* Leonides 33):

> We broach the drink of a different fountain in order to enjoy the marvellous poetry of the bard Leonides. For the couplets equal each other in their tallies. But you, Blame, begone, and harm others with your sharp bite.

Each Greek letter from alpha to omega doubles up as a numeral in mathematics – alpha is one, beta is two, and so on, stepping up to tens at iota and hundreds at rho; omega, the last letter of the alphabet, thus doubles as the numeral for eight hundred. Therefore every word and sentence is potentially also a larger number, the sum of its letters.

Leonides' poems are almost all of four lines each: two elegiac couplets. Add up all the letters in the first couplet and you arrive at a very large number indeed; repeat the sum for the second, and you get *the exact same number*. Or rather, you get the same number once the ingenious modern editor has repaired the received text (which hardly ever *does* add up) through extensive and bold emendation.

These are poems that suffer in transmission – any tiny slip ruins the maths – and that by definition lose everything that made them distinctive when read in translation. Doing the sums on them drives modern scholars to distraction.[5] Even the standard modern text of their Greek original is the product of a scholarly party trick that naughtily mimics the 'perverse ingenuity' of Leonides' original 'parlour game', play for play.[6] To show how it is done, the virtuoso editor Denys Page randomly selects a non-Leonidean *Anthology* poem and *makes* it isopsephic by tinkering with spellings and changing a couple of words, replicating Leonides' feat 'at the cost of a few minutes' experimenting'. Pick an epigram, any epigram, and note that there is absolutely nothing up his sleeves. Page then applies his talents to the poems of Leonides and succeeds in making their numbers add up too – although whether this is isopsephy recreated or invented from scratch is hard to say. A typical editorial intervention 'is not wholly pleasing, but the restoration of *isopsephia* at so trifling a cost is a strong argument in its favour'. Page is too dry a critic to allow himself irony quotes around 'restoration'.[7]

Epigram's brevity encourages other types of parlour game too. Nicodemus of Heraclea writes about works of art; his unique selling point is that each poem can be read backwards.[8] Nicodemus' ingenuity, combined with the properties of Greek as an inflected language, creates semi-palindromes that make sense – and fit the elegiac metre – in both directions simultaneously. His poems are even less translatable into English than Leonides'. (For an idea of how awful a literal version would be, read the words in this sentence in reverse order.)

Another new variety seems much less odd to modern readers, and probably less odd than it should. This is skoptic epigram, discussed in our last chapter. In its Roman reception by Martial, and more or

---

[5] Page in *FGE* pp. 508–10 on errors in modern editions.
[6] 'Perverse ingenuity': J. Powell 1917: 143. For the ancient parlour game and modern editorial intervention, see Page in *FGE* pp. 504–6.
[7] Page in *FGE* p. 523.
[8] *AP* 6.314–20 and perhaps also 6.323, attributed to Leonides; for discussion, see *FGE* pp. 541–5.

less by accident, skoptic epigram became the Latin West's paradigm for the genre of epigram from Late Antiquity onwards; it established the expectation of a satirical punch line or twist. At the time, though, these poems were probably unprecedented. At the very least, they were developed on an unprecedented scale as a distinct specialism, something they had never been before.[9]

### An altar for Hadrian: Greek culture in a Roman world

It is surely no accident that these new varieties of epigram are also the ones that speak explicitly of, and to, Roman power in a Greco-Roman world. The more established types of poem maintained the antiquarian focus and local feel of their Hellenistic models; they typically addressed the interface between cultures only obliquely, if at all.[10] Epigram in this period is almost always composed in Greek, and operates within a Hellenic, and typically nostalgic, frame of reference. This regardless of whether the individual writer is 'Greek' or 'Roman' – and most are both, by citizenship and/or acculturation.

One of Hadrian's officials, for instance, writes a pattern-poem – a classic Hellenistic literary game made famous by Simias and Theocritus in the fourth and third centuries BCE.[11] The poems are descriptions (*ekphrases*), written in the shape of the objects they describe: Simias' *Egg* is ovoid, Theocritus' *Syrinx* is shaped like a shepherd's pipe, and so on. These poems can now be found in *AP* 15, Cephalas' book of miscellaneous odds and ends.[12] Like these famous Hellenistic poems, Vestinus' poem (*AP* 15.25) must use several different metres in order to keep its shape when written out on the page. This convenient and concise advertisement of the author's literary education, versatility, and skill also helps Vestinus align himself with fashionable Callimachean poetics. No translator rises to the challenge of replicating the effect in English, and this has to be a good thing. Like Leonides' isopsephic epigrams, these poems are all about the visual and cognitive effect

---

[9] On the absence of Hellenistic skoptic epigram, see Nisbet 2007b.

[10] Readers interested in seeing how Second Sophistic rhetoric made space for implicit political comment through allegory should begin with the valuable and accessible treatment by Whitmarsh 2005: 57–73.

[11] On Vestinus as Hadrianic functionary, see briefly Bowie 1990: 61. The poem also comes down under the variant name 'Besantinus', preferred by the Loeb edition.

[12] These examples by Simias and Theocritus are at *AP* 15.21 and 27; cf. 15.22 and 24, also by Simias.

of the *written* text in the papyrus roll. As puzzles, they expect an individual reader with time and ingenuity to spare – and a very careful copyist; anyone who merely listens in misses the point. This is about as far as we can get from the sympotic ideal of Hellenistic epigrams on life, love, and wine.

Vestinus' *Altar* takes its shape and inspiration from a famous Hellenistic pattern-poem by Dosiadas of Rhodes, but is constructed on a grander scale – twenty-six lines to Dosiadas' eighteen. ('Typical Roman!' a contemporary reader might have thought, 'always having to go one better.') The author also works in an acrostic, meandering down the line-beginnings of the altar's left-hand side. It is a prayer, and one highly appropriate to its context: 'Olympian, may you offer sacrifices for many years to come'. The Olympian deity is surely Hadrian, flattered as a good emperor (and thus destined for posthumous deification) with specifically Greek sympathies; Vestinus prays for the long life of his emperor and boss. Perhaps this pattern-epigram was presented in lieu of a birthday present, like Leonides' isopsephic poem; or perhaps it was written to accompany a real gift, like Martial's *Xenia* and *Apophoreta* (collections of gift-tag epigrams presented in modern editions as Books 13 and 14).

We present the top half of Vestinus' *Altar* as an example of the kinds of Roman-era material that Cephalas found so hard to categorize – a poem as far from the traditional elegiac epigram as can be imagined. In a sense it is the ultimate faux-inscriptional epigram, supplying a cut-out template for building the object it is supposed to adorn:

Ὀλὸς οὔ με λιβρὸς ἱρῶν
Λιβαδέσσιν, οἷα κάλχη
Ὑποφοινίῃσι τέγγει·
Μαύλιες δ' ὕπερθε πέτρης Ναξίας θοούμεναι
Παμάτων φείδοντο Πανός· οὐ στροβίλῳ λιγνύϊ
Ἰξὸς εὐώδης μελαίνει τρεχνέων με Νυσίων.
Ἐς γὰρ βωμὸν ὁρῇς με μήτε γλούρου
Πλίνθοις, μήτ' Ἀλύβης παγέντα βώλοις·
Οὐδ' ὃν Κυνθογενὴς ἔτευξε φύτλη
Λαβόντε μηκάδων κέρα,
Λισσαῖσιν ἀμφὶ δειράσιν
Ὅσσαι νέμονται Κυνθίαις,
Ἰσόρροπος πέλοιτό μοι.

...

The acrostic can be read down the wiggly left margin: *ΟΛΥΜΠΙΕ* ('Olympian'), etc. A few lines down, the altar widens again to form a slanted base. The metres are various and obscure, and the difficult Greek is full of learned allusion to local cult. Look at this poem in Paton's Loeb if you get the chance (Paton 1916–18): he gives it no fewer than nine footnotes, far more than any other poem in his five volumes, and his faithfully literal English translation is practically unreadable.

I am not the sort of altar on which beasts are sacrificed, says this first part of the *Altar*; no smoke rises from me, and I am not built of gold, silver, or horn. (Not that Vestinus *says* silver; instead he makes an incredibly obscure Homeric reference – even most professional scholars would be lost without the Loeb footnote. Ancient readers would not have got very far without an expert knowledge of Callimachus either.) The next four lines of the poem identify its builders: the text *seems* to specify the Muses, but in such a tortuous way that even Paton (a very skilled and perceptive reader of epigram) is hard pressed to explain exactly how Vestinus gets there. The topos of presenting a clever epigram as a bloodless sacrifice of course recalls Leonides' dedication of his book of newfangled isopsephic poems to the emperor Nero; so Vestinus expects a readership well enough versed in recent genre history to get the reference. The remaining nine lines, progressively lengthening to form the base of the *Altar*, compliment Hadrian as a fellow poet – again in a very roundabout way.

### Epigram and the sophists

Hadrian is himself attested as a newfangled skoptic epigrammatist – and as a 'satirical' one, in Latin.[13] But he is also the author of epigrams in the oldest Greek varieties of all, dedicatory and funerary epigram. These poems are not merely inscriptional in form; we know that some were actually inscribed. A rare example of epigram in hendecasyllables from Thespiae in Boeotia (*FGE* Hadrian 5 = *IG* VII 1827) commemorates a bear hunt, and may relate to the foundation of the city of Hadrianoutherae. From an inept transcript of an ancient stone copy comes a conventional and touching epitaph (*FGE* Hadrian 7 = *IG* XIV 1089), composed for inscription on the newly restored

---

[13] In Greek: *FGE* Hadrian 3. In Latin: Courtney 1993: 375–5.

tomb of the Hellenistic poet Parthenius.[14] The historian Dio attributes
to Hadrian a verse epitaph for Pompey, which also survives in the
*Anthology* (*FGE* Hadrian 4 = *AP* 9.402).[15] Pompey was murdered
between ship and shore, and his headless corpse was buried in an
unmarked grave. Hadrian thus dramatically declaimed his single
hexameter line; there was no monument on which to inscribe it. His
response to Roman epic treatment of Pompey's death scene has long
been noted, but Hadrian's quasi-inscriptional performance also evokes
fictional epitaphs for the shipwrecked dead of the type we find in the
new Posidippus:

> He had the lion's share of temples; how great a loss that he should have no
> tomb.

Hadrian's range as a poet advertises his mastery of *paideia* while
simultaneously alluding to Republican elite traditions of witty light
verse.[16] Epigram makes him not just a good Greek sophist but
also a good Roman senator. Hadrian's background is atypical but
symptomatic of his age: an emperor who is also a former archon
of Athens; a career soldier with a Greek-style younger boyfriend in
whose memory, Alexander-like, he founds a city (Antinoöpolis, the
City of Antinous).

Hadrian's fellow Greek intellectuals are drawn to epigram as an
established element of the sympotic culture that, in their eyes, unites
them with the revered classical past. Their ideas of how epigram
really fits into this tradition are perhaps a little confused. Plutarch's
*Table-Talk*, a voluminous work of commentary on the culture of the
symposium, ignores epigram completely – it is not part of *his* idea of
the ideal dinner party, so he leaves it out. (Presumably the sticking-
point, as in education at the time, was its lack of a copper-bottomed
classical pedigree. Contrastingly, Plutarch often quotes funerary
epigrams – which *do* have such a pedigree – in his parallel biographies
of famous Greeks and Romans, the *Lives*.) Perhaps at around the same
time, the anonymous author of the *AP* 11 preface goes to the other
extreme, representing skoptic epigram in particular as a subgenre that
had always been at the heart of the symposium among 'the ancients'.

---

[14] For a brief discussion, see Nisbet 2007a: 553–4. On Parthenius, see the modern
commentary by Lightfoot 1999.

[15] The line is ascribed to Hadrian in both *AP* and *APl*. See also Pompey in Lucan: 9.789–
822, recently discussed by Spencer 2005.

[16] Nisbet 2007a; on Hadrian as Greek poet, see Bowie 1990.

This is clearly a desperate piece of fudging, as we saw in Chapter 1; but Plutarch is probably no better. Veiling prescription as description, each of these prose writers makes a case for (or, in Plutarch's case, implicitly against) epigram's place, status, and pedigree.

Other authors attempt to rewrite genre history through more direct intervention, composing a spurious back catalogue of erotic epigrams for the philosopher Plato:[17]

> As I kissed Agathon, I held back my soul at my lips; the naughty thing was trying to pass through and enter him.

> I throw you an apple; if you really love me, girl, pick it up, and give me your virginity in exchange. But if you are thinking what you should not be, take this very same apple and consider how fleeting is the prime of youthful beauty.

> I am an apple: the one who throws me, loves you. Please consent, Xanthippe; both you and I are subject to decay.

The thrown apple is a standard love offering in Hellenistic poetry. Many of the pseudo-Platonic poems must be Hellenistic themselves; Meleager boasts in his preface that his *Garland* includes 'the golden bough of ever-divine Plato'. The third example seems a likely case in point: in its unlikely conceit of an epigram 'upon' an apple it resembles one of Martial's poetic gift tags, but the still more improbable idea of incision into the apple's skin chimes with the playful meta-inscriptionality of the new Milan text. In fact, this third epigram can now be ascribed with some confidence to Philodemus of Gadara, writing (as we saw in our chapter on Hellenistic epigram) in imitation of Hellenistic models in the first century BCE, on the cusp of empire.[18] Others will be imperial in date, minor props in the Second Sophistic's consensual hallucination of its Attic heritage. Working out contemporary erotics against the backdrop of a utopian past fleshed out from Plato's own classic texts – Xanthippe is the wife of his teacher Socrates (*Phaedo*), and Agathon is the host of the *Symposium* – they bear close comparison to prose texts such as Lucian's *Dialogues of Courtesans*.[19]

---

[17] These examples are at *AP* 5.78–80. *FGE* 'Plato' (note Page's irony quotes) runs to twenty-three poems.

[18] Sider 1997: 64–7, citing as evidence the papyrus incipit list, P.Oxy. LIV 3724.

[19] On literary treatment of sexual desire and relationships in the Second Sophistic, see Goldhill 1995.

The culture fans who retroactively concocted a corpus of epigrams for Plato can never seriously have expected or intended to fool fellow aficionados; they are paying witty homage and displaying rhetorical virtuosity. Nevertheless, as we will see in our final chapter, the modern critical literature on epigram found advantage in postponing the final death of Plato-the-poet until quite recently.[20] The ancient consumers of these epigrams will have been in on the joke, deriving a pleasurable kick from the fantasy of the Father of Philosophy mastered by Eros. A similar story – sadly post-classical – has Aristotle robbed of reason and ridden like a donkey by another famous *hetaira*; more germanely, the Epicurean and literary critic Philodemus had earlier written funny epigrams on his own helplessness (so contrary to the strictures of his philosophical master) in the face of sexual desire.[21]

Viewed in this light, many of the pseudo-Platonic epigrams are perhaps not so much fakes in our modern sense (composed in earnest to deceive) as exercises in the sophists' favourite game of virtuoso rhetorical impersonation, *prosopopoeia* (literally, something like 'pulling faces'). Not being fooled was the payoff, confirming the reader's worth and wit as an educated person (*pepaideumenos*). Only a careless and imperfectly acculturated reader would swallow such a line, becoming a figure of fun for the *pepaideumenos* in the process. Nero famously fell for such tall stories (or was said to have done) on more than one occasion; for Greek authors in particular, his naïve readings marked him as a poor student of the Hellenism that he made such a show of pursuing.[22] So the epigrams of Plato reveal nothing about Plato but plenty about how the sophists of the early centuries CE fashioned their ideal – and always already ironized – classical past.

They also used epigram to jostle for position in the present. Ammianus, a puzzle addict in second-century Smyrna, gouges away at the public reputation of a local VIP in a series of skoptic epigrams preserved in *AP* 11. Marcus Antonius Polemo was a descendant of local royalty and a friend of emperors, but Ammianus' epigrams cut him down to size. As with Leonidas' poems, they lose a lot in

---

[20] The attributions in Paton's Loeb (Paton 1916–18) are a case in point. Page in *FGE* smites wishful predecessors who took the ascriptions at face value: 'It is remarkable that some modern scholars have been caught in the web...ascription to Plato is plainly false...[the content] absolutely condemns the ascription' (161–2, 169).

[21] For Aristotle ridden by Alexander's mistress, Phyllis, see Tatum 1994: 1–2. Examples of Philodemus in love include Philodemus 1 (see above, p. 000), 4 (love as 'madness'), 5, and 7.

[22] On dissimulation and fakes under Nero, see the contemporaneous monographs of Bartsch 1994 and Bowersock 1994.

translation. Typically Ammianus lops bits off his target's proper name to reveal a hidden Greek word, and thus the ugly truth of their identity. This process has affinities with the pseudoscience of the contemporary physiognomists (famously including Polemo), who diagnosed the hidden truths of individual and ethnic character by reference to details of physical appearance – the shape of the head, the distance between the eyes, or, in extreme cases, the relative length of finger joints.[23] In one poem (*AP* 11.181), the reader is instructed to subtract the first three letters of the target's name. Cutting three letters from his Roman *nomen* Antonius (*Antōnios* in Ammianus' Greek) gives *ōnios*, meaning up for sale – Polemo's financial irregularities were notorious:

> We all knew, Polemon, that your name was Antonius; how do you suddenly find yourself three letters short?

Other poems by Ammianus skewer the pretensions of contemporary intellectuals generally. *AP* 11.157, for instance, ridicules sophists whose public performances aspire to recreate the flawless fifth-century Greek of the canonized Attic orators, cramming in as many obscure archaisms as they can find (or invent); Paton's Loeb translation (Paton 1916–18) does a good job of conveying the flavour. Numerous epigrams by Lucian do the same.[24]

Other sophists dip into epigram only occasionally, at least as far as we can see from what survives. The surviving handful of poems attributable to major sophistic figures are intricate in their intertextual play with ancient and modern genre figures. Philostratus compresses into a nutshell (*AP* Appendix 110) dense allusion to his landmark literary achievement, the *Imagines* ('Images' – *ekphrases* of the paintings in an art gallery), transposing for this purpose Meleager's pederastic clichés into a new context of art criticism. Fronto constructs erudite and very smutty double entendres, riffing on Ammianus, Strato, and Callimachus *all in the same poem* (*AP* 12.174) while naming none of them (we are expected to keep up). In his other surviving poem (*AP* 12.233), which owes much to Lucillius, Fronto turns the canonical plays of New Comedy (all set texts in the ancient schoolroom) into

---

[23] For context and an accessible overview, see Gleason 1995, précised by Whitmarsh 2005: 29–32; also Barton 1994.

[24] For a thorough and lucid account of Atticism, see Swain 1996: 17–42; Whitmarsh 2005: 41–52 is accessible and lively. On Ammianus and Lucian, see generally Nisbet 2003a: 134–81.

an increasingly pornographic chat-up routine to get a schoolboy into bed:[25]

> ...Time will make you *The Despised One*, and then *The Ploughman*, and then you will crave *The Clipped Woman*.

In other words, with the onset of puberty the boy will find himself suddenly spurned (*The Despised One*) by the male admirers who now surround him; he will shift role from passive beloved (*erōmenos*) to active lover (*erastēs*), no longer pursued but pursuing (*The Ploughman* – attested in Old Comedy as an agricultural metaphor for penetrative sex).[26] Shockingly, he will even become interested in women, specifically *hetairai* (whose shaving of intimate areas was a source of fascination to male customers.) So he might as well submit now, while Fronto is still interested. This is heady stuff and loses much in the explanation, to say nothing of translation; in any case, these isolated survivals can give little to no indication of how epigram was being used in more run-of-the-mill contexts. The same applies to the most famous site of inscriptional epigram-production in the Second Sophistic: the singing Colossus of Memnon at Thebes in Egypt.

## Colossal graffiti

The Colossus started life in the mid-fourteenth century BCE as half of a matched pair of large sandstone statues of an enthroned Amenhotep III, a pharaoh of the Eighteenth Dynasty. During the reign of Augustus the right-hand statue was broken in two, perhaps by an earthquake. Amenhotep's story was long forgotten, and the fractured stump took on a new identity: Memnon, son of the dawn goddess, Eos. This famous Ethiopian warrior king and ally of Troy was well known from art and literature; his exploits and death in a duel with Achilles were related in the *Aethiopis*, the Cyclic epic that picked up where Homer's *Iliad* left off. Now his name became attached to a statue that lay perhaps not too far from his Ethiopian homeland – although Homer had been vague as to which 'Ethiopia' he meant.[27] The wrecked colossus often

---

[25] For a fuller discussion of these poems, see Nisbet 2007c.

[26] Henderson 1991: 166 – only the one example, suggesting that Fronto anticipates either a very well-read or a very dirty-minded reader, and the context seems to link ploughing to vaginal rather than anal penetration; but cf. ibid.: 168, on the more common 'digging' metaphor.

[27] On antiquity's two Ethiopias, see Romm 1992: 45–60.

made a hollow knocking noise as it warmed up in the sun: this was explained as Memnon greeting his mother, the Dawn. As word of Memnon spread, Thebes began to do very well out of its new tourist attraction; by Hadrian's time, its legs and base were quickly filling up with the erudite graffiti of important visitors. These often expertly inscribed texts were almost all epigrams.

Hadrian's entourage visited Memnon in November CE 130. Hadrian, whose boyfriend Antinous had recently drowned in the Nile, does not seem to have composed a poem – but a member of his entourage left several. She was Julia Balbilla, the travelling companion and perhaps the lover of the emperor's wife, Sabina. Balbilla is a fascinating instance of hybrid identity in the Mediterranean world of the early centuries CE: one of her grandfathers was the last independent ruler of the Hellenized Mesopotamian kingdom of Commagene (gobbled up by Roman Syria), the other a Roman tribune with an Egyptian background who played an important role in Claudius' invasion of Britain and was later appointed head of the Museum in Alexandria. Her brother Philopappus was a friend of Hadrian from his time in Athens; there is still a monument to him there. Balbilla's epigrams on Memnon extravagantly praise Sabina's beauty, in a poetic dialect designed to recall the Lesbian poet Sappho. This one is on the statue's left ankle:[28]

When on the first day we did not hear Memnon.

Yesterday Memnon greeted the husband in silence, so that the lovely Sabina might make her way again to this place. For the desirable beauty of our queen delights you. But he greeted her arrival with a divine cry, lest the emperor should grow angry with you: for too long now you have fearlessly detained his august and wedded wife. Yes, Memnon himself, fearing the wrath of great Hadrian, suddenly gave voice; and hearing it, she was delighted.

Balbilla *seems* to be hinting at a lesbian relationship in the imperial household, but it could be a literary game – Hadrian was after all a fellow poet with a shared penchant for antiquarianism. Readings of the Balbilla poems dominate modern discussions of the Memnon graffiti.

[28] Bernand and Bernand 1960: text 30.

They reflect our own predilections back at us – scholarly (postmodern metafiction), popular (lesbian chic), or often both at once.[29]

## Latin epigram (long) after Martial

The Latin inscriptions on Memnon are in dull, semi-official prose.[30] Latin literary epigram, too, is largely silent in this period. A major topos of Martial's poetics is that he was exploiting his genre to its breaking point and perhaps beyond, just as Ovid had for elegy; perhaps through anxiety of influence, no major literary author took it up again until the fourth century CE.[31] The new poets of Late Antiquity looked back less to Martial than to Hellenistic and Imperial Greek collections, including the two *Garlands*; they may have known these sources only through an intermediary proto-Anthology of their own era.[32] Epigram was now one literary accomplishment among many, not a lifetime specialization as it had been for Martial, and many of these later writers were active in prose as well as verse.

Ausonius, a politician in the consciously classicizing late Roman milieu of fourth-century Gaul, was particularly fond of epigrams on works of art in imitation of classic Greek models; he also embraced the skoptic epigram of the immediately preceding centuries. He was not just an epigrammatist: Kay, his most accessible modern editor, reasonably calls him 'the dominant literary figure of the Latin West in the fourth century'.[33] Ausonius invokes Martial as a pretext for writing rude poems but finds ways around Martial's own obscene vocabulary, and is keener to flag up his adherence to non-epigrammatic Latin verse heroes including Vergil, Catullus, Horace, and post-Augustan Latin poets – all the while surreptitiously ripping off Martial's back catalogue.[34]

---

[29] On Memnon visitors, including Balbilla, see briefly Bowie 1990: 61–6; on Balbilla in reception, see Nisbet 2007a: 555–8.

[30] Bernand and Bernand 1960: texts 1–10, 13–17, 24–6.

[31] The very thin evidence for Latin epigram in the centuries-long gap between Martial and Ausonius is usefully summarized by Kay 2001: 21–2.

[32] Cameron 1993: 78–96, densely argued.

[33] Kay 2001: 23, concluding a serviceable summary account of Ausonius' life and literary career.

[34] Ibid.: 18 for correspondences with the skoptic epigrammatists; 19–20 on Martial and other Latin models. Kay confidently detects allusions only to Catullus' longer and polymetric poems, not his elegiac epigrams.

He also wrote epigrams in Greek, and sometimes showed off with alternate lines of Latin *and* Greek, maintaining seamless metricality and syntax across the join. The following epigram responds closely to Hellenistic and Imperial Greek epideictic epigrams from *AP* 7 and 9 – Sappho was a favourite subject for literary epitaphs – but its explicit bilingualism has hardly any antecedents.[35] The visual juxtaposition of alphabets dramatizes Ausonius' virtuosity in handling the inherited literary traditions of Greece and Rome alike; careful choice of words advertises his ability to blend them harmoniously. (The *Pierides*, named in Latin, are Greek Muses; the *Aonidae*, named in Greek, are Latin ones.) We include the text to illustrate the transition between languages. Epigram had never looked like this before:

> *Lesbia Pieriis Sappho soror addita Musis*
> εἴμ᾽ ἐνάτη λυρικῶν, Ἀονίδων δεκάτη.

> I, Sappho of Lesbos, who was added as a sister to the Muses of Pieria,
> *suis la neuvième poète lyrique, et la dixième fille d'Aon.*[36]

At least one Ausonian juxtaposition, poems 64–5 in Kay's edition, ratchets up the tension between Greek and Latin literary *and* cultural codes. The first of these poems tackles a very familiar Hellenistic theme, centuries on – Myron's *Cow*:

> Why do you butt against the chill udders of your brazen mother, little calf, and why try to suck nourishing milk from bronze? I would supply this too, if a god had fashioned my inside as finely as Myron my outside.

The second, immediately following the first, invokes a famous Greek artificer but evokes Martial:

> Daedalus, why do you exhaust your labour in pointless craftsmanship? Instead offer me to the bull with Pasiphae inside.[37]

---

[35] A couple of Ammianus' plays on words are self-consciously provocative by being even *implicitly* bilingual: Nisbet 2003a: 137–52. The closest precedent we know for Ausonius' explicit bilingualism is a literary self-epitaph by the renowned Meleager (1 *HE* = *AP* 7.419), which places the poet at the crossroads of not two but three distinct linguistic cultures. Meleager's poem greets potential passers-by in Syrian ('Salam!') and Phoenician ('Naidius!'), as well as in Greek – but he presents these greetings *in* Greek, and does not introduce a 'foreign' alphabet and syntax.

[36] Kay 2001: poem 35, with useful notes on Greek models at 150–1. Our use of French flags up the linguistic shift – for readers without it, the second line means '(I) am the ninth of the Lyric poets, and the tenth of the daughters of Aon'.

[37] In myth, Pasiphae, cursed by Poseidon to fall in love with a bull, had the legendary Athenian craftsman Daedalus construct a hollow artificial cow so that she could satisfy her

Compare Martial *de Spectaculis* 6:

> Believe that Pasiphae was offered to the Dictaean bull: we have seen it,
> and the ancient myth is now believed. But venerable antiquity should not
> marvel at itself, Caesar: whatever Fame sings of, the arena supplies to you.

Complex webs are being woven here. The two Ausonian poems are
placed within an elaborate and teasing sequence exploring the interplay
of reality-effect and sexual desire; within it, legendary Greek special-
effects technicians come and go.[38] Kay's poem 57 inaugurates the
sequence. Niobe, in myth turned to stone, is polished by Praxiteles'
wandering hands into a lifelike and thus a 'living' work of art.[39] Or
rather, not; this is an ekphrastic cliché in praise of a canonical sculptor's
verisimilitude. Praxiteles' skill might easily fool you into thinking that
you were looking at the real Niobe:

> I was once alive; then I was made stone. Buffed by Praxiteles' hands I live
> once more – Niobe. The hand of the artificer restored everything except
> sense; but I already lacked that, when I insulted the gods.

Poem 58 is Niobe again, riffing for genre-bending effect on the famous
eleventh line of Vergil's *Aeneid* – an epic that itself borrows repeatedly
from epigram for its own internal epigraphic habit.[40] The earlier Niobe
of poem 57 had calmly announced that she was a statue without *sensus*
(variously 'sense impressions', 'common sense', and 'sensitivity'). In
contrast, this second Niobe is a creature of pure *sensus* – pain, tears,
and grief – without visible form. Her *imago* (likeness, appearance,
death mask, phantom, copy, reflection...) has long since vanished:

> ...
> What wickedness! *Can the hearts of the gods be so angry?*
>    A mother's grief endures to this day; her image has perished.

In poem 59, a Venus clad in armour (and thus resembling a statue
herself) scores points off Minerva; Ausonius works in a reference to
the local cult of armed Aphrodite at Sparta, known from Pausanias
(3.15.10). In poem 60, Lais, the most famous *hetaira* of all time, hangs

---

passion – the result of their unnatural union was the Minotaur.

[38] On Ausonius' fascination with reality-effect and its deconstruction, see the excellent essay
by Nugent 1990: 240–7.

[39] Niobe was *silex*, 'hard stone' but also proverbially lacking feeling and emotion (*OLD silex*
3); Ausonius' choice of words plays upon this figurative meaning.

[40] On the *Aeneid*'s relation to epigram, see e.g. Dinter 2005.

up her mirror – another maker of uncanny visual copies – as a thank-offering at a temple of Venus, much as a successful mercenary might dedicate his shield; the epigram invites us to imagine inscription, by a long-dead Greek woman, in Latin. Both of these poems are close variations on Hellenistic models, but their selection and juxtaposition by Ausonius create new effects. Poem 61 takes us to the birth (from a three-yolked egg) of Helen, ancient pin-up and doom of Troy – in hexameters, appropriately enough for the face that launched a thousand ships and several epics. In poem 62, the goddess Venus faces off against her world-famous statue, the Venus of Cnidus, and playfully accuses its maker, Praxiteles, of spying on her in the nude; just as playfully, he bats the accusation away. (Praxiteles has used iron tools; iron is in the care of Mars, Venus' husband; Mars knows what he likes Venus to look like.) Parallels identified by Kay make it clear that the charge and its rebuttal are both clichés from earlier Greek epigram.[41]

Poem 63 focuses the sequence specifically on Myron's *Cow*, ticking off all the clichés:

> I am the heifer made by the chisel of my father Myron; in my opinion I was not made, but born. This is why the bull mounts me, why the nearby heifer moos to me, and why the thirsty calf seeks my udders. Are you surprised that I deceive the herd? Even the herdsman tends to count me as one of his livestock.

It is tempting to read this epigram against the elaborate metapoetics of genre already evident in the Milan Posidippus' epigrams on gems, and elaborated in translation by Martial. Ausonius' ekphrasis speaks not just for the artwork it describes but for his own practice as a latecomer to a massively imitative genre; it dramatizes its own interpolation as a Latin impostor into the 'herd' of Hellenistic Greek epigrams on the *Cow*.

Poems 64–5 immediately follow. The first, as we have seen, modifies the stereotyped scenario of poem 63 by refocusing on a distinction already explored in some Greek models: interior/exterior (bearing in mind that ancient bronze statues were hollow).[42] The second poem crosses over into the bronze heifer's interior to summon up a Roman arena scenario out of Martial. Martial's *de Spectaculis* is all about the gladiatorial games and other shows that inaugurated the Flavian

---

[41] Kay 2001: 195–6.
[42] For parallels see ibid.: 203.

Amphitheatre, better known today as the Colosseum. Ausonius in his poem 65 alludes to its sixth epigram, describing one of Domitian's famous executions dressed up as scenes from myth – 'fatal charades'.[43] Ausonius transposes Myron's work of art onto the bloody sand at Rome's heart, and turns it into a pretentious killing machine.

He also creates effects of *indirect* juxtaposition. Any reader intrigued enough by Ausonius' manipulation of tone to follow up on the allusion to *de Spectaculis* will find that Martial's sixth poem sits in a sequence of its own, between two others that add nuance to the Ausonian series. The fifth poem of *de Spectaculis* brags of Domitian's purge of informers from Rome. It becomes a kind of *sphragis*, a poetic signature for Ausonius' distinctive poetics of citation ('Ausonia' is a poetic name for Italy):

> The fugitive informer is exiled from the *Ausonian* city [*Ausonia...ab urbe*]; one may add this item to our emperor's expenses.

*De Spectaculis'* seventh poem is plausibly read by its modern editor as praising Domitian for introducing the novelty of women gladiators. Reconfigured through Ausonian allusion, it now ties Venus and Mars, the omnipresent divinities of Ausonius' sequence, to the emperor's pleasure. Greek technology of illusion meets Roman appetite in the service of imperial power:[44]

> That Mars serves you in unconquered arms, Caesar, is not sufficient: Venus herself serves you too.

Ausonius' sequence is not yet over. His business with Myron's *Cow* will not conclude until the closing words of poem 71: 'because I did not want to follow the other heifers'. Metapoetics again? Ausonius' intricate art of allusion and juxtaposition advertises his mastery of genre, and illustrates in miniature his virtuosity in crafting an original response to the classical literary inheritance that he shares with his peers in the Gallo-Latin elite. The sequence discussed above is self-consciously palimpsestic; the active reader must tease out its meaning

---

[43] Coleman 1990.

[44] Shackleton Bailey 1993 *ad loc*; on Ausonius' creative 'misreading' of canon texts, see Nugent 1990.

against the precisely segmented virtual backdrop of Martial's juvenilia. 'Ausonius comfortably inhabits the work of his predecessors.'[45]

## Playing in the wreckage: late antique Latin epigram

Later Latin poets continued in the Ausonian tradition. In sixth-century Africa under the Vandals, Luxorius and the anonymous poet of *Anthologia Latina* 78–188 published books of epigrams.[46] The latter opens with an epigram addressing the reader, closely recalling the programmatic poems and sequences in which Martial tells his readers how to use his books. The allusion ties the poet to a specifically Roman tradition of dry wit associated with Republican free speech – *sal*, literally 'salt'. Edgy and urbane, *sal* defines the Latin genre of hexameter satire, and becomes a measure of success for Latin epigram in the hands of Catullus and Martial; subsequently, Hadrian co-opts their street cred by writing satirical epigrams of his own.[47] Here, though, *sal* is assigned to Greek Muses (*Pieridae*) in a cultural balancing-act that recalls Ausonius' own:[48]

> The games of my childhood, the passions of my youth, the bombast
> of a garrulous tongue seasoned with Pierian wit [*sale Pierio*]: this work
> encompasses them all. And you, reader, apply an expert mind to weigh
> them all up and pick out the ones you enjoy.

Several poems in the early part of the book praise bath-houses – perhaps a bigger deal in sixth-century Africa than in Martial's cosmopolitan Rome of five centuries earlier. Christian and pagan mythologies rub alongside one another.[49] The temptation is strong to

---

[45] Nugent 1990: 249 and see also 248: 'A kind of Joycean exuberance makes of the late antique poet an intellectual *bricoleur*, assembling creations to delight and astound his friends, from the *disiecta membra* of the poetic corpus they share.'

[46] *Anthologia Latina* is misleadingly named: it is not an organic collection like *AP* but a modern miscellany of ancient Latin verse compiled by a nineteenth-century editor who does not restrict himself to epigrams. A concise account is given in Kay 2006: 20–2. Luxorius' poems are at *Anth. Lat.* 291–375; scholars place him in Carthage. For reasons to place the anonymous poet of *Anth. Lat.* 78–188 in Africa, see Kay 2006: 5–7.

[47] See *OLD sal* 6, citing e.g. Hor. *Sat.* 1.10.3 (on Lucilius, pioneer of Latin satire), Catull. 16.7 (linking *sal* to *lepos*, 'charm'), and Mart. 12.95.2 ('pages tinged with prurient *sal*').

[48] Poem 79 in Kay 2006, whose numbering is again used in what follows; on Luxorius' very similar opening sequence, see Kay 2006: 65–6; on Martial and *sal*, see 66 n. 2.

[49] Contrast e.g. poems 81–2 (an epitaph for a Christian child and a poem on the judgement of Solomon – clearly designed to be read as a pair) to poems 86–7 (Bellerophon and the Chimaera – likewise).

read for social history; old civic and religious infrastructure is falling apart in this book. As romantic moderns, reading with a hindsight not available to the poet or his original readers, we cannot help anticipating barbarians at the gates. Twelve epigrams in, a pagan temple has been pulled apart to supply stone for city fortifications – the poet's objectification of Mars and Venus may recall Ausonius:[50]

> ...Mars has saved himself the trouble of long yearning; now Venus seeks her temple [*sua templa*] amid his walls.

Later in the book a former library has become a pick-up joint; the Muses who stood for its amassed learning, Latin ones this time (*Camenae*), have been driven out. Verbal repetition (*sua templa*) invites us to 'read back' to the Mars/Venus poem, and the Cyprian goddess is of course Venus under a well-known cult name, a regular patron of this bar-*cum*-brothel in her capacity as goddess of sexual desire. Bromius is a cult name for Bacchus, the Roman Dionysus, god of intoxication and half-brother to Apollo, the patron of literature and the arts:[51]

> *On a library turned into a bar:*

> This building, until recently dedicated to the nine Camenae, is now held by Bacchus – he calls it his temple [*sua templa*]. For in the place that preserved so many writings of men of old, the Cyprian delights in quaffing sweet wines. The shrine continues to be occupied by a god related to its former owner: where Phoebus lived, now lives Bromius!

As we saw in Chapter 3, this is exactly the kind of quasi-topographic literary factoid that drives a certain kind of Martial scholar to start sticking pins into a large-scale map of ancient Rome. Faced with an anonymous poet in an unknown city, though, the pressure is off. We can read outwards from the urban detail to track larger social concerns, or simply enjoy the text as a literary game of connections and allusions.

---

[50] Poem 89; we translate the final couplet, lines 5–6.
[51] Poem 115.

## Icons and heretics: epigram in Byzantium

Greek epigram continues under Byzantium. Cephalas is not merely an antiquarian; he reports a living tradition. The very first Book of the *Anthology* is headed 'The Epigrams of the Christians'. A subtitle clarifies Cephalas' intent: 'Let the pious and godly epigrams of the Christians be placed first, even if the Hellenes are displeased.' He writes here like a sophist, in perfect Attic Greek, with one exception. Hellene now means not Greek but 'pagan', a negative sense found in Christian authors from Late Antiquity onwards.[52]

*AP* 1 is unusually varied in its content. The opening poem celebrates the restoration of icons to the great cathedral of Hagia Sophia following a phase of iconoclasm (in its literal sense of the doctrinally motivated destruction of religious images); subsequent epigrams attest the partial rebuilding of dilapidated churches by emperors and other powerful patrons. *AP* 1.4 nicely illustrates the mix of Christian sentiment and pagan offices. It runs to three lines of hexameters, bypassing the epigram tradition of the pagan Hellenes to touch base with Homer (long read allegorically). To a modern readership, the juxtaposition of epic diction, pious devotion, and late Roman bureaucracy is jarring, but clearly it worked for its intended readership:[53]

Τοῦτον Ἰωάννῃ, Χριστοῦ μεγάλῳ θεράποντι,
Στούδιος ἀγλαὸν οἶκον ἐδείματο· καρπαλίμως δὲ
τῶν κάμεν εὕρετο μισθόν, ἑλὼν ὑπατηΐδα ῥάβδον.

Studius built this splendid house for John, Christ's great servant; and he swiftly found the reward for which he toiled, taking up the consular *fasces*.

Many other *AP* 1 epigrams pursue this alternative literary pedigree. Homer was still a staple of the schoolroom, he had been read allegorically for hundreds of years, and his themes were redeemable for the Church.[54] Later in the Book (*AP* 1.56), within a long sequence by the compiler of the *Cycle*, Agathias Scholasticus, an epigram in two hexameter lines celebrates Christ's harrowing of Hell. Literary

---

[52] LSJ Ἕλλην 5, with examples of usage including the Christian emperor Julian (fourth century CE).

[53] Worth following up for Homeric associations are: ἀγλαός ('splendid'), δέμω ('build'), καρπάλιμως ('swiftly'), θεράπων ('servant'), κάμνω ('toil').

[54] The contributors to Lamberton and Keaney 1992 address instances of allegorical exegesis of Homer by Neoplatonists, Stoics, and other interested parties ranging from antiquity to the Renaissance; see also Lamberton 1986.

association merges the Christian Hell with the underworld of pagan epic:

> Christ, being a god [or 'being God'], took all the dead out of Hades;
> Hades alone, bane of men, he left behind lifeless.

'Bane of men' (*brotoloigos*) is an impressively rare Homeric epithet; the *Iliad* and *Odyssey* each use it once of Ares, god of war. Agathias' epigram re-imagines Christ's redemption of the dead as a heroic *aristeia*, his most glorious feat of arms. Hades is of course the pagan god, brother to Zeus and Poseidon, to whose underworld so many Homeric heroes are bloodily despatched: 'to Hades' halls' is a common formula in the *Iliad*'s death scenes. Here the tables are turned, and Hades himself becomes the opponent whom Christ slays: 'lifeless' (*akērios* – lacking *kēr*, 'a heart') is a characteristically Iliadic description of a fallen enemy on the battlefield. Moreover, there may be a double sense: *kēr* can also mean 'death spirit', and Christ's self-sacrifice has deprived Hades of its power over the faithful. To die in Christ is not true death but the way to everlasting life.

Homer himself could even become a sacred text if properly reordered. Towards the end of Book 1, a hexameter poem by Ignatius (*AP* 1.119) celebrates another, larger hexameter poem that unfortunately does not survive in its original form: a Homeric cento by Patricius, an otherwise unknown fourth-century bishop. This book-length epic, narrating the story of Christ from birth to resurrection and ascension, consisted entirely of lines taken from the *Iliad* and *Odyssey*. The cento was a popular late antique form: Ausonius had composed a *Nuptial Cento*, the closing part of which turned lines from Vergil into obscene double entendres (this still survives, and includes a handy preface setting out the rules of cento composition), but they were typically religious.[55] The pagan source text conferred canonical prestige on the Christian theme, and was in turn Christianized by lending service. (Cento would later become a favoured form of the Renaissance, as it explored its own problematic relation to rediscovered antiquity.) Patricius' cento was

---

[55] Ausonius introduces the closing section of the *Cento* with a Digression (*Parecbasis*) in which he humorously apologizes for turning Vergil into an obscene poet: 'Up to this point I have veiled the mystery of marriage in paraphrase and circumlocution, to make it fit to be heard by chaste ears... Stop reading here, if you like, and leave the remainder to the curious.' See Green 1991: 132–9 (text) and 518–26 (useful and detailed discussion and commentary).

particularly famous: the empress Eudocia paid homage by composing an expanded and corrected version.[56]

Ignatius praises Patricius as a 'God-fearing priest' who has 'performed a mighty deed', composing a 'highly prized song of renowned words'. Patricius' deed wins him a warrior's glory, τιμή (timē). All of these words and ideas come straight out of Homer – surprisingly even 'God-fearing' (θεουδής), which occurs frequently in the *Odyssey* and hardly anywhere else in ancient literature. Ignatius keeps the act up for all twenty-eight lines of this poem about a poem made out of two other poems. Herod seeks the Iliadic 'doom' of the infant Christ (οἶτος, line 11) – the deadly fate that awaits a warrior in battle or a city under siege. Resurrected, the crucified Jesus arises on the 'early-born' (ἠριγένεια, line 27) third morning, borrowing a standard epithet of the goddess of dawn (Eos) in the *Odyssey*; and harrows Hades, just as in Agathias. Cephalas is underselling his material; the Hellenes would not have been so displeased after all. Because we go to the *Anthology* primarily as a source for the Greek epigrams of classical antiquity, we tend to downplay the extent to which it reflects a tradition that was still creatively alive.[57]

---

[56] On the cento in late antiquity, and Eudocia's (still extant) expansion of Patricius, see Usher 1998 and briefly Plant 2004: 198–9. Usher 1997: 305 concisely reports the rare examples of the cento in classical antiquity.

[57] Epigram was still being composed long after Cephalas' own time. For an eye-opening account that takes Greek inscriptional epigram into the fourteenth century, see Talbot 1999.

# V ANCIENT EPIGRAM IN RECEPTION

'Reception', the study of how the present recognizes and constructs its past, has developed from sober origins (the literary hermeneutics of Gadamer and Jauss) into a hot topic in contemporary classical studies. This rapidly changing field resists stable definition of methodology or subject matter, and elicits firebrand rhetoric. Some practitioners are explicitly confrontational, exposing the historically recent 'uses and abuses of antiquity' perpetrated in the service of reactionary ideologies, and critiquing the disciplinary sleights of hand by which classics itself has come into being.[1] Others use reception terminology to repackage *Nachleben*, the post-classical afterlives of ancient texts, or a broader 'classical tradition': the conventional study (blurring at times into optimistic hagiography) of the enduring influence of antiquity in literature and the arts. Recent trends are thoughtfully surveyed in Lorna Hardwick's New Survey, *Reception Studies* (Hardwick 2003).

Our closing chapter stakes out its own interpretative space within this contested domain by examining epigram in reception. The project demands clarification. Throughout this book, we have seen that the genre of epigram has always blurred any distinction that critics might wish to impose between the interpretation and use of a literary work. The meaning of an epigram, as of any text, is always subject to context, and in the particular case of epigram this context is always liable to rapid sequential change. Individual poems flit from stone to papyrus; from papyrus to the symposium, and back again; from the authored book into commonplace books, collections, and anthologies. Each reconfiguration of context refashions the epigram as a different aesthetic object, altering *what, how,* and *for whom* the poem 'means'. To take an example discussed earlier, the Milan Posidippus changes the nature of each of the previously known poems that it contains – each such poem has the same *text* as before (more or less), but becomes a different *work* when approached as a compositional element within the teasingly self-referential Milan book-roll.[2]

---

[1] Classicists' discussion of 'uses and abuses' looks back to Wyke and Biddiss 1999; for examples of disciplinary auto-critique see Stray 1999, Winterer 2002.

[2] Mukařovský's theory and terminology of the 'aesthetic object' (1979) apply extremely well here; see also Obbink 2004 and, on the difference made by what *sort* of book we think the Milan

In this sense, epigram's history of meaning is *nothing but* reception – and always has been (and always will be?). The *Anthology* of Constantine Cephalas is the obvious end product of one particularly dense reception strand, codifying epigram's miscellaneous hand-me-downs as a completed tradition – a ready-made canon-within-a-canon. But this seeming end point is in turn the starting point for subsequent reading communities. Its re-emergence enables new and surprising reconfigurations of the ancient genre, as we will see.

Viewed within the confines of classical tradition, ancient epigram has an afterlife well worth studying. An established trend in Latin epigram scholarship traces the influence of Martial on the vernacular traditions of European verse from the Renaissance onwards.[3] As these studies make clear, the West has historically understood epigram (whether ancient, modern or somewhere in between) in terms dictated by Martial's own, highly idiosyncratic creative choices. This process has been continuous since his re-emergence as a poetic model in Late Antiquity (see Chapter 4). Martial's insistence on closing his poems with a satirical 'point' has been so pervasive in its influence that genuine Greek epigram struck many early modern connoisseurs as frustratingly un-epigrammatic. 'Martial has wit, and is worth looking into sometimes; but I recommend the Greek epigrams to your supreme contempt', wrote Lord Chesterfield in a letter to his son. Chesterfield's correspondence aimed at, and achieved, a pithy quotability that itself owed much to Martial's particular model of epigrammatic point.[4] Greek epigram has exercised a much more localized and less enduring influence as a literary model for Western authors than has its unusual Latin imitator; the story that we tell here is thus not 'classical tradition' in a conventional, grand-narrative sense.

Instead, we focus on one particular phase in the reception history of the *Anthology*: the late nineteenth century, when Greek epigram, previously the playground of a small educated elite, first impacted on the new literate mass culture of industrialized Britain. We will see that the mediation and promotion of this unlikely genre to the new popular readership through translations and handbooks was at least as much a process of reinvention as of rediscovery. The mobility and flexibility

---

roll was, Gutzwiller 2005b. On theorizing internal allusion and patterning, see Sharrock and Morales 2000.

[3] The obvious starting point is the final chapter of Sullivan 1991.

[4] Quoted at Neaves 1874: 2, probably from the edition controversially published the year after Chesterfield's death (1774) by his daughter-in-law Eugenia Stanhope.

of epigram were pressed into service once more, to concoct a version
of ancient Greece that flattered and responded to contemporary
priorities and concerns. However, we will see that this reclamation of
epigram for mainstream social convention only became necessary in
response to an initial radical appropriation from within a marginalized
subculture. The following discussion characterizes this response as
'conservative' – a convenient shorthand, but this is not (or not just) a
narrowly political backlash against socially progressive self-expression.
Some of the critics rushing to the defence of Hellas' respectability were
political liberals whose revolution had been hijacked; they needed an
ancient Greece that reflected their own progressive vision for society
as a whole, and were unwilling to see it dirtied by association with
what was then seen as a criminal minority.[5] This stampede of late
Victorian men of letters should instead be seen as a species of broader
moral panic – a hasty and overblown exercise in damage limitation,
aimed at containing a dangerously subversive reception of a revered
classical past.[6]

### The Uranian *Anthology*

The source of this subversion was John Addington Symonds,
'Soddington Symonds', the aesthete and essayist who put homosexuality
into the dictionary. Today Symonds is remembered as a pioneer of
the emergent gay male subculture of the late nineteenth century. His
treatises, *A Problem in Greek Ethics* (1883) and *A Problem in Modern
Ethics* (1891), are placed among the founding texts of modern gay and
lesbian studies: they broke new ground in asserting that homosexuality
was neither sin nor disease, but a natural identity. In its best form
it was even morally superior to the heterosexual norm. (*Greek Ethics*
identified the 'heavenly' or Uranian pederasty of the Greeks as their
distinctive contribution to mankind – and we use the gendered term
advisedly; profane Pandemic Eros could be had anywhere, whether
with men or women.) The fame of the *Problem* treatises was a long

---

[5] On Hellenism as a vehicle for Britain's liberal intelligentsia – 'a discursive language of social
renewal' – see Dowling 1994: 35.

[6] Foundational to study of ancient Greece in Victorian reception are Jenkyns 1980 and
Turner 1981; Dowling 1994 runs with their ideas and is of wider applicability than her title
suggests. Whitmarsh 2005: 6–8, concisely analysing the 'invention' of the Second Sophistic in
racialist German scholarship, is thought-provoking on how the nineteenth century negotiated
antiquity's 'late' periods and cultural hybridities.

time coming, however: in Symonds' lifetime they circulated *sub rosa* in tiny, privately printed editions. *Greek Ethics* is reported to have run to ten copies, and it took him years to gather the nerve to print even these.[7]

This was a Symonds that the Victorian reading public never knew. *Their* Symonds was a well-connected public intellectual, famous for two major works of popular scholarship: *The Renaissance in Italy* (1875–6) and *Studies of the Greek Poets*, first published as two 'Series' in 1873 and 1876.[8] These well-priced and accessible handbooks were bestsellers for decades: the third edition of *Studies* was reissued as late as 1920.[9] Largely forgotten today even by classicists, it initiated generations of readers into the glories of Greek literature, coaching them in a proper reverence for canonical authors including Homer, Pindar, and Sophocles.

Unfortunately, Symonds added the *AP* 12 poets Meleager and Strato to the list, turning aspirational outreach into barely closeted homosexual apologetics.

### Black sheep of the Anglo-Hellenic empire

This was a blow for the conservatives who wished to keep Greece sexually pure. It was an article of faith that the Victorians were new-and-improved ancient Greeks. In one favoured formulation, popularized by Matthew Arnold, the British character struck exactly the right balance between free-thinking Hellenism (creativity and logic) and morally sound Hebraism (monotheistic piety).[10] This added ingredient would safeguard Britain from the eventual political and moral decline of Greece's Hellenistic era, enabling the robust racial

---

[7] Holliday 2000: 94–5.

[8] For wry comment on his public mask as 'the author of *Renaissance in Italy* and *Studies of the Greek Poets*', see Symonds 1984: 29.

[9] For convenience, all subsequent references are to this final version: it unites what were previously two volumes, regularizing their pagination, and is the easiest to find second-hand.

[10] Jenkyns 1980: 69–72 wittily picks apart the polarity. According to Butcher 1893: 38, Hellenic rationality – 'reasonable, fearless, temperate' – blatantly anticipated Britain's modern technological triumphs; and 'The Greek precocity of mind in this direction, unlike that of the Orientals, had in it the promise of uninterrupted advance in the future – of great discoveries' (12).

essence of Hellenism (a 'pervading and quickening spirit') to inspire an empire without end.[11]

Hellenism was thus defined in 'our' own terms, and its boundaries were carefully policed – especially for the new mass readership. Approaching the ancient texts through the shortcuts of translation and paraphrase, the aspiring masses were held to lack the mental discipline and moral fibre instilled by a linguistically based classical education; they might thus jump to rash conclusions about the exemplary past.[12] Entire genres and periods were accordingly ruled out, especially anything un-classically late: standard accounts of Greek literature often ended with Euripides. With their unmanly intellectualism and flattery of despots, Hellenistic authors were not like us, or as we wished to be; so they were not really Greek. Theocritus, for instance, became notorious – less for anything he actually said in his poems than because gay Victorians used his name as a kind of semi-secret password to identify themselves to others in the know. Greece was pure, but *some* Greeks were the late-nineteenth-century equivalent of a hanky code – with classical education as a primitive gaydar.[13]

Even some properly classical authors and texts – the *Symposium* and *Phaedrus* of Plato, for example, with their ill-considered talk of love between men – attracted an undesirable fringe readership, and required careful exegesis to protect the nation's youth from getting inappropriate ideas about their meaning.[14] School editions and mass-market translations of such texts were frequently censored;

---

[11] Jebb 1893: 273 (and see also 280): '[in] the province of religion and morals Hellenism alone is not sufficing... Yet there is no inherent conflict between true Hellenism and spiritualized Hebraism, such Hebraism as has passed into Christianity'. Butcher 1893: 1 declares that 'Hellenism [alone] has not given us enough to live by'.

[12] Jebb 1893: 279 praises the classical languages as moral and intellectual tonic – 'Hellenism... supplies a medicine for diseases of the modern mind, a corrective for aberrations of modern taste' – but on the next page warns of the moral dangers of a 'superficial or defective' understanding of the Greeks. (Acquired by reading translations, or by believing Symonds?)

[13] On Theocritean allusion as a subcultural code, see e.g. Jenkyns 1980: 290, a teasingly indirect example picked up on by Dowling 1994: 26–8. 'The colours of the [hanky] code... function less as signals for something precise than as...signs that a code exists and, more importantly, that a practice exists and is shared...use of the code presupposes difference': Worton 1994: 53. Aldrich 1993: 22–3 naïvely reproduces the nineteenth-century myth of gay Theocritus, egregiously misreading *Idyll* 2 (of which the narrating persona is explicitly female) as an expression of male same-sex desire.

[14] Gay love in the *Phaedrus* provokes the famous line by a classics tutor in E. M. Forster's *Maurice*, written in 1913–14 but only published posthumously in 1971: 'Omit: a reference to the unspeakable vice of the Greeks' (61). After the class Maurice and Clive identify each other as potential romantic partners by talking about the *Symposium* (62).

Aristophanes very frequently indeed.[15] Other authors were better not read at all – and now Symonds came, dragging the mire of Strato's *Mousa Paidikē* into plain view.

Symonds' timing was excellent. Greece was in vogue, and public taste was beginning to move away from Martial, seeing him as the mercenary lackey of a corrupt urban regime. Martial's Greek models could be presented as quite literally a breath of fresh Hellenic air. Symonds' canonization of the genre appropriated and modified an established Victorian rhetoric: it was an article of faith that the classics of Greek literature possessed marvellous health-giving qualities.[16] Symonds made it axiomatic that Greek epigram was intrinsically superior to its grubby Roman imitator; indeed, it sank to its lowest when it deigned to resemble him.[17]

Symonds' chapter on epigram was his biggest from the outset, and grew larger and more effusive with each new edition. Its position towards the end of *Studies* was notionally based on chronology, but also had the effect of making epigram the grand finale of the series. In it, the author singles out the erotic poems of Meleager for particular praise. *AP* 5 and *AP* 12 poems are mixed in indiscriminately, as though – unthinkably – one sort of desire was every bit as good as the other. Meleager's love is nobler, purer, and more beautiful than the heterosexual norm:

Of all the amatory poets of the Anthology, by far the noblest is Meleager... The first great merit of Meleager as a poet is limpidity. A crystal is not more transparent than his style; but the crystal to which we compare it must be coloured with the softest flush of beryl or of amethyst...

These quotations are sufficient to set forth the purity of Meleager's style, though many more examples might have been borrowed from his epigrams on the cicada, on the mosquitoes who tormented Zenophila, on Antiochus,

---

[15] Dover 1979; and see also Stray 2007b: 82–4 on Jebb's argument for prioritizing the moral 'purity' of a text over its philological 'integrity' in the preface to his bowdlerized Theophrastus. This included a running translation; rather than leave gaps in this where the content was unsuitable for the non-classically educated public, Jebb cut the relevant passages from the Greek as well. On censorship in this period generally, see the highly entertaining Perrin 1992.

[16] Sullivan 1991: 308 on distaste for Martial. Cf. Jenkyns 1980: 170–1: 'Youth, light and clear southern skies were blent together to represent the Greek genius as a kind of lithe, buoyant athleticism...clean fresh air became a symbol of the Hellenic spirit'.

[17] 'In Lucillius the Hellenic muse has deigned for once to assume the Roman toga, and to show that if she chose, she could rival the hoarse-throated satirists of the empire on their own ground. But she has abandoned her lofty eminence, and descended to a lower level' (Symonds 1920: 521).

who would have been Eros if Eros had worn the boy's petasos and chlamys... Meleager had a soul that inclined to all beautiful and tender things.[18]

Strato was a borderline case. Meleager's pederastic Eros was discreetly Uranian – the ideal expression of Symonds' own anxious yearnings and relentless self-critique;[19] but Strato was a lusty Pandemic, the sort of brilliant bad boy who might give the movement a bad name. Symonds damned him in terms calculated to excite the admiration of Byron fans – 'the firmness of his touch, the cynicism of his impudicity':

...there are few readers who, even for the sake of his pure and perfect language, will be prepared to tolerate the immodesty of his subject-matter. Straton is not so delicate and subtle in style as Meleager; but he has a masculine vigour and *netteté* of phrase peculiar to himself. It is not possible to quote many of his epigrams. He suffers the neglect which necessarily obscures those men of genius who misuse their powers...[20]

And Symonds dropped broad hints to the privileged minority that this was all about the here and now, mangling Strato's coda (*AP* 12.258) to ventriloquize his own lifelong desires. To readers who knew their Greek, Symonds' root-and-branch revisions of what Strato actually wrote were a tacit declaration of the inherent and enduring nature of homosexual *eros*, and of a subculture with a future in which Symonds himself would be remembered as an important pioneer (this bit more or less worked out as he had hoped). Strato's original brags of its author's commercial adaptability in writing pederastic epigrams – 'these trifles', he calls them – to order, 'for various boy-lovers'. Symonds' reworked version slips in a token female object of desire as well. This veneer of deniability reinforces the strong implicit point made in his eulogy of 'noble' Meleager. Homosexual love is an inherent and lifelong identity, equal in nature to its heterosexual equivalent and perhaps actually surpassing it in value (the emphases indicate places where the Greek is deliberately mistranslated):

Here, lastly, is an Envoy, slightly altered in the English translation from Straton's original:—

---

[18] Ibid.: 521–4.
[19] On Symonds' intellectual and moral struggle to come to terms with his sexual identity, see now Kemp 2000 and, reflecting on her 1964 biography of Symonds, Grosskurth 2000.
[20] Symonds 1920: 528, 525.

'It may be in the years to come
That *men who love shall think of me,*
And reading o'er these verses *see*
*How love was my life's martyrdom.*

'Love-songs I write *for him and her,*
Now this, now that, *as Love dictates*;
One birthday gift alone *the Fates*
Gave me, to be Love's scrivener.'[21]


## Holding the pass

No-one had presented Greek epigram to a mass public before – and certainly not like this. Symonds' *Studies* were, if anything, greater eulogies of gay identity than the *Problem* treatises; they just avoided calling it by name, and countless common persons were reading him. Displacing gay love into the distant past made Symonds' ideas *more* dangerous, not less. This was the past that, by overwhelming consensus, stood in as Victorian Britain's own ideal prototype.

Thus it is that in the years following *Studies* we see a massive conservative backlash against Symonds' liberal reading of the *Anthology*. Previous popularizing critics had not bothered to write about the *Anthology* at all, and still less for a mass market; the genre was un-classically late and unashamedly minor. Like the more popular Latin epigram of Martial it had some small use as a linguistic teaching tool at the better public schools, and this had eventually spawned a messily edited mass-market translation, but the selection of poems in Bohn's edition had been safe enough, and no case had been put for the public taking the *Anthology* seriously.[22] Until Symonds, ancient Greek epigram could be safely ignored. From time to time, in the more upmarket literary magazines, gentleman scholars showed off their linguistic education in one-off compositions and translations; but

[21] A more neutral translation: 'Perhaps someone in time to come, listening to these boyish light verses of mine, will think that all these erotic πόνοι ['labours', 'exertions'; perhaps 'pains'?] were my own – but actually I'm forever penning assorted poems for various boy-lovers, since some god gave me this talent.'

[22] The Bohn edition: Burges 1854. On comparable school editions of Martial and the use of Latin epigram in composition exercises, see Sullivan 1991: 283, 304. In stark contrast to the series' *Greek Anthology*, Bohn's 1860 translation of Martial was complete and unexpurgated: ibid.: 304–5.

there was no *scholarship* on epigram.[23] Now the critics had no choice, if ancient Greece was to be rescued from pederastic degeneracy: 'how greatly they misread the mind of Greece who think to become Hellenic by means of eccentricity tinged with vice'.[24]

Symonds had turned the genre's shortcomings into virtues. He had packaged Greek epigram as a rational recreation ideally suited to a nation of nature-lovers, package tourists, and devotees of Alpine spas. No other genre presented the ancient Greeks as they really were and always had been – exactly like us:

> The Anthology may from some points of view be regarded as the most valuable relic of antique literature which we possess…it is coextensive with the whole current of Greek history… Many subjects of interest in Greek life…are here fully and melodiously set forth. If we might compare the study of Greek Literature to a journey in some splendid mountain region, then we might say with propriety that, from the sparkling summits where Aeschylus and Sophocles and Pindar sit enthroned, we turn in our less strenuous moods to gather the meadow-flowers of Meleager, Palladas, Callimachus… [They] tell us that the Greeks of Athens or of Sidon thought and felt exactly as we feel. Even the *Graffiti* of Pompeii have scarcely more power to reconstruct the past and summon as in dreams the voices and the forms of long-since buried men.[25]

In Symonds' hands, the 'we' in 'exactly as we feel' was daringly inclusive. These ordinary Greeks of Athens (always the focal point of Victorian culture's identification with Hellas) took differing sexualities calmly on board as a fact of human nature.

Symonds' combination of selective translation and exegesis with a universalizing sales pitch was tactically convenient for his subcultural agenda, but it could very easily be turned around. The guardians of Greece's purity were caught in a double bind, unable to warn against Symonds' implications without drawing public attention to them. All they could do was to hint darkly at the 'unhealthy tendencies' and decadent 'fashion' of certain unspecified moderns whose grasp of the Hellenic genius was somehow 'defective'.[26] But the problem of epigram offered its own solution. If all human life was in the *Anthology*, then critics could present any version of it as the essential truth of our nature. All they had to do was to pick the right handful from its

---

[23] Stray 1998: 65–8 on classical quotation and the solidarity of the male elite, and 68–74 on composition in elegiacs as a 'heroic' attainment within that group. I view epigram translation in the magazines as an extension of this.
[24] Butcher 1893: 1, quoted with approval by Jebb 1893: 280.
[25] Symonds 1920: 499–500.
[26] Jebb 1893: 280.

thousands of poems and arrange them to tell the right story – just as Symonds had. Symonds had actually been relatively faithful in his presentation of categories – his one major deception was to start with Book Six and take it from there, skipping not only the weird first four Books but also the heterosexual Book Five. His successors were less scrupulous in reporting the *Anthology*'s structure: instead they freely imposed their own categories and chronologies to justify including some poets and excluding others. New section headings knocked the *Anthology*'s Greeks into shape as a model family of proto-Victorians: sentimental devotees of home, God, and country.

### Go tell it to the Victorians

Funerary and related categories were placed prominently within these schemes. Poems written as witty literary pastiches of the epigraphic habit were now reconfigured to deliver earnest moral closure as a presentist *memento mori*. The new schemes of arrangement attributed to the Greeks a glimmering of awareness that, without Hebraism, they could never *quite* become like us; pagan Hellenism itself would not be enough in the long haul. Rome was there to decline and fall for us in godless, heedless excess; Greece, to sensitize us through decorous reflection on its own beautiful death:

[The] Greek genius kindled before the vision of life and death into a clearer flame... [I]n all of the best period there is a common note, mingled of a grave tenderness, simplicity, and reserve... There is...none of the ugliness of dying; with calm faces and undisordered raiment they rise from their seats and take the last farewell...so piercing and yet so consoling in its quiet pathos.[27]

In this sentimental image, Mackail's Greeks – Victorians before the fact, except in the crucial matter of faith – calmly take their leave, bequeathing to an intuited future the fearless Hellenic rationality that dimly foresees its own nineteenth-century resurrection and union with Hebraism. Beyond 'the bright and brief space of life' they perceive 'far away a shadowy and beautiful country to which later men were to give the name of Heaven'.[28]

---

[27] Mackail 1890: 65, 67. On the topos of Roman decline in Victorian reception, see Vance 1997 and 1999.

[28] Mackail 1890: 66. This prescient Hellas is clearly operating as a generic quasi-Christian fantasy space. Compare Frodo's vision of the Grey Havens as he passes into the West at the close

The structure of Butler's influential *Amaranth and Asphodel* (1881) is indicative. The Greeks are there to fall in love; to offer sincere, but sadly misdirected prayers; to stop and smell the flowers; and to reflect on their own mortality for posterity's benefit:

> Love Poems
> Life, Time, and Moralities
> Temple Offerings
> Poems on Nature and on Art
> Poems on Death.

A later scheme outdoes Butler for nature worship and morbid piety:

> Religious
> Historical
> Dead Cities
> Seafaring and Fishermen
> Sailor's Graves
> Other Graves
> Life and Death
> Fountains and Wayside Gods
> Pastoral
> Grasshoppers and Crickets
> Love and Ladies
> Works of Art
> Miscellaneous.[29]

### Redrawing the borders

The timeline could also be rearranged. Symonds had proposed a genre history of rise, peak, and decline, knowing that no-one could argue with his basic outline. The art historian Johannes Winckelmann had devised this now familiar story-shape to explain phases in classical sculpture, and the Victorians applied it indiscriminately to past, present, and future phenomena in human culture. The histories of nations, races, and literary genres all followed the same bell curve, often at more than one level. In standard Victorian accounts of Greek

---

of Tolkien 1966: 310: 'white shores and beyond them a far green country under a swift sunrise'.
   [29] Butler 1881; Fry 1915.

civilization, Athenian literature of the fifth century was the pinnacle of Greek culture; tragedy was the pinnacle of Athenian literature; and Sophocles was the pinnacle of tragedy – a curve within a curve within a curve. The genre thus contained its own micro-trajectory of rise (Aeschylus), peak (Sophocles), and decline (Euripides, 'a herald of death to the art around which he threw [his] novel splendours'). Careers of individual authors could do the same.[30]

For Symonds, literary epigram ascended late (the Hellenistic era – full points for accuracy) and, as we have seen, peaked with Meleager. Strato occupied the Euripides role, as the brilliant and cynical harbinger of the genre's fall into decadence. After Strato, the phase of decline was populated by degenerate and disgusting latecomers, 'corrupted by the lusts of Rome and the decadence of the East' – coincidentally, all authors of heterosexual love poems:

Very pale and hectic are the hues which give a sort of sickly beauty to their style... [A] man need be neither a prude nor a Puritan to turn with sadness and with loathing from these last autumnal blossoms on the tree of Greek beauty. The brothel and the grave are all that is left for Rufinus and his contemporaries.[31]

Pandemic heterosexuality is sick. Specifically, it is 'hectic' – a word that specifically suggests tuberculosis, 'hectic fever', the corrosive inner decay of the big city; but it is also figured as syphilitic, the link between the 'brothel and the grave'. By modern estimates, Strato and Rufinus may well have been contemporaries – both of them much earlier than was previously thought – but Symonds pushes the aggressively heterosexual poet centuries into the future to join Macedonius and Paulus Silentiarius (incidentally two favoured authors of the schools-derived Bohn translation) in a desolate post-Hellenic wasteland.[32]

One obvious conservative response was to move the bell curve back in time towards the classical period, cutting off Strato and other morally dubious writers of the Roman era. The ersatz epigrams at the symposium in Becker's *Charicles* are an isolated and eccentric foretaste of the full-blown trend of purposeful manipulation in the wake of Symonds' *Studies*; Mackail wrote, 'One sees [in the *Garland*

---

[30] For a lively introduction to Winckelmann's art-historical ideas see Beard and Henderson 2001: 68–74. For purely Hellenic spirit, see Jebb 1893: 216; and for 'herald of death', ibid.: 239. On Jebb's quasi-religious 'commitment to Sophoclean perfection' and avoidance of Euripides, see Stray 2007b: 80–1, 85.

[31] Symonds 1920: 527–8.

[32] On relative dating, see most recently the judicious summary by Coleman 2006: xxiii–xxiv.

of Philip] the decline of art from its first exquisiteness.'[33] This often involved some tenuous special pleading – Symonds had been right about literary epigram's relation to the Hellenistic age, and denial of this easily shaded into overstatement and outright fibbing. Even Meleager could edge towards lateness: 'After [the Alexandrian era] comes nothing new but the jokes of Rome'.[34] Or away from Greekness, which amounted to the same thing: in this view, the passing of time and assimilation to Alexander's East had sapped the racial strength of Hellas and created a morbid mulatto identity.[35] The post-classical Greek epigrammatist 'has drunk of the wine of the Orient, but it holds no nepenthe against the thought of death'.[36] Touched with the tar-brush and already 'acute in his susceptibilities', Meleager becomes an opium addict:[37]

Meleager was born in a Syrian town and educated at Tyre... In Meleager, the touch of Asiatic blood creates a new type, delicate, exotic, fantastic. Art is no longer restrained and severe. The exquisite austerity of Greek poetry did not outlive the greatness of Athens... The atmosphere is loaded with a steam of perfumes.[38]

In Meleager, a native of Gadara in Palestine...whose temperament and genius are not without some Asiatic quality, love becomes a new and almost mystical ardour...though the antique simplicity is wanting. The colouring is richer, the imagery is often fantastic; the fragrance of oriental spices, the scents of lilies and roses are shed over the things of the heart.[39]

## Whole classes of epigrams could be excluded on the same basis:

Of the great mass of [AP 12] epigrams no selection is possible or desirable. They belong to that side of Greek life which is akin to the Oriental world, and remote and even revolting to the western mind. And on this subject the common moral sense of civilised mankind has pronounced a judgment which requires no justification as it allows of no appeal.[40]

---

[33] Mackail 1890: 17.

[34] Lothian 1920: n.p.

[35] The classic discussion of 'Orientalism', the Western construction of the East as its barbaric Other, is Said 1978.

[36] Soutar 1939: 246, a posthumously published 1890s doctoral dissertation.

[37] On Meleager's susceptibilities, see Neaves 1874: 6. On Classics' implication in colonial discourse, see Goff 2005; the very useful Hingley 2000 concentrates on the Roman side of this reception history.

[38] Mackail 1890: 33–4.

[39] Butcher 1893: 307–8.

[40] Mackail 1890: 36.

## Digging for victory

This Orientalist fantasy of diseased mysticism rewrote Symonds' Greek love as racially Other in explicitly presentist terms. Stamping out pederasty in the *Anthology* became part of Britain's civilizing mission as an imperial power, viewed in the same terms as eradicating white slavery and the harem.[41] Contamination by Eastern blood had turned the Greece of the *Anthology* into a Levantine shambles, in urgent need of colonial intervention and sprucing up. Its irrational structures of organization were tottering relics; enlightened modern administration swiftly brought order to the text.

These translators aimed to do the *Anthology* a favour by weeding and pruning it to remove racial impurity and reveal its wholesome original design. For the purposes of this scheme, a selectively read Meleager – elsewhere 'the voluptuous Syrian singer' – becomes the last 'good' epigrammatist.[42] His *Garland* is a tidy cottage garden, sadly spoilt by post-classical landfill.

As we saw in the Introduction, Cephalas' *Anthology* is in plain fact the end product of a millennium of endlessly repeated sifting, sorting, selection, and exclusion – to say nothing of loss. Each poem has been chosen, chosen, and chosen again by successive compilers. In late Victorian reception, however, the *Anthology* becomes its own polar opposite: the municipal dump of unwanted late-Greek culture:

The Greek Anthology is no garden of chosen flowers... It is a garden full of roses, of waste ground, of rubbish heaps confused together. But it began as a flower garden, with the Wreath which Meleager made...[43]

The misrepresentation of the *Anthology* as a muddle of rubbish heaps is surely an inspired appropriation of the breaking news in textual studies: the excavation of thousands of Greek papyri from the genuinely confused rubbish mounds of Oxyrhynchus, the lost metropolis of Greco-Roman Egypt that we first encountered in our Introduction.[44] These tattered fragments of books and documents, thrown away as

---

[41] 'Both nations belong to one great and elevated family of the human race', and stand united against 'female degradation' (Neaves 1874: 80), and see also the harem fantasy at Mackail 1890: 37. For some striking examples of racialist fabulation in popular and scholarly reception of Greco-Roman Egypt, see Montserrat 1998.

[42] Soutar 1939: 249.

[43] Lothian 1920: n.p.

[44] For orientation see above, p. 18 n. 31; for images of the mounds, see Bowman, et al. 2007: 5, 8, and their Plate X.

broken or useless by the ancient inhabitants of the provincial city, randomly sampled its textual production and consumption. Epigram was now imagined to be in the same sorry state of affairs:

> The Greek Anthology is a mass of heterogeneous material which may well dismay anything but the hardihood of scholars and editors... [A]s it stands, [it] is not a selection, in any proper sense – it is simply a vast reservoir, with some subdivision...a garden run to weeds in which the weeds predominate with varying degrees of worthlessness and noisomeness.[45]

Dross was mixed indiscriminately with gold, the former hugely outweighing the latter, and it was the job of the expert to pronounce on which was which. Translators bought into the new sub-papyrological idiom enthusiastically. The *Anthology* was not a selection of selections, but a discard pile; the bulk of its poems were accidental and unworthy survivors. Papyrology's scientific cachet as an all-new, technical sub-discipline of philology lent gravitas and objectivity to the task of epigram translation.

If translators were unable to find the proper flowers for their new Garlands among the aesthetic-*cum*-moral detritus of the *Anthology*, others could legitimately be brought in. The degenerate dross of the 'rubbish heaps' was no fit basis for a panoptic display of properly understood human nature. New blood was needed:

> The Greek Anthology, therefore, in its largest sense...may now be considered as consisting, not merely of the collections of Cephalas and Planudes, but also of a large number of other short poems...which it is likely that Meleager, Philippus, or Agathias, if we had them entire, would be found to have inserted in their collections, or might reasonably have done so.[46]

The new and morally improved *Anthology* would be anything its translators and exegetes wanted it to be. In their rhetoric of presentation, the 'garland' of cut flowers (always so quick to fade) blurred imperceptibly into a 'garden' that could be set right for perpetuity. They became avid plantsmen in the mould of J. W. Mackail, the 'Capability' Brown of epigram's afterlife in translation as an English country garden. His text-with-translation of *Select Epigrams from the Greek Anthology* was the Chatsworth of modern anthology-making – a landmark in garden design, endlessly discussed, praised, and imitated.

---

[45] Anonymous review of Mackail 1890, *The Nation* 55.1425 (1892): 304.
[46] Neaves 1874: 13–14.

Like Brown's landscapes, Mackail's improvements swept away what had gone before, erasing the *Anthology*'s historic design. For English readers and writers, *Select Epigrams* now simply *was* the *Anthology*. Its selection of 500 best poems included everything of value – 'according to the editor's best judgment, all which are of the first excellence in any style' – and was laid out in a design that gave the impression of always having been there.[47] Reproduced as our front-cover illustration, the book's frontispiece shows a no-nonsense female gardener-*cum*-anthologist at work on her drifts: it could be Vita Sackville-West at Sissinghurst.

### After Mackail

Mackail's categories comprehended all human life – all that was fit to print. Epigram was now wholesome, sentimental, and patriotic, but not over-serious or intellectualizing; it ideally expressed the late Victorian and Edwardian craze for 'muscular Christianity'. The elegiac couplets of the reduced *Anthology* were

a metre which could refuse nothing, which could rise to the occasion and sink with it, and be equally suited to the epitaph of a hero or the verses accompanying a birthday present, a light jest or a profound moral idea, the sigh of a lover or the lament over a perished Empire.

The editor's rhetoric of selection excluded later authors ('in any collection of Greek epigrammatic poetry these authors [of the Roman period] naturally sink to their own place'), and found room for honourable early outsiders such as Mimnermus and Theognis.[48]

Subsequent translators went to Mackail's Greek text and no further, transposing his distinctive landscape design and planting scheme into their own modest suburban plots. They proudly advertised his influence on their philosophy of epigram cultivation. Even the token departures from Mackail's selection were applications of his method:

The pleasure which I derived from Mr. Mackail's *Select Epigrams*...is the origin of this little book. I have freely used his text, his notes, his bibliography and above all his translations. All the epigrams here translated are to be found in his selection, with the

---

[47] Mackail 1890: vii.
[48] Ibid.: 3, also the source of the 'lament'.

solitary exception of the poem to the Grasshopper from the Anacreontica, which is not really an epigram, but a short lyric...[49]

It was just as I completed the usual scholastic training of our Universities, that Mr. Mackail's lesser volume of Selections came into my hands; and for some years it was my custom in leisure times to carry these little poems about with me, not in my pockets only, but in my head and heart... Of about half of [my translations from Mackail] I have in this book made a Garland after the ancient fashion, picking a flower here, another there...adding also a few things curious or characteristic, which took my fancy... I have rarely troubled to go behind his notes.[50]

The 'lesser volume' was the Greek text without translation or notes, in a smart and keenly priced pocket edition; a translation-only edition in the same format sold in yet greater numbers. All references were now to Mackail; *AP* dropped off the map, replaced with *M*.

Mackail's response to the Uranian threat is foundational to the subsequent reception of Greek epigram in the English language. The equation of epigram's decline with racial miscegenation (half-breed Meleager), the shifting of the bell curve, the search for the point at which the rot set in – all the tropes we have been tracking originate with him.

## The *Anthology* in the twentieth century

'First you tell the lie, then you make it true.'[51] Mackail's decorous revisionism won the mainstream battle and set the terms for epigram's future use. Paton's solidly useful Loeb (1916–18) still churns over the Symonds-bashers' rhetoric: homosexuality is the effete 'fashion' of an age of decline, and 'much misunderstanding has been caused by people quoting anything from the "Greek Anthology" as specifically "Greek"'.[52] As late as 1929, a major translator of the *Anthology* was still reproducing Symonds' rhetoric of the brothel and the grave. Shane Leslie implicitly buys into *Greek Ethics'* binary of Pandemic and Uranian *Eros* to deny Symonds' point about naturally inherent sexual identities:

---

[49] Fry 1915: vii.
[50] Lothian 1920: n.p.
[51] Perrin 1992: 229.
[52] Paton 1918 vol. 4: 280–1, introducing *AP* 12; and vol. 1: x, general preface.

In dealing with the Erotic, a frank cleavage has been made between the natural and unnatural... Too many Epigrams [in *AP* 12] had better been tied to a mill-stone and dropped into the sea... The apples of Sodom are generally omitted in Greek studies, but such of their dead blossoms as survive in the Anthology turn to dust in modern taste... No doubt [this love] was often too strong to be anything but Platonic. Its weaker side was gross.[53]

Leslie is still tinkering with the genre's Winckelmann curve – epigram's fifth-century inscriptional rise is now implausibly also its literary peak:

With Simonides the Greek Epigram reached an immediate height, to which it never reascended, but the decadence of Alexandria and Constantinople was strewn with the intellectual and the ingenious.[54]

And his *Anthology* is still most definitely a random rubbish heap:

Herein was stored flower and fungus, wreath and rubbish... All the vices, all the virtues, all the arts are represented and descend side by side. The scrap-heap of Greece survives in a scrap-book.[55]

Throughout the twentieth century, translators carry forward the Victorian insistence that the *Anthology* must be pruned and grafted for its own good – and is best translated very loosely:

Many of the translations came to me as I turned the Greek poem over in my head, with no text at all. Along with the epigrams of the *Anthology* are a few lyric fragments and some bits of Latin... In a few cases, what might seem to the pedant to be mistranslations are deliberate *jeux d'esprit*. I know what the Greek says.[56]

In the spirit of a Beat cut-up, this 1962 version of the *Anthology* by Kenneth Rexroth includes snippets of the archaic lyric poet Archilochus, the ubiquitous Martial (humiliatingly lumped in with his Greek models), Sappho, Petronius, and the mediaeval Latin lyrics of *Carmina Burana*. Epigram turns Rexroth into Kerouac: 'on the freight trains of my youthful years of wandering, in starlit camps on desert and mountain ranges...[epigrams] have been my constant companions'. Despite himself, the translator echoes the romantic Victorian insistence that Greek poetry is canned fresh air – and particularly that elegiac composition is best done on the hoof. The exercise of epigram-work

---

[53] Leslie 1929: 27. Strato is Pandemically 'gross' also at Paton 1916–18: *ad loc.*
[54] Ibid.: 10.
[55] Ibid.: 30–1.
[56] Rexroth 1962: n.p.

unites the rail-riding Beat poet with the Oxbridge undergraduate reading party among the Lakes.[57]

There is still no complete translation into English, and probably never will be;[58] and the story of Soddington Symonds is part of why. For a time, he made epigram too hot to handle; then it sank back into unmarketable obscurity. The genre's profile in modern perception of Greek literature tracks Symonds' own posthumous Winckelmann curve. With Uranian Love a mere historical curiosity, it no longer seems to matter how or whether the public at large reads Strato and Meleager. Translators who would *like* them to must compete for attention with flashier contemporary pleasures – one translator of erotic epigram, struggling to come across as edgy and worldly wise, brags of inclusion in seedy men's magazines.[59]

### 'Grass of Parnassus'

Even the specialized scholarship continues to carry faint echoes of the Mackail method (and occasionally reproduces it verbatim); but what else are scholars to do?[60] The 'here's another pretty one' approach is probably less avoidable than ever before: it ideally complements the modern academic production line of journal articles and chapters in edited volumes, advertising philological acumen in a convenient nutshell. Scholars today show off with epigram much as earlier generations did. Besides, opportunities to study ancient epigram in its 'original' literary contexts have only now begun to appear – along with plenty of new pretties to distract us with their shine.

Nor is it terribly helpful to scoff at Mackail et al. as misguided in their educated instinct for repression; all being well, what *we* do with epigram (and with classics) will seem every bit as odd in a hundred years' time as opium-addict Meleager does now. Bits of this

---

[57] Ibid.; his rhetoric bears close comparison to, for example, Bowen's 'knapsack tour' and Butler's 'mountain walks, in solitary hours', quoted by Stray 1998: 67 and 71.

[58] Even Paton's Loeb – at five volumes, unlikely to be replaced any time soon – puts some poems into Latin instead of English: see e.g. *AP* 5.35, 36, 38, 49, 54, 55, etc. Book 5 is much more sexually explicit than Book 12, but Paton may also be trying to reinforce his editorial line that homosexuality is not so much a real sexual identity as a temporary accommodation to social pressures. 'In [Meleager's homoerotic epigrams], if I err not, we miss the distinguishing note of passion, which his other love-poems so often have... [They are] rather a matter of fashion' (Paton 1918 vol. 5: 281).

[59] Kelly 1986: 8.

[60] Littlewood 2005: 53 calls the *Anthology* 'a garden with possibly more weeds than flowers'.

strange nineteenth-century back story even achieve a kind of topsy-turvy fidelity, replicating the steps of epigram's ancient reception history. Those early Victorian gentlemen's magazines are uncannily like the ancient symposium in their relaxed solidarity and keen eye for a class divide; it is hard to imagine a more congenial or indeed a more authentic space for the resurrection of classical epigram in translation and composition. The motives of a Mackail or Neaves in cutting Cephalas down to size were very nearly identical to those of their fourteenth-century hero, Planudes: they sincerely believed (and contemporary reviewers agreed) that they were doing the ancients a favour by winnowing their texts. By the standards of their time, they were if anything moderates in their approach to censorship of the classics.[61] Indeed, their claim to interfere was greater than Planudes'; they came from a nation of avid gardeners. Censors of classical literature had long characterized their activity as horticultural, separating flowers from weeds – 'rank tares and poisonous roots' – so an ancient genre that explicitly announced itself as flower-like was especially well suited by nature to enthusiastic hoeing, thinning out, and potting on.[62] These activities restored epigram, and the ancient world it represented, to their proper selves. When as modern scholars we restore what our predecessors cut, we feel the same warm glow of communion with the spirit of the classic – but they felt it more deeply.

One of their main advantages lay in possessing the skills to take this communion further, closing the loop. We supply no fresh translation of the following epigram because the Latin *is* the translation – the source text is in English:

'*Stemmata quid faciunt?*'

*Incluta multorum per nomina, Pontice, patrum*
   *Deducta est ad te linea clara diu:*
*Sic uia deducta est Romanis incluta fabris;*
   *Sic in stagnanti desiit illa luto.*

---

[61] An influential American moral reformer, Anthony Comstock, was at this time pressing for a ban on *all* classical literature in translation; see Beisel 1997: 162–4, and cf. Perrin 1992: 6 on extreme attitudes to censorship of the eighteenth-century novel. Comstock was an authoritarian conservative with religious backing; Mackail, a liberal socialist. On Mackail's politics, see briefly Stray 1998: 229–30. For close parallels to various epigram-censors quoted in this chapter, see Perrin 1992: 25, 37, 84, 200.

[62] On the gardening metaphor, see Perrin 1992: 63; for rank tares, see 200.

This classic example of elegiac epigram was composed by an Oxonian, Charles Gepp, and was selected for inclusion in a mid-nineteenth-century Anthology – *Sabrinae Corolla*, 'The Garland of the Severn'. This latter-day Garland (which ran to four editions) was one of several that collected miscellaneous poems in Latin and Greek by alumni of prominent public schools, in this case Shrewsbury.[63] Almost every poem is a translation into Greek or Latin of an excerpt from an English author, interspersed with occasional German romantics such as Schiller. The book is laid out like a Loeb in reverse (not that the Loebs existed then) – English on the left-hand page, Latin or Greek on the right. There is a great deal of Shakespeare (whose 'small Latin and less Greek' is thereby remedied) and almost as much Tennyson. A genuine epitaph for a child buried in Meole Churchyard becomes a Greek funerary epigram – Ὦ Θάνατε παιών! Time and again, English epigrams in the manner of Martial are transformed into Latin ones that might as well *be* by him. The reception supplements and supplants its ancient model – itself, of course, always already a reception *too*.

In this case the English original is by Robert Burns (1793):

> Bright ran thy line, O Galloway,
>   Through many a far-famed sire:
> So ran the far-famed Roman Way,
>   So ended in the mire.

This epigram was originally part of a run of topical poems by Burns, all targeting a dissolute contemporary landowner. Gepp (or the anonymous editors) fit it for inclusion in the *Corolla* as a stand-alone piece by assigning a generalizing heading and thus a broader moral application: 'Virtue alone is true nobility'. This newly manufactured title is then loosely 'translated' into a genuinely classical Latin tag, which becomes the title of Gepp's Latin version on the facing page: *Stemmata quid faciunt?*, 'What use are family trees?' (referring to the visual displays of ancestry in the atria of elite Roman households). This famous and much-quoted *sententia* (moralizing sound bite) opens the schoolroom-friendly eighth hexameter *Satire* of Martial's contemporary, Juvenal.

---

[63] By curious coincidence, Frederick Metcalfe (the translator of Becker's *Charicles*) was a Shrewsbury old boy. *Sabrinae Corolla* is anonymously edited; I cite from the third edition (1867): 314–5. On these local Garlands, and epigram composition as a badge of scholarly virtuosity, see respectively and very briefly Stray 1998: 69, and McKitterick 2007: 8.

Moving on from the title into the text of Gepp's version, it is evident that the habits of Latin verse composition instilled at Shrewsbury have stuck. There are echoes of cleaned-up Catullus (*multorum per... patrum*, cf. *Carmen* 101.1), perhaps of the opening lines of Ovid's *Metamorphoses* (his *carmen deductum*), and certainly of Martial, Gepp's main model. 'Ponticus' is one of Martial's metrically convenient stock names for comic targets.[64] The effect of its substitution here is uncanny. An epigram that could easily be mistaken for a classical original instead looks backwards in time, from a distinctly modern perspective, to classical culture's predetermined end point – the decline and fall of pagan Rome. To successive generations of readers, Burns's 'far-famed Roman Way' was doubly resonant. Laid bare for the edification of day-trippers by the new science of archaeology, famous Roman roads such as the Fosse Way connected nineteenth-century Britain to the infrastructural and administrative prototype of its own expanding empire; but the 'Roman Way' also called to mind the Roman *way* of doing things – slaves, gladiators, and orgies. This figurative path could only end in the 'mire' of Rome's moral and political collapse, a favourite cautionary tale diagnosed by Burns's older contemporary Edward Gibbon and busily embroidered ever since by popular entertainments.[65] *Sabrinae Corolla* is careful to steer us away from this pagan road to ruin: it ends with a section of Christian hymns, prayers, and psalms.

As consumers of epigram who are not also its producers, we cannot share the vertiginous frissons of the Victorians' literary correspondence with the classical past – except vicariously, through them. A Victorian translator of epigram could hail the 'Grass of Parnassus, flower of my delight!' and mean the heathers of his native Scotland, straightforwardly and without straining taste or tolerance;[66] but the old hallucinatory overlay of classical education and allusion (the 'virtual reality' of our Prologue) is forever lost to us. The most that we can hope for is to be usefully aware of our own situatedness as consumers and producers of 'classics' – and again, Mackail and Symonds and the rest were there before us: open-eyed, clear-headed, and surprisingly honest in their attempts to fit ancient texts to modern

---

[64] Mart. 2.32, 82; 3.60; 4.85, etc; for metrical equivalents, see e.g. 'Postumus' and 'Rusticus' in the invaluable 'Index of Names' at the back of Shackleton Bailey 1993 vol. 3.

[65] On Rome and the British imperial imaginary from 1860, see Hingley 2000. On Roman decline and fall in popular theatre, see Mayer 1994; in the novel, Turner 1999.

[66] Andrew Lang in the title poem of his collection (1892), which also includes a 'Little Garland' of thirty-five 'versions from' the *Anthology*; where in it, he does not say.

needs. We would no sooner call Plato an epigrammatist than Dickens a blogger, for identical and soundly scholarly reasons – with the result that the symposium of Becker's *Charicles* reads strangely to modern eyes; but the late Victorians, knowing almost as much as we do, resumed an authentically classical game of let's pretend. Like ancient readers, they played along. They entertained the pleasant fantasy that Plato the philosopher-poet was 'one of us', a kindred spirit invisibly present at the symposium, gentleman's club, school reunion – or Decadent salon. Then as now, and as it always had, the past was seen to suffuse and motivate the present; and epigram supplied any and every past that could be desired. It still does.

# BIBLIOGRAPHY

## Collections of epigrams and other reference works for which abbreviations are used

Austin, C. and Bastianini, G. (eds.) 2002. *Posidippi Pellaei Quae Supersunt Omnia.* Milan, LED. = AB.

Gow, A. S. F. and Page, D. L. (eds.) 1965. *The Greek Anthology. Hellenistic Epigrams.* 2 vols, Cambridge, Cambridge University Press. = *HE*. (References by page number to *HE* refer to vol. 2, which contains the commentary.)

———— (eds.) 1968. *The Greek Anthology. The Garland of Philip.* 2 vols, Cambridge, Cambridge University Press. = *GPh*. (References by page number to *GPh* refer to vol. 2, which contains the commentary.)

Hansen, P. A. 1983. *Carmina Epigraphica Graeca Saeculorum VIII-V A. Chr. N.* Berlin, Walter de Gruyter. = *CEG* I.

———— 1989. *Carmina Epigraphica Graeca Saeculi IV A. Chr. N.* Berlin, Walter de Gruyter. = *CEG* II.

Kühner, R. and Gerth, B. 1898–1904. *Ausführliche Grammatik der griechischen Sprache. Zweiter Teil: Satzlehre I–II.* Hanover and Leipzig, Hahn. = KG.

Meiggs, R. and Lewis, D. (eds.) 1988. *A Selection of Greek Historical Inscriptions, to the End of the Fifth Century BC. Revised edition.* Oxford, Clarendon. = M.-L.

Page, D. L. (ed.) 1975. *Epigrammata Graeca.* Oxford Classical Texts. Oxford, Oxford University Press. = OCT.

———— (ed.) 1981. *Further Greek Epigrams. Epigrams Before A.D. 50 from the Greek Anthology and Other Sources Not Included in 'Hellenistic Epigrams' or 'The Garland of Philip'.* Revised and prepared for publication by R. D. Dawe and J. Diggle. Cambridge, Cambridge University Press. = *FGE*.

## Abbreviations for corpora of inscriptions and other epigraphic publications

For a straightforward introduction to such publications, with references to more specialist works, see Bodel 2001: 153–74.

IG = *Inscriptiones Graecae*
IGASMG = *Iscrizioni greche arcaiche di Sicilia e Magna Grecia*
SEG = *Supplementum Epigraphicum Graecum*

# Bibliography

Acosta-Hughes, B. and Barbantani, S. 2007. 'Inscribing Lyric', in Bing and Bruss 2007a: 429–57.

Acosta-Hughes, B., Kosmetatou, E., and Baumbach, M. (eds.) 2004. *Labored in Papyrus Leaves. Perspectives on an Epigram Collection Attributed to Posidippus (P. Mil. Vogl. VIII 309)*. Washington, DC, Center for Hellenic Studies.

Aldrich, R. 1993. *The Seduction of the Mediterranean. Writing, Art and Homosexual Fantasy*. London, Routledge.

Algra, K., Barnes, J., Mansfeld, J., and Schofield, M. (eds.) 1999. *The Cambridge History of Hellenistic Philosophy*. Cambridge, Cambridge University Press.

Allen, T. W. (ed.) 1963. *Homeri Opera*. Oxford Classical Texts. Volume 5, 1912, Oxford, Oxford University Press.

Aloni, A. 2009. 'Elegy: Forms, Function and Communication', in Budelmann 2009: 168–88.

Ambühl, A. 2002. 'Zwischen Tragödie und Roman: Kallimachos' Epigramm auf den Selbstmord der Basilo (20 Pf. = 32 Gow-Page = *AP* 7.517)', in Harder, Regtuit, and Wakker 2002: 1–26.

——— 2007. 'Tell, All Ye Singers, My Fame: Kings, Queens and Nobility in Epigram', in Bing and Bruss 2007a: 275–94.

Argentieri, L. 2007. 'Meleager and Philip as Epigram Collectors', in Bing and Bruss 2007a: 147–64.

Arnush, M. F. 1995. 'The Career of Peisistratos Son of Hippias', *Hesperia* 64: 135–52.

Baldwin, B. 1980. 'More Love with Doris', *Mnemosyne* 33: 357–9.

Barton, T. S. 1994. *Power and Knowledge. Astrology, Physiognomics, and Medicine under the Roman Empire*. Ann Arbor, MI, University of Michigan Press.

Bartsch, S. 1994. *Actors in the Audience. Theatricality and Doublespeak from Nero to Hadrian*. Cambridge, MA, Harvard University Press.

Battezzato, L. 2003. 'I viaggi dei testi', in L. Battezzato (ed.), *Tradizione testuale e ricezione letteraria antica della tragedia greca*. Amsterdam, Hakkert: 7–31.

Baumbach, M., Petrovic, I., and Petrovic, A. (eds.) in press. *Archaic and Classical Greek Epigram*. Cambridge, Cambridge University Press.

Beard, M. and Henderson, J. 2001. *Classical Art. From Greece to Rome*. Oxford, Oxford University Press.

Becker, W. 1895. Translated by F. Metcalfe. *Charicles, or Illustrations of the Private Life of the Ancient Greeks. With Notes and Excursuses*. New edition, London, Longmans.

Beisel, N. 1997. *Imperiled Innocents. Anthony Comstock and Family Reproduction in Victorian America*. Princeton, NJ, Princeton University Press.

Bernand, A. and Bernand, É. (eds.) 1960. *Les inscriptions grecques et latines du Colosse de Memnon*. Paris, Institut Français d'Archeologie Orientale au Caire.

Beta, S. 2007. 'Lysianassa's Skills: Philodemus, *Anth. Pal.* 5.126 (= Sider 22)', *CQ* 57: 312–14.

Bettenworth, A. 2007. 'The Mutual Influence of Inscribed and Literary Epigram', in Bing and Bruss 2007a: 69–93.

Bing, P. 2002. 'The Un-read Muse? Inscribed Epigram and its Readers in Antiquity', in Harder, Regtuit, and Wakker 2002: 39–66.

——— 2005. 'The Politics and Poetics of Geography in the Milan Posidippus, Section 1: On Stones (AB 1–20)', in Gutzwiller 2005c: 119–40.

——— and Bruss, J. S. (eds.) 2007a. *Brill's Companion to Hellenistic Epigram down to Philip*. Leiden, Brill.

——— 2007b. 'Introduction', in Bing and Bruss 2007a: 1–26.

Bodel, J. (ed.) 2001. *Epigraphic Evidence. Ancient History From Inscriptions*. London and New York, Routledge.

Boedeker, D. and Sider, D. 1996. 'The New Simonides: Introduction', *Arethusa* 29: iii–vi.

Bohn, H. G. (ed.) 1860. *The Epigrams of Martial Translated into English Prose. Each Accompanied by One or More Verse Translations from the Works of English Poets, and Various Other Sources*. London, Bell.

Booth, J. 2001. 'Moonshine: Intertextual Illumination in Propertius 1.3.31–3 and Philodemus, *Anth. Pal.* 5.123', *CQ* 51: 537–44.

Bowersock, G. W. 1994. *Fiction as History. Nero to Julian*. Berkeley, CA, University of California Press.

Bowie, E. L. 1990. 'Greek Poetry in the Antonine Age', in D. A. Russell (ed.), *Antonine Literature*. Oxford, Clarendon Press: 53–90.

——— 2007. 'From Archaic Elegy to Hellenistic Sympotic Epigram?', in Bing and Bruss 2007a: 95–112.

Bowman, A. K., Coles, R. A., Gonis, N., Obbink, D., and Parsons P. J. (eds.) 2007. *Oxyrhynchus. A City and its Texts*. Graeco-Roman Memoirs 93. London, Egypt Exploration Society for the Arts and Humanities Research Council.

Boyle, A. J. 1995. 'Evaluating the Unexpected Classic', *Ramus* 24: 82–101.

Braund, S. H. 1989a. 'City and Country in Roman Satire', in Braund 1989b: 23–48.

——— (ed.) 1989b. *Satire and Society in Ancient Rome*. Exeter, Exeter University Press.

Bravi, L. 2006. *Gli epigrammi di Simonide e le vie della tradizione. Filologia e critica 94*. Rome, Edizioni dell'Ateneo.

Bridge, R. T. and Lake, E. D. C. (eds.) 1906. *Select Epigrams of Martial. Spectaculorum Liber and Books I–VI. Edited from the Text of Professor Lindsay*. Oxford, Clarendon Press.

Bruss, J. S. 2002/3. 'A Program Poem of Alcaeus of Messene: Epigram 16 G-P (= *A.P.* 7.429)', *CJ* 98: 161–80.

——— 2005. *Hidden Presences. Monuments, Gravesites, and Corpses in Greek Funerary Epigram*. Hellenistica Groningana 10. Leuven, Paris, and Dudley, MA, Peeters.

Bryson, N. 1994. 'Philostratus and the Imaginary Museum', in S. Goldhill and R. Osborne (eds.), *Art and Text in Ancient Greek Culture*. Cambridge, Cambridge University Press: 255–83.

Budelmann, F. (ed.) 2009. *The Cambridge Companion to Greek Lyric*. Cambridge, Cambridge University Press.

Burges, G. (ed.) 1854. *The Greek Anthology. As Selected for the Use of Westminster, Eton and Other Public Schools. Literally Translated into English Prose, Chiefly by George Burges. To which are added Metrical Versions by Bland, Merrivale, and Others, and an Index of References to the Originals*. London, Henry G. Bohn.

Burnikel, W. 1980. *Untersuchungen zur Struktur des Witzepigramms bei Lukillios und Martial. Philologus* Supplement 22(2). Wiesbaden, Steiner.

Butcher, S. H. 1893. *Some Aspects of the Greek Genius.* Second edition, London, Macmillan.

Butler, A. J. 1881. *Amaranth and Asphodel. Songs from the Greek Anthology.* London, C. Kegan Paul & Co.

Cameron, A. 1993. *The Greek Anthology. From Meleager to Planudes.* Oxford, Clarendon Press.

―――― 1995. *Callimachus and his Critics.* Princeton, NJ, Princeton University Press.

Carey, C. 2009. 'Iambos', in Budelmann 2009: 149–67.

Clayman, D. L. 2007. 'Philosophers and Philosophy in Greek Epigram', in Bing and Bruss 2007a: 497–517.

Coleman, K. M. 1990. 'Fatal Charades: Roman Executions Staged as Mythological Enactments', *JRS* 80: 44–73.

―――― (ed.) 2006. *Martial. Liber Spectaculorum. Edited with Introduction, Translation, and Commentary.* Oxford, Oxford University Press.

Connor, W. R. 1979. 'Pausanias 3.14.1: A Sidelight on Spartan History, c. 440 BC?', *TAPA* 109: 21–7.

Courtney, E. (ed.) 1993. *The Fragmentary Latin Poets. With Commentary.* Oxford, Clarendon Press.

Cribiore, R. 2001. *Gymnastics of the Mind. Greek Education in Hellenistic and Roman Egypt.* Princeton, NJ, Princeton University Press.

Dalby, A. 2000. *Empire of Pleasures. Luxury and Indulgence in the Roman World.* London and New York, Routledge.

Daux, G. 1975. 'Notes de lecture', *Bulletin de Correspondance Hellénique* 99: 145–71.

Day, J. W. 1989. 'Rituals in Stone: Early Greek Grave Epigrams and Monuments', *JHS* 109: 16–28.

―――― 1994. 'Interactive Offerings: Early Greek Dedicatory Epigrams and Ritual', *HSCP* 96: 37–74.

―――― 2000. 'Epigram and Reader: Generic Force as (Re-)Activation of Ritual', in M. Depew and D. Obbink (eds.), *Matrices of Genre. Authors, Canons, and Society.* Cambridge, MA, Harvard University Press: 37–57.

―――― 2007. 'Poems on Stone: The Inscribed Antecedents of Hellenistic Epigram', in Bing and Bruss 2007a: 29–47.

Demoen, K. 1988. 'The Date of the Cyzicene Epigrams: An Analysis of the Vocabulary and Metrical Technique of *AP* III', *AntCl* 57: 231–48.

Derderian, K. 2001. *Leaving Words to Remember. Greek Mourning and the Advent of Literacy.* Leiden, Brill.

Diggle, J. (ed.) 2004. *Theophrastus. Characters.* Cambridge, Cambridge University Press.

Dinter, M. T. 2005. 'Epic and Epigram: Minor Heroes in Virgil's *Aeneid*', *CQ* 55: 153–69.

Dover, K. J. 1979. 'Expurgation of Greek Literature', in W. den Boer (ed.), *Les études classiques aux XIXe et XXe siècles. Leur place dans l'histoire des idées.* Entretiens sur l'Antiquité 26. Vandoeuvres and Geneva, Fondation Hardt pour l'Étude de l'Antiquité Classique: 55–89.

Dowling, L. 1994. *Hellenism and Homosexuality in Victorian Oxford.* Ithaca, NY, Cornell University Press.

Edwards, C. 1996. *Writing Rome. Textual Approaches to the City*. Cambridge, Cambridge University Press.

—— (ed.) 1999. *Roman Presences. Receptions of Rome in European Culture, 1789–1945*. Cambridge, Cambridge University Press.

Elsner, J. 2001. 'Describing Self in the Language of the Other: Pseudo(?) Lucian at the Temple of Hierapolis', in Goldhill 2001: 123–53.

Erbse, H. 1998. 'Zu den Epigrammen des Simonides', *RhM* 141: 213–30.

Erskine, A. 1989. 'Culture and Power in Ptolemaic Egypt: The Museum and Library of Alexandria', *G&R* 42: 38–48.

—— (ed.) 2003. *A Companion to the Hellenistic World*. Malden, MA, Oxford, and Carlton, Victoria, Blackwell.

Fantuzzi, M. 2004a. 'Performance and Genre', in Fantuzzi and Hunter 2004: 1–41.

—— 2004b. 'The Epigram', in Fantuzzi and Hunter 2004: 283–349.

—— 2007. 'Epigram and the Theater', in Bing and Bruss 2007a: 477–95.

—— and Hunter, R. 2004. *Tradition and Innovation in Hellenistic Poetry*. Cambridge, Cambridge University Press.

Faraone, C. 1996. 'Taking the Nestor's Cup Inscription Seriously: Conditional Curses and Erotic Magic in the Earliest Greek Hexameters', *ClAnt* 15: 77–112.

Ferguson, J. 1970. 'The Epigrams of Callimachus', *G&R* 17: 64–80.

Fitzgerald, W. 2007. *Martial. The World of the Epigram*. Chicago, IL, University of Chicago Press.

Fletcher, I. (ed.) 1980. *Decadence and the 1890s*. Stratford-upon-Avon Studies 17. New York, Holmes & Meier Publishers.

Ford, A. 2002. *The Origins of Criticism. Literary Culture and Poetic Theory in Classical Greece*. Princeton, NJ, and Oxford, Princeton University Press.

Fordyce, C. J. (ed.) 1961. *Catullus. A Commentary*. Oxford, Clarendon Press.

Forster, E. M. 1971. *Maurice*. London, Edward Arnold.

Fowler, D. P. 1995. 'Martial and the Book', *Ramus* 24: 31–58.

Fry, E., with Fry, M. and Fry, A. 1915. *A Century of Greek Epigrams. Done into English Verse*. Letchworth Garden City Press.

Gavrilov, A. K. 1997. 'Techniques of Reading in Antiquity', *CQ* 47: 56–73.

Gigante, M. 1995. *Philodemus in Italy. The Books from Herculaneum*. Translated by D. Obbink. Ann Arbor, MI, University of Michigan Press.

Gleason, M. 1995. *Making Men. Sophists and Self-presentation in Ancient Rome*. Princeton, NJ, Princeton University Press.

Goff, B. (ed.) 2005. *Classics and Colonialism*. London, Duckworth.

Goldhill, S. 1995. *Foucault's Virginity. Ancient Erotic Fiction and the History of Sexuality*. Cambridge, Cambridge University Press.

—— (ed.) 2001. *Being Greek under Rome. Cultural Identity, the Second Sophistic and the Development of Empire*. Cambridge, Cambridge University Press.

Green, R. (ed.) 1991. *The Works of Ausonius*. Oxford, Clarendon.

—— (ed.) 1999. *Ausonii. Opera*. Oxford Classical Texts. Oxford, Clarendon Press.

Grosskurth, P. 1964. *John Addington Symonds. A Biography*. London, Longmans.

—— 2000. 'Bringing Symonds Out of the Closet: Some Recollections and Reflections', in Pemble 2000: 170–7.

Gutzwiller, K. J. 1993. 'Callimachus and Hedylus: A Note on Catullus 66.13–14', *Mnemosyne* 46: 530–2.

———— 1998. *Poetic Garlands. Hellenistic Epigrams in Context.* Berkeley, CA, University of California Press.

———— 2002. 'Art's Echo: The Tradition of Hellenistic Ecphrastic Epigram', in Harder, Regtuit, and Wakker 2002: 85–112.

———— 2004. 'A New Hellenistic Poetry Book: P.Mil.Vogl. VIII 309', in Acosta-Hughes, Kosmetatou, and Baumbach 2004: 84–93.

———— 2005a. 'Introduction', in Gutzwiller 2005c: 1–16.

———— 2005b. 'The Literariness of the Milan Papyrus or "What Difference a Book?"', in Gutzwiller 2005c: 287–319.

———— (ed.) 2005c. *The New Posidippus. A Hellenistic Poetry Book.* Oxford, Oxford University Press.

———— 2007a. *A Guide to Hellenistic Literature.* Malden, MA, Oxford, and Carlton, Victoria, Blackwell.

———— 2007b. 'The Paradox of Amatory Epigram', in Bing and Bruss 2007a: 313–32.

Habicht, C. 1997. *Athen. Die Geschichte der Stadt in hellenistischer Zeit.* Munich, Verlag C. H. Beck. Translated by D. L. Schneider with minor revisions as *Athens from Alexander to Antony*, Cambridge, MA and London, Harvard University Press, 1997.

Hammond, M. 1980. 'A Famous "Exemplum" of Spartan Toughness', *CJ* 75: 97–109.

Harder, M.A. 2007. 'Epigram and the Heritage of Epic', in Bing and Bruss 2007a: 409–28.

————, Regtuit, R.F., and Wakker, G.C. (eds.) 2002. *Hellenistic Epigrams.* Hellenistica Groningana 6. Leuven, Paris, and Sterling, VA, Peeters.

Hardwick, L. 2003. *Reception Studies.* Greece and Rome New Surveys in the Classics 33. Oxford, Oxford University Press for the Classical Association.

Harris, W.V. 1989. *Ancient Literacy.* Cambridge, MA, Harvard University Press.

Hatzilambrou, R. 2007. 'P.Oxy. XVIII 2192 Revisited', in Bowman et al. 2007: 282–6.

Haynes, K. 2007. 'The Modern Reception of Greek Epigram', in Bing and Bruss 2007a: 565–84.

Henderson, Jeffrey 1991. *The Maculate Muse. Obscene Language in Attic Comedy.* Second edition, New York, Oxford University Press.

Henderson, John 2006. *'Oxford Reds'. Classic Commentaries on Latin Classics.* London, Duckworth.

Henrichs, A. 2003. 'Writing Religion: Inscribed Texts, Ritual Authority, and the Religious Discourse of the Polis', in Yunis 2003: 38–58.

Highet, G. 1954. *Juvenal the Satirist. A Study.* Oxford, Clarendon Press.

Hingley, R. 2000. *Roman Officers and English Gentlemen. The Imperial Origins of Roman Archaeology.* London, Routledge.

Hoffman, G. 2004. 'An Archaeologist's Perspective on the Milan Papyrus', in Acosta-Hughes, Kosmetatou, and Baumbach 2004: 302–8.

Holliday, P. J. 2000. 'Symonds and the Model of Ancient Greece', in Pemble 2000: 81–101.

Hopkinson, N. 1988. *A Hellenistic Anthology.* Cambridge, Cambridge University Press.

Hunter, R. 2004a. 'The Aetiology of Callimachus' *Aitia*', in Fantuzzi and Hunter 2004: 42–88.

———— 2004b. 'Notes on the *Lithika* of Posidippus', in Acosta-Hughes, Kosmetatou, and Baumbach 2004: 94–104.

Hurwit, J. M. 2007. 'The Human Figure in Early Greek Sculpture and Vase Painting', in H. A. Shapiro (ed.), *The Cambridge Companion to Archaic Greece*. Cambridge, Cambridge University Press: 265–86.

Inwood, B. (ed.) 2003. *The Cambridge Companion to the Stoics*. Cambridge, Cambridge University Press.

Janko, R. 1988. 'Vergil, *Aeneid* 1.607–9 and the Midas Epigram', *CQ* 38: 259–60.

Jebb, R. C. 1893. *The Growth and Influence of Classical Greek Poetry. Lectures Delivered in 1892 on the Percy Turnbull Memorial Foundation in the Johns Hopkins University.* London, Macmillan & Co.

Jenkyns, R. 1980. *The Victorians and Ancient Greece*. Cambridge, MA, Harvard University Press.

Kaczko, S. 2009. 'From Stone to Parchment: Epigraphic and Literary Transmission of Some Greek Epigrams', *Trends in Classics* 1: 90–117.

Kaibel, G. 1876. 'De Callimachi Epigrammate XLIII ed. Schneid', *Hermes* 10: 1–6.

——— ed. 1885. *Philodemi Gadarensis Epigrammata*. Greifswald.

——— 1896. 'Zu den Epigrammen des Kallimachos', *Hermes* 31: 264–70.

Katz, J. 2005. 'The Indo-European Context', in Foley, J. M. *A Companion to Ancient Epic*. Malden, MA, Oxford, and Chichester, Blackwell Publishing: 20–30.

Kay, N. M. (ed.) 2001. *Ausonius. Epigrams. Text with Introduction and Commentary.* London, Duckworth.

——— (ed.) 2006. *Epigrams from the Anthologia Latina. Text, Translation and Commentary.* London, Duckworth.

Kelly, M. 1986. *Jousts of Aphrodite. Erotic Verse Translated from the Original Greek.* London, Forest Books.

Kemp, J. 2000. 'A Problem in Gay Heroics: Symonds and l'Amour de l'impossible', in Pemble 2000: 50–61.

Ker, W. C. A. (ed.) 1919–20. *Martial. Epigrams. With an English Translation.* Loeb Classical Library. 2 vols, London, Heinemann. Reissued Cambridge, MA, Harvard University Press, 1968.

Knox, B. M. W. 1968. 'Silent Reading in Antiquity', *GRBS* 9: 421–35.

Köhnken, A. 2007. 'Epinician Epigram', in Bing and Bruss 2007a: 295–312.

König, J. 2005. *Athletics and Literature in the Roman Empire*. Cambridge, Cambridge University Press.

Kovacs, D. 1995. 'Paralipomena Euripidea', *Mnemosyne* 48: 565–70.

Krevans, N. 2005. 'The Editor's Toolbox: Strategies for Selection and Presentation in the Milan Epigram Papyrus', in Gutzwiller 2005c: 81–96.

——— 2007. 'The Arrangement of Epigrams in Collections', in Bing and Bruss 2007a: 131–46.

Kuttner, A. 1995. 'Republican Rome Looks at Pergamon', *HSCP* 97: 157–78.

——— 2005. 'Cabinet Fit for a Queen: The Λιθικά as Posidippus' Gem Museum', in Gutzwiller 2005c: 141–63.

Lamberton, R. 1986. *Homer the Theologian. Neoplatonist Allegorical Reading and the Growth of the Epic Tradition.* Berkeley, CA, University of California Press.

——— and Keaney, J. J. (eds.) 1992. *Homer's Ancient Readers*. Princeton, NJ, Princeton University Press.

Lang, A. 1892. *Grass of Parnassus. First and Last Rhymes.* New edition, London, Longmans & Co.

Larmour, D. H. J. and Spencer, D. (eds.) 2007. *The Sites of Rome. Time, Space, Memory*. Oxford, Oxford University Press.

Lattimore, R. 1962. *Themes in Greek and Latin Epitaphs*. Urbana, IL, University of Illinois Press.

Lauxtermann, M. 1998. 'What is an Epideictic Epigram?', *Mnemosyne* 51: 525–37.

Lavelle, B. M. 1986. 'The Dating and Patronage of the Archedike-Epigram', *Hermes* 114: 240–4.

Leslie, S. 1929. *The Greek Anthology. Selected and Translated with a Prolegomenon*. London, Ernest Benn.

Lightfoot, J. L. (ed.) 1999. *Parthenius of Nicaea. The Poetical Fragments and the Ero tika Pathe mata. Edited with Introduction and Commentaries*. Oxford, Clarendon Press.

Lissarague, F. 1999. 'Publicity and Performance: *Kalos* Inscriptions in Attic Vase-painting', in S. Goldhill and R. Osborne (eds.) *Performance Culture and Athenian Democracy*. Cambridge, Cambridge University Press: 359–73.

Littlewood, A. R. 2005. 'Anthology, Greek', in N. G. Wilson (ed.), *Encyclopedia of Ancient Greece*. London, Routledge: 52–3.

Livingstone, N. (ed.) 2001. *A Commentary on Isocrates' Busiris*. Leiden, Brill.

Livrea, E. 1990. 'Tre Epigrammi Funerari Callimachei', *Hermes* 118: 314–24.

Lloyd-Jones, H. 2001. 'Notes on P. Mil. Vogl. VIII 309', *ZPE* 137: 6.

Lorenz, S. 2001. Review of C. Henriksén (ed.) 1999, *Martial Book IX. A Commentary*, *CR* 51: 262–4.

———— 2004. 'Waterscape with Black and White: Epigrams, Cycles, and Webs in Martial's *Epigrammaton Liber Quartus*', *AJP* 125: 255–78.

Lothian, A. 1920. *The Golden Treasury of the Greeks. Being 250 Pieces from the Anthology Rendered in English*. Oxford, Basil Blackwell.

Luck, G. 1959. 'Kids and Wolves', *CQ* 9: 34–7.

Mackail, J. W. (ed.) 1890. *Select Epigrams from the Greek Anthology. Edited with a Revised Text, Introduction, Translation and Notes*. London, Longmans & Co.

McKitterick, D. 2007. 'Publishing and Perishing in Classics: E. H. Barker and the Early Nineteenth-century Book Trades', in Stray 2007a: 7–33.

Magnelli, E. 2007. 'Meter and Diction: From Refinement to Mannerism', in Bing and Bruss 2007a: 165–83.

Männlein-Robert, I. 2007. 'Epigrams on Art: Voice and Voicelessness in Ecphrastic Epigram', in Bing and Bruss 2007a: 251–71.

Mayer, D. 1994. *Playing Out the Empire. Ben-Hur and Other Toga Plays and Films, 1883–1908. A Critical Anthology*. Oxford, Clarendon Press.

Merkelbach, R. and Stauber, J. (eds.) 2001. *Steinepigramme aus dem griechischen Osten. Bd. 2: Die Nordküste Kleinasiens (Marmarasee und Pontos)*. Munich and Leipzig, K. G. Saur.

———— 2007. 'The Act of Reading and the Act of Writing in Hellenistic Epigram', in Bing and Bruss 2007a: 187–210.

Mitsis, P. 2003. 'The Institutions of Hellenistic Philosophy', in Erskine 2003: 464–76.

Montserrat, D. 1998. 'Unidentified Human Remains: Mummies and the Erotics of Biography', in D. Montserrat (ed.), *Changing Bodies, Changing Meanings. Studies on the Human Body in Antiquity*. London, Routledge: 162–97.

Mukařovský, J. 1979. *Aesthetic Function, Norm and Value as Social Facts*. Translated by M. E. Suino. Michigan Slavic Contributions 3. Ann Arbor, MI, Dept of Slavic Languages and Literature, University of Michigan.

Munn, M. H. 2006. *The Mother of the Gods, Athens, and the Tyranny of Asia. A Study of Sovereignty in Ancient Religion*. Berkeley, CA, University of California Press.

Murgatroyd, P. 1979. '*Militia Amoris* and the Roman Elegists', *Latomus* 34: 59–79.

———— 1995. 'The Sea of Love', *CQ* 45: 9–25.

Murray, O. 1985. 'Symposium and Genre in the Poetry of Horace', *JRS* 75: 39–50.

Neaves, C. 1874. *The Greek Anthology*. Edinburgh, William Blackwood & Sons.

Newby, Z. 2005. *Greek Athletics in the Roman World. Victory and Virtue*. Oxford, Oxford University Press.

Nisbet, G. 2000. Review of Sider 1997, *CR* 50: 416–7.

———— 2003a. *Greek Epigram in the Roman Empire. Martial's Forgotten Rivals*. Oxford, Oxford University Press.

———— 2003b. 'A Sickness of Discourse: The Vanishing Syndrome of *Leptosune*', *G&R* 50: 191–205.

———— 2006. '"That's Not Funny": Advice in Skoptic Epigram', in D. J. Spencer and E. Theodorakopoulos (eds.), *Advice and its Rhetoric in Greece and Rome*. Bari, Levante: 159–77.

———— 2007a. 'Roman Receptions of Hellenistic Epigram', in Bing and Bruss 2007a: 543–63.

———— 2007b. 'Satiric Epigram', in Bing and Bruss 2007a: 353–69.

———— 2007c. 'Sex Lives of the Sophists: Epigrams by Philostratus and Fronto', in J. Elsner, S. J. Harrison, and S. Swain (eds.), *Severan Culture*. Cambridge, Cambridge University Press: 114–24.

Nixon, P. 1927. *Martial and the Modern Epigram*. New York, Longmans, Green and Co.

Nugent, S. G. 1990. 'Ausonius' "Late-antique" Poetics and "Post-modern" Literary Theory' in A. J. Boyle (ed.), *The Imperial Muse. Ramus Essays on Roman Literature of the Empire. Flavian Epicist to Claudian*. Bendigo, Victoria, Aureal Publications: 236–60.

Obbink, D. 2004. '"Tropoi" (Posidippus AB 102–103)', in Acosta-Hughes, Kosmatatou, and Baumbach 2004: 292–301.

Osborne, R. and Pappas, A. 2007. 'Writing on Archaic Greek Pottery', in Z. Newby and R. Leader-Newby (eds.), *Art and Inscriptions in the Ancient World*. Cambridge, Cambridge University Press: 131–55.

Paley, F. A. and Stone, W. H. (eds.) 1868. *M. Val. Martialis Epigrammata Selecta. Select Epigrams from Martial with English Notes*. London.

Papalexandrou, N. 2004. 'Reading as *Seeing*: P. Mil. Vogl. VIII 309 and Greek Art', in Acosta-Hughes, Kosmatatou, and Baumbach 2004: 247–58.

Parsons, P. J. 2007. *City of the Sharp-nosed Fish. Greek Lives in Roman Egypt*. London, Weidenfeld & Nicolson.

Paton, W. R. (ed.) 1916–18. *The Greek Anthology. With an English Translation*. Loeb Classical Library. 5 vols, London, Heinemann. Reissued Cambridge, MA, Harvard University Press, 1979.

Patterson, J. R. 1992. 'The City of Rome: From Republic to Empire', *JRS* 82: 186–215.

Pelliccia, H. 2009. 'Simonides, Pindar and Bacchylides', in Budelmann 2009: 240–62.

Pemble, J. (ed.) 2000. *John Addington Symonds. Culture and the Demon Desire.* Basingstoke, Macmillan.

Perrin, N. 1992. *Dr Bowdler's Legacy. A History of Expurgated Books in England and America.* Enlarged edition, Boston, MA, David R. Godine.

Petrovic, A. 2007a. 'Inscribed Epigram in Pre-Hellenistic Literary Sources', in Bing and Bruss 2007a: 49–68.

—— 2007b. *Kommentar zu den simonideischen Versinschriften.* Leiden and Boston, MA, Brill.

—— and Petrovic, I. 2003. 'Stop and Smell the Statues: Callimachus' Epigram 51. Pf. Reconsidered (Four Times)', *MD* 51: 179–208.

Pfeiffer, R. 1968. *The History of Classical Scholarship. From the Beginnings to the End of the Hellenistic Age.* Oxford, Clarendon Press.

Plant, I. 2004. *Women Writers of Ancient Greece and Rome. An Anthology.* London, Equinox.

Potter, R. A. 2007. *Arctic Spectacles. The Frozen North in Visual Culture, 1818–1875.* Seattle, WA, University of Washington Press.

Powell, B. B. 1991. *Homer and the Origin of the Greek Alphabet.* Cambridge, Cambridge University Press.

Powell, J. U. 1917. Review of vol. 1 of Paton 1916–18, *CR* 31: 142–4.

Prauscello, L. 2006. 'Sculpted Meanings, Talking Statues: Some Observations on Posidippus 142.12 A-B (= XIX G-P) *ΚΑΙ ΕΝ ΠΡΟΘΥΡΟΙΣ ΘΗΚΕ ΔΙΔΑΣΚΑΛΙΑΝ*', *AJP* 127: 511–23.

Preston, R. 2001. 'Roman Questions, Greek Answers: Plutarch and the Construction of Identity', in Goldhill 2001: 86–122.

Prior, R. E. 1996. 'Going Around Hungry: Topography and Poetics in Martial 2.14', *AJP* 117: 121–41.

Ramsby, T. R. 2007. *Textual Permanence. Roman Elegists and the Epigraphic Tradition.* London, Duckworth.

Rexroth, K. 1962. *Poems from the Greek Anthology. Translated.* Ann Arbor, MI, University of Michigan Press.

Richlin, A. 1983. *The Garden of Priapus. Sexuality and Aggression in Roman Humor.* New Haven, CT, Yale University Press.

Rodríguez Almeida, E. 2003. *Terrarum Dea Gentiumque. Marziale e Roma. Un Poeta e sua Città.* Rome, Unione Internazionale degli Istituti di Archeologia Storia e Storia dell'Arte in Roma.

Roman, L. 2001. 'The Representation of Literary Materiality in Martial's Epigrams', *JRS* 91: 113–45.

Romm, J. S. 1992. *The Edges of the Earth in Ancient Thought. Geography, Exploration, and Fiction.* Princeton, NJ, Princeton University Press.

Rosen, R. M. 2007. 'The Hellenistic Epigrams on Archilochus and Hipponax', in Bing and Bruss 2007a: 459–76.

Rossi, L. 2002. 'Composition and Reception in *AP* 9.1–583: *Aphegeseis, Epideixeis* and *Progymnasmata*', in Harder, Regtuit, and Wakker 2002: 151–74.

Ruskin, J. 1860. *Modern Painters. Volume V.* London, Smith, Elder, and Co.

Rutherford, I. 1996. 'The New Simonides: Towards a Commentary', *Arethusa* 29: 167–92.

Said, E. W. 1978. *Orientalism*. New York, Pantheon Books.

Schrier, O. J. 1979. 'Love With Doris. Dioscorides, *Anth. Pal.* V 55 (= 1483–1490 Gow-Page)', *Mnemosyne* 32: 307–26.

—— 1982. 'Doris' Love Again', *Mnemosyne* 35: 146–8.

Scodel, R. 2003. 'Two Epigrammatic Pairs: Callimachus' Epitaphs, Plato's Apples', *Hermes* 131: 257–68.

Shackleton Bailey, D. R. (ed.) 1993. *Martial. Epigrams. Edited and Translated*. 3 vols, Cambridge, MA, Harvard University Press.

Sharrock, A. and Morales, H. (eds.) 2000. *Intratextuality. Greek and Roman Textual Relations*. Oxford, Oxford University Press.

Shipley, G. 2000. *The Greek World After Alexander, 323–30 BC*. London and New York, Routledge.

Sickinger, J. P. 2007. 'The Bureaucracy of Democracy and Empire', in L. J. Samons II (ed.), *The Cambridge Companion to the Age of Pericles*. Cambridge, Cambridge University Press: 196–214.

Sider, D. 1997. *The Epigrams of Philodemos. Introduction, Text, and Commentary*. Oxford, Oxford University Press.

—— 2006. 'The New Simonides and the Question of Historical Elegy', *AJP* 127: 327–46.

—— 2007. '*Sylloge Simonidea*', in Bing and Bruss 2007a: 113–30.

Sourvinou-Inwood, C. 1995. '*Reading' Greek Death to the End of the Classical Period*. Oxford, Clarendon Press.

Soutar, G. 1939. *Nature in Greek Poetry*. London, Oxford University Press.

Spencer, D. J. 2005. 'Lucan's Follies: Memory and Ruin in a Civil War Landscape', *G&R* 52: 46–69.

Stanzel, K.-H. 2007. 'Bucolic Epigram', in Bing and Bruss 2007a: 333–351.

Steiner, A. 2002. 'Private and Public: Links Between *Symposion* and *Syssition* in Fifth-century Athens', *ClAnt* 21: 347–80.

Steiner, D. 1999. 'To Praise, Not to Bury: Simonides fr. 531P', *CQ* 49: 383–95.

Stephens, S. and Obbink, D. 2004. 'The Manuscript: Posidippus on Papyrus', in Acosta-Hughes, Kosmetatou, and Baumbach 2004: 9–15.

Stray, C. 1998. *Classics Transformed. Schools, Universities, and Society in England, 1830–1960*. Oxford, Clarendon Press.

—— (ed.) 1999. *Classics in 19th and 20th Century Cambridge. Curriculum, Culture and Community*. PCPS Supplement 24. Cambridge, Cambridge Philological Society.

—— (ed.) 2007a. *Classical Books. Scholarship and Publishing in Britain since 1800*. BICS Supplement 101. London, Institute of Classical Studies.

—— 2007b. 'Jebb's Sophocles: An Edition and its Maker', in Stray 2007a, 75–96.

Sullivan, J. P. 1991. *Martial. The Unexpected Classic. A Literary and Historical Study*. Cambridge, Cambridge University Press.

—— and Boyle, A. S. (eds.) 1996. *Martial in English*. London, Penguin.

Svenbro, J. 1993. *Phrasikleia. An Anthropology of Reading in Ancient Greece*. Translated by J. Lloyd. Ithaca, NY, and London, Cornell University Press.

Swain, S. 1996. *Hellenism and Empire. Language, Classicism, and Power in the Greek World, AD 50–250*. Oxford, Clarendon Press.

Symonds, J. A. 1920. *Studies of the Greek Poets*. Single-volume reprint of third edition, London, A. & C. Black.

—— 1984. *The Memoirs of John Addington Symonds*. Edited and introduced by P. Grosskurth. London, Hutchinson.

Talbot, A.-M. 1999. 'Epigrams in Context: Metrical Inscriptions on Art and Architecture of the Palaiologan Era', *Dumbarton Oaks Papers* 53: 75–90.

Tarán, S. L. 1979. *The Art of Variation in the Hellenistic Epigram*. Leiden, Brill.

Tatum, J. 1994. 'Introduction', in J. Tatum (ed.), *The Search for the Ancient Novel*. Baltimore, MD, Johns Hopkins University Press: 1–19.

Thomas, Rosalind. 1992. *Literacy and Orality in Ancient Greece*. Cambridge, Cambridge University Press.

Thomas, Richard. 2004. '"Drownded in the Tide": the Nauagika and some "Problems" in Augustan Poetry', in Acosta-Hughes, Kosmetatou, and Baumbach 2004: 259–75.

Thomson, G. 1941. *Aeschylus and Athens. A Study in the Social Origins of Drama*. London, Lawrence & Wishart.

Tolkien, J. R. R. 1966. *The Return of the King*. Second edition, London, Allen and Unwin.

Tsagalis, C. C. 2008. *Inscribing Sorrow. Fourth-century Attic Funerary Epigrams*. Berlin, Walter de Gruyter.

Tueller, M. A. 2008. *Look Who's Talking. Innovations in Voice and Identity in Hellenistic Epigram*. Hellenistica Groningana 13. Leuven, Paris, and Dudley, MA, Peeters.

Turner, F. M. 1981. *The Greek Heritage in Victorian Britain*. New Haven, CT, Yale University Press.

—— 1999. 'Christians and Pagans in Victorian Novels', in Edwards 1999: 173–87.

Usher, M. D. 1997. 'Prolegomenon to the Homeric Centos', *AJP* 118: 305–321.

—— 1998. *Homeric Stitchings. The Homeric Centos of the Empress Eudocia*. Lanham, MD, Rowman & Littlefield.

Vance, N. 1997. *The Victorians and Ancient Rome*. Oxford, Blackwell Publishers.

—— 1999. 'Decadence and the Subversion of Empire', in Edwards 1999: 110–24.

West, S. 1985. 'Herodotus' Epigraphical Interests', *CQ* 35: 278–305.

—— 1994. 'Nestor's Bewitching Cup', *ZPE* 101: 9–15.

White, P. 1974. 'The Presentation and Dedication of the *Silvae* and *Epigrams*', *JRS* 64: 40–61.

Whitmarsh, T. 2005. *The Second Sophistic*. Greece and Rome New Surveys in the Classics 35. Oxford, Oxford University Press.

Wilder, T. 1948. *The Ides of March*. London, Longmans, Green & Co.

Winterer, C. 2002. *The Culture of Classicism. Ancient Greece and Rome in American Intellectual Life, 1780–1910*. Baltimore, MD, Johns Hopkins University Press.

Wiseman, T. P. 1985. *Catullus and his World. A Reappraisal*. Cambridge, Cambridge University Press.

—— 1995. *Remus. A Roman Myth*. Cambridge, Cambridge University Press.

Wissman, J. 2002. 'Hellenistic Epigrams as School-texts in Classical Antiquity', in Harder, Regtuit, and Wakker 2002: 215–30.

Worton, M. 1994. 'You Know What I Mean? The Operability of Codes in Gay Men's Fiction', *Paragraph* 17: 49–59.

Wyke, M. and Biddiss, M. (eds.) 1999. *The Uses and Abuses of Antiquity*. Bern, Peter Lang.

Yunis, H. (ed.) 2003. *Written Texts and the Rise of Literate Culture in Ancient Greece.* Cambridge, Cambridge University Press.

Zanker, G. 2004. *Modes of Viewing in Hellenistic Poetry and Art.* Madison, WI, and London, University of Wisconsin Press.

———— 2007. 'Characterization in Hellenistic Epigram', in Bing and Bruss 2007a: 232–49.

## Useful websites

Classics@: http://chs.harvard.edu/ under 'Publications'
Issue 1 of this electronic periodical publishes a regularly updated, downloadable electronic text of the 'New Posidippus', as well as translations into various languages, a bibliography, and other resources.

Packard Humanities Institute Greek Epigraphy: http://epigraphy.packhum.org/
This is a well-designed, highly searchable (and concordance-generating) database containing the texts from the most important corpora of Greek inscriptions, region by region. Greek text only (at time of writing), but with some functionality even for those with limited knowledge of Greek: clicking on an inscription removes letters reconstructed by epigraphists, revealing how much can actually be read on the stone.

# INDEX

Aeschines 41
  3 *Against Ctesiphon* 18: 41 n. 54
Aeschrion 53
  1 *HE*: 93–94
Aeschylus
  *Agamemnon* 36–37: 95
*Agamemnon* 106: 29 n. 23
Agathias 10–11, 13, 137–8
Agis
  1 *HE*: 60 n. 26
Alcaeus of Messene (Hellenistic epigrammatist) 53
  16 *HE*: 92–93
Alexandria 5, 48–49
Ammianus 126–7, 131
*Anthology, Greek* 1, 7–13, 15, 21, 106–7, 141, 147–9, 153–6, 159: see also epigram, collection and selection of
*Anthology, Latin* 21, 135–6
Antipater 8–9, 15
Anyte 53
  16 *HE*: 84–85
  18 *HE*: 85
Apollonius of Rhodes 12
Archilochus 10, 62 n. 30, 157
  F 196a West: 81–82
Asclepiades 4, 53, 97
  1 *HE*: 84
11: 72–74, 77
Athens 23
Ausonius 20–21, 112, 130–6
Balbilla, Julia: see Memnon, Colossus of
Besantinus: see Vestinus
bilingualism: see Ammianus; Ausonius
Burns, Robert 160–1
'Cadmean letters' 31
Callimachus 4, 6, 10, 12, 16, 49–50, 53, 57–58, 102, 123, 127
  8 *HE*: 52, 74–77
  13: 71–72
  22: 55–57
  25: 52, 55
  29: 90–92
  30: 90–92
  31: 94–96
  33: 95 n. 89
  46: 88–89
  63: 73–77
Catullus 7, 16, 101–4, 114–15, 130, 161
  7: 86

*CEG* (*Carmina Epigraphica Graeca*) 22
  24: 28–30
  28: 24
  72: 23–24
  80: 24 n. 9
  108: 24 n. 9
  286: 25
  305: 39–40
  326: 26
  432: 68
  454: 68–69
  519: 41 n. 54
  776: 41 n. 54
censorship 1–3, 12–13, 106, 112–13, 116, 144–5, 151–2, 159; see also sexuality
cento 138–9
*Charicles* (didactic novel) 1–4, 14, 16, 151, 160, 162
Christodorus of Thebes 11
Cleobulus of Lindos 43–44
collections: see epigram, collection and selection of
comedy, Greek 3, 107
Cyzicene epigrams 11, 99–101
Demosthenes 41
  7 *On the Halonnesus* 40: 41 n. 54
  18 *On the Crown* 289: 41 n. 54
Diogenes Laertius
  1.90: 44
Diogenianus 10–11
Dioscorides 9, 53
  5 *HE*: 80–82
Dipylon oinochoe (vessel inscribed with epigram) 68
Donne, John
  *The Sunne Rising* 87–88
ekphrasis 99–101, 121–3, 127, 133: see also Cyzicene epigrams; epigram, ecphrastic; *tekhnopaignia*
elegy: see epigram, Greek, and archaic elegy
epigram, Greek
  amatory and erotic 68–88
  by anonymous authors 4, 7, 9
  and antiquarianism 5–6, 137: see also *paideia*
  and archaic elegy 14, 47, 69–70
  in Byzantium 11, 20–21, 137–9: see also *Anthology, Greek*